Coaching, Counseling & Mentoring

Second Edition

Coaching, Counseling & Mentoring

How to Choose & Use the Right Technique to Boost Employee Performance

Second Edition

Florence M. Stone

AMACOM

American Management Association

New York • Atlanta • Brussels • Chicago • Mexico City • San Francisco
Shanghai • Tokyo • Toronto • Washington, D.C.

Special discounts on bulk quantities of AMACOM books are available to corporations, professional associations, and other organizations. For details, contact Special Sales Department, AMACOM, a division of American Management Association, 1601 Broadway, New York, NY 10019.
Tel: 212-903-8316. Fax: 212-903-8083.
E-mail: specialsls@amanet.org
Website: www.amacombooks.org/go/specialsales
To view all AMACOM titles go to: www.amacombooks.org

This publication is designed to provide accurate and authoritative information in regard to the subject matter covered. It is sold with the understanding that the publisher is not engaged in rendering legal, accounting, or other professional service. If legal advice or other expert assistance is required, the services of a competent professional person should be sought.

Library of Congress Cataloging-in-Publication Data

Stone, Florence M.
    Coaching, counseling & mentoring : how to choose & use the right technique to boost employee performance / Florence M. Stone.—2nd ed.
        p. cm.
    Includes bibliographical references and index.
    ISBN-10: 0-8144-7385-7
    ISBN-13: 978-0-8144-7385-6
    1. Mentoring in business. 2. Employees—Coaching of. 3. Employees—Counseling of. 4. Employees—Training of. I. Title. II. Title: Coaching, counseling and mentoring.

    HF5385.S76   2007
    658.3′ 124—dc22   2006024994

Printing number

10 9 8 7 6 5 4 3 2 1

Contents

Coaching, Counseling & Mentoring

Second Edition

Three Ways to Develop High-Performance Employees

IF YOUR ORGANIZATION IS TO SUSTAIN its competitive advantage, it needs employees who are motivated and eager to learn and adapt as their roles change along with the organization. Today's companies need people who, at the least, meet their goals and, when given the opportunity, exceed those goals, demonstrating initiative and creativity. If you have strong people skills, you can build a high-performing team that can be relied on to make major contributions to your organization's strategic plan.

What is your role in this? It is to have competency in three key people skills: coaching, counseling, and mentoring. Because it means better bottom-line results, organizations look for managers with these abilities. On a personal level, being a good coach, counselor, and mentor could be your ticket to advancement.

With escalating time pressures and constant change, upper management has their eye out for managers who can recruit capable employees, develop the skills they need to do today's jobs, and prepare them to handle tomorrow's jobs; who recognize their obligation to confront poor performers and who will work with these people to find a solution or make the tough decisions to terminate those who are dragging down the rest of the team; and who can keep their superstars shining even when there is little opportunity for advancement or dollars for increased performance.

In short, organizations want and reward managers who are skilled at the managerial tasks of coaching, counseling, and mentoring. Note that they are referred to here as "managerial responsibilities" with good rea-

1

son: coaching, counseling, and mentoring are very much a part of a manager's job—and have always been so. The demands on organizations, however, have made them critical skills today. This is why this book has been developed. It not only describes each responsibility but also tells when to use which critical skill and how to most effectively use it—something many managers aren't always sure about doing.

Clearing Up the Mystery

Confusion about these three management skills abounds. A review of the management literature would suggest that the confusion is only semantic, with *coaching* confused with *counseling* or *mentoring*, and *mentoring* confused with coaching or counseling. But the confusion goes deeper. All managers pay lip service to these terms, many managers think they are good at these skills, but very few managers are actually doing them. Managers and team leaders may have a general idea about how to coach, how to counsel, and/or how to mentor people, but for the most part they are unaware of the various roles involved in each task and the best way of proceeding. Nor do they know all the problems they may encounter if they don't do these things right.

In this book you will find answers to all the questions you might have about coaching, counseling, and mentoring, including the descriptions of the traps you could fall into and, more important, how to avoid these traps.

What Are the Differences Between Coaching, Counseling, and Mentoring?

To help you get the terminology straight, in this book the term *coaching* refers to the task of continually developing employees so that they do their jobs well. Comparable to the work of a professional coach, managerial coaching involves not only assessment of development needs and subsequent training but also making good hires to begin with. Good coaches recruit only the best athletes, and they train newcomers to close whatever skill gaps remain as well as help more experienced workers update their skills and increase their employability. Managers should also communicate the organization's values and mission to ensure that the staff is empowered and even shares the leadership responsibilities.

There are mistakes you can make along the way—mistakes that can turn a capable newcomer into a troublesome employee or an employee with a personal problem into a problem employee. Either situation demands *counseling,* defined here as a four-step process, of which one-on-one communication is most important since the success of these meetings could mean the difference between an employee's continued employment or not.

The hard work of the team can be undone by just one employee who doesn't carry his or her weight. Consequently, poor performance can't be tolerated. Employees who are working ineffectively need to know it, and they need your help to make the necessary improvements. In today's tough antidiscrimination legal climate, managers need to demonstrate how they have expended every reasonable effort to help employees perform well. A manager should have documentation to show that a suspended or discharged employee was warned and that help was available. This book will show you how to conduct effective counseling sessions, keep written records of these sessions, and develop an action plan—the necessary evidence you will need should an aggrieved employee take legal action against your organization. Some managers think they can avoid counseling traps just by ignoring performance problems, but that can be the biggest career mistake of all, should litigation result from this failure to act.

Whereas counseling is concerned with your poorer performers, *mentoring* is an activity directed to coaching your best performers not only in their jobs but also in their career development. A manager can become role model, coach, broker, and advocate for the outstanding performers so as to sustain their motivation despite limited opportunities for advancement, as well as give these employees opportunities to utilize their abilities for their own benefit and that of the organization. Managers can also mentor up-and-coming employees within the organization, sharing their knowledge and skills.

You don't have to be a part of a corporate mentoring program to mentor, but increasingly corporations are setting up formal mentoring efforts in which managers can participate. As you will read here, such participation can add to your toolkit of managerial skills as well as give you greater visibility in your organization. Companies are looking for managers who are willing to add to corporate continuity and strength by sharing their knowledge with new and talented workers.

Through mentoring, you may gain personally as well. Besides the pride you will feel in helping a staff member grow, you will have someone who can take on important projects or assume some of your mundane tasks, which will in turn free you to work on more rewarding, high-visibility projects. Done right, mentoring can motivate not only the employees but also others on the staff or in the organization as a whole, as you demonstrate that you truly care about people. On the other hand, if done incorrectly, mentoring can create jealousies, suspicion about your motives, charges of discrimination, and many more troubles.

How This Book Is Organized

Section I of this book is devoted to coaching, Section II to counseling, and Section III to mentoring. The first chapter in each section provides an overview of the managerial process. The second chapter zeroes in on critical elements of the process to ensure that you maximize its benefits. The third chapter in each section provides additional scenarios and actual scripts for modeling conversations with employees. The fourth and final chapter in each section presents those traps and problems associated with the process.

What's in It for Me?

Since you picked up this book, I have to assume that you either have a specific problem with an employee and hope that you can find a solution here or you suspect that your department could be more productive than it is and hope that you will find ways to boost the output of your average staff members, turn your good employees into better ones, and transform your best workers into super-performers.

Whichever your reason, you should find the answer here. Better yet, when you succeed in effectively applying this trio of skills, create your own total performance management process, and boost your employees' performance, you will get the attention from upper management that your people-management efforts will merit.

Some Cases in Point

To demonstrate just how valuable the advice in this book can be to improve your department's or team's productivity, let me share ten "people situations." Very likely, you've encountered several situations like these; if you haven't, you probably know people in your organization who have. They are the situations that continually frustrate and can cause manager burnout today. In this book, you'll discover the solutions to such problems that will enable you to handle these "people situations" confidently the next time or, better yet, prevent their recurrence.

• *Situation 1.* Deidre is expected to begin work at 8:30 A.M. By arriving a half hour early each day, she can leave a half hour early to pick up her daughter from school. It seems a fair arrangement for Deidre and the organization, except for one major problem: while Deidre arrives at 8:30, even a little before, she truly doesn't get to work until 9:15, sometimes 10:00 A.M. Rather than take her coat off, sit down, and start entering sales figures into the computer system, she visits with her friends in the employee lounge. Although her co-workers often put in extra time after 5:00 P.M. to make up for time spent over coffee in the morning, Deidre promptly leaves at 4:30, regardless of the time she truly begins work. Should you talk solely to Deidre or to all those who gather in the lounge in the morning? Are you wrong to count on Deidre's professionalism to get her to abide by her promise to start work as soon as she came into the office?

• *Situation 2.* The company has set aside Friday for casual dress. Your women employees are abiding by company rules. Your problem is with Bill. Since the program began, he has come into the office in tight pants and bright-colored shirts opened to the third button or in teeshirts with promotional graphics. The women in your department have asked you why you allow Bill to get away with a provocative look while they have to wear pant suits and slacks, not jeans. You started to talk to Bill but he treated it as a joke: "Do you think I look too sexy?" he asked. What are you going to do?

• *Situation 3.* Arlene is one of your fastest data-entry operators when you keep at her. In crises, she also pulls herself together and gets everything done. But if you ease off, focusing on your own work rather than constantly monitoring her performance, she begins to fiddle with her hair or pull out a book and let the work sit on her desk. She's been warned twice, but each time after her performance improved, she was taken off warning and the slack behavior began again. What would you do?

• *Situation 4.* Lee was transferred to your marketing department a month ago to fill the position of proofreader. She wasn't an experienced proofreader, but she was given the job when her previous job as typist for the law department was eliminated. Since she had to proof copy in that job, the personnel department offered her the opening in your department as an alternative to being laid off. Your problem is that Lee used to rely on another staff member to help proof the legal documents—one person read the original aloud while the other read the typed copy. Lee never proofed copy on her own, and she isn't improving with on-the-job practice. She also seems out of place in the department. Should you suggest transfer to another department or lay her off?

• *Situation 5.* Nick is one of your best employees, but he's been moping about since you announced that his pet project would have to be discontinued. There are other projects he could oversee, but he lacks some people skills that are important for the success of these initiatives. What would you do?

• *Situation 6.* Bill's performance appraisal review is not going well. You have some specific subjects you want to discuss, yet he keeps chattering about this situation or that, almost as if he suspects you have problems you want to discuss. What would you do?

• *Situation 7.* Maxine has the potential to take on much more work than she currently has—at least you believe so—but right now her output ranges from poor to average. You realize that the job is pretty monotonous for someone with her experience (she had been transferred from another department to avoid downsizing her) and the current position is much simpler than the previous one. What would you do?

• *Situation 8.* Linda, a manager, is being pressured by her boss, Tom, to put Sylvia, one of Linda's staff members, on warning. Tom doesn't like Sylvia's attitude. Sylvia is a loner, uncomfortable in team settings. And Tom feels that she should speak up more at meetings and, given her three years with the organization, should have more knowledge about the organization than she does. Linda doesn't agree with Tom's concerns. She knows about and can document some problems with Sylvia's performance, and she could use those points to justify putting Sylvia on warning, but other employees with similar problems first went through counseling. Tom doesn't want to waste the time with counseling; he wants Sylvia out and someone else who better fits the company's new culture put in her place. What would you do?

• *Situation 9.* Andrea, a customer service rep, lost her temper with customers on several occasions and consequently was placed in counseling. She continues to have problems with customers on the phone, but today you observed her helping an older customer with a billing problem when she took over the front customer desk. Her behavior was quite unusual for her: she was patient and considerate. This incident shows that Andrea could develop the right behavior. On the other hand, one good incident seems insignificant when weighed against the three or four bad ones when she snapped at callers. What would you do?

• *Situation 10.* Your organization is updating its recordkeeping system, and senior management expects the changeover to be completed within a few more weeks. Today, you learned that the project is not proceeding fast enough to suit your boss. He has asked you to talk to each of your staff members and critique their work in order to speed up the change process. This request puts you on the spot because it means you have to talk to Grace about her work performance. She is very sensitive to criticism and is easily hurt. Only a week ago, she burst into tears when you questioned her about her handling of the new system. She also seems uncomfortable when her co-workers talk about the new setup. How can you handle your boss's request? Or do you have a bigger problem demanding your attention?

• • •

If you want to solve problems like these, you have to understand whether coaching, counseling, or mentoring is called for and how best to use the technique. That way, not only can you solve the specific dilemmas but you can move beyond them to continue performance improvement—and win management's recognition.

Coaching

CHAPTER 1

Your Role as Coach

COACHING IS THE PROCESS by which individuals gain the skills, abilities, and knowledge they need to develop themselves professionally and become more effective in their jobs. When people are coached, they can increase both their performance in their current jobs and their potential to do more in the future.

Coaching has received much attention in recent years, as companies hire professional coaches—usually retired executives or consultants with psychological training—to prepare managers and executives with high potential to take on greater responsibility within their organizations. Experts estimate that there are more than 10,000 professional coaches worldwide. A 1999 study of human resources professionals found that 90 percent of U.S. companies offered some form of coaching to top executives, for the purpose of leadership development and/or ensuring success after promotions or hire. Other uses for coaching are improved teamwork, improved relationships with peers, and reduced conflict.

Not only are companies offering coaches to executives and managers, but they are being asked for them by their employees. At one time, needing an industrial psychologist as an executive coach might be an indictment of poor management or leadership capability. No more. Managers and executives have come to recognize how a coach, internal or external, can help them identify their strengths and weaknesses, set goals, and discover creative answers to operational problems. Some gurus have attributed the interest of managers in having their own coach to the use of 360-degree feedback programs that identify unexpected interpersonal shortcomings. Whatever has prompted this importance placed on coaching, it is also responsible for greater recognition of the manager's role in employee job success.

Managers who master the skill of coaching find that it can boost the performance of workers by making clear to them what they should do and how they should best do it (think *instruction*), positively reinforce good work (think *praise*), and find ways to redesign jobs or increase employee contribution (think *empowerment* or *shared leadership*).

But increased employee performance isn't the sole benefit of coaching. When employees receive regular feedback from you, you won't have to worry about their being surprised and defensive at performance appraisal time. And the good rapport that coaching creates should help reduce complaints from your employees. Everything should run more smoothly—or, at least, as well as it can in today's leaner organizations where crisis management is often the order of the day. Certainly, you won't have to worry so much about getting demerits from senior management for "people problems."

Instead, upper management will likely recognize your people skills. While it might seem that people skills don't get the attention they deserve, so long as they result in high productivity, which translates into decreased operating costs or increased income, then coaching can enhance your reputation.

Your Beliefs About People

Coaching begins with an assumption: Most employees are eager to do well, to please their managers, and to achieve as high a position as they can with the company. As coach, you can ensure that your employees do all three. Should this approach to performance management be contrary to your own mindset about your employees—that is, should you believe that, on the contrary, your employees don't care about their work, have no interest in pleasing you, and are quite happy going nowhere in their careers—then you may want to stop reading this section of the book and proceed to Section II, on counseling. Better still, continue to read.

Motivational research conducted by psychologist Abraham Maslow and others shows that most people have a genuine interest in bettering themselves and in achieving all that they can. You don't have to threaten or force employees to get them to increase their performance so long as you give them reason to do so. You don't have to offer financial rewards or promotions. Instead, by giving your employees the opportunity to increase their employability, by offering them assignments and providing training to help them grow beyond their current positions, and by creating an environment in which they feel free to share their ideas and will get recognition for those ideas and their efforts to implement them, you are contributing to that sense of job satisfaction that can increase job performance.

And managers who are willing to coach their employees to realize their full potential and build their confidence will gain loyalty and respect. If you doubt the worth of this statement, what do you think is the value of the following?

- Employees who are oriented to corporate values and business intent and strategies
- Employees who are clear about your expectations for their performance and their priorities
- Employees who accept responsibility for their performance and are motivated to exceed their current performance

These benefits, too, come from coaching.

Managerial Resistance

Many managers argue that they don't have the time to coach employees. But coaching is not time-intensive; rather, the problems that result from *not* coaching can become time-intensive. If you don't continually work to develop your employees' skills, the additional work of operating in a leaner organization will wind up on your shoulders.

Another reason managers give for not coaching is that their employees don't need the added attention; they already know what is expected of them. But ask yourself, How little will it cost me to confirm this by assuming the role of coach in meetings with my employees? Or, put another way, How much will it cost me if I am wrong and my employees truly don't have a clear idea of my expectations or priorities?

Still another excuse that managers give for not coaching is that their employees should take responsibility for their own job development and their own careers. Yes, employees *are* ultimately responsible for their job development and careers. But managers who help to increase employees' employability receive two benefits: employees are better prepared to take on more responsibility, and they gain employee loyalty. Efforts to train employees beyond the level of their current jobs have been found to build greater employee commitment to corporate values and mission, as well as build a better relationship between employees and supervisors.

It doesn't matter if the employee is on-site every day of the week or just one day of the week. Just as you can supervise by phone and e-mail a worker who operates from home, you can coach that individual by phone or e-mail (assuming there are no serious work problems or bad habits that need to be addressed in a face-to-face conversation). Think of those practices that are important for supervising someone off-site: (1) you have to set clear expectations, (2) you need to agree on performance standards and how results will be monitored, (3) you need to provide feedback on performance, and—most important—(4) you need to communicate, communicate, communicate. The first two practices enable you to provide the telecommuter with the third practice, feedback (think *coaching*). The work insights all depend on the last practice—the quality and frequency of your communications with the individual.

Put down that report you were reading and concentrate on what the off-site worker is telling you. Show the individual the respect he or she deserves by not doing anything else when you're on the phone with him or her. If you discover a problem in the making, then set a quiet time for you and the telecommuter to talk on the phone or, better yet, ask the individual to come to the office. Even better, if it is possible, schedule one day each month to meet the individual in person so he or she has the same in-person coaching time with you as you give on-site employees.

And for managers who argue that coaching has no place in today's horizontal organizations characterized by teamwork, that's not so. With today's cross-functional teams, coaching is the responsibility not only of every team leader but also of every team member. All team members have a responsibility to facilitate the work of other members by helping them understand the scope of the project, assisting them in fulfilling their responsibilities to the group, and sharing their experiences and insights to help get the tasks done.

As coach, team leaders help create the mission statement and the ground rules by which the team will operate to achieve its mission. Often, too, team leaders are responsible for the group's administrative details, like drawing up meeting agendas and recording and then distributing the minutes of each session. But, most important, team leaders need to help the group overcome any obstacles in achieving the goal— just as you as coach help your staff members accomplish their jobs by monitoring their progress on each assignment.

The Five Principles of Coaching

As a manager, you need five principal coaching skills. These are the same skills that the best sports coaches have.

1. *Ability to Gather Information.* A good coach knows how to get information from an individual without making that person feel as if he or she were being interrogated. Information is important in making numerous decisions, ranging from whether to hire a particular job candidate to identifying a skill deficiency, to uncovering confusion about how to do a particular job, to finding out an employee's interests and aspirations so as to redesign the job and thereby stimulate above-standard performance.

2. *Ability to Listen to Others.* Asking the right questions means little if you don't listen to the replies. A good coach is able to listen with a "third ear," paying as much attention to the speaker's nonverbal signals and body posture as to his or her words in order to determine the feelings behind the response as well as its truthfulness. That same coach also knows how to use body language to communicate interest in what the speaker has to say. Throughout this book, there will be many guidelines offered about what to say and how to say it, whether you are coaching, counseling, or mentoring. Remember that verbal or body language means little if you don't truly listen to the person on the other side of the conversation.

Listening falls into three categories: (1) listening in bursts of energy, tuning in when the other party touches on a subject of interest or agreement, and then tuning out as he or she moves on to a point of disinterest or disagreement; (2) listening to the words spoken but not hearing their implications or the feelings behind the words; and (3) listening empathetically, hearing not only the words but also making an effort to grasp the speaker's thoughts and feelings. The best coaches practice *empathetic listening.* (As you will read later, the best counselors and mentors also suspend their own thoughts and feelings to give full attention to the individuals with whom they are talking.)

3. *Awareness of What's Happening Around You.* You should talk frequently to your employees to see if there are morale problems or other causes of distress in the workplace that could lower productivity or generate attitudinal problems or, better, notice signs that an employee is not only willing but also ready and able to assume more responsibility. Let's see how one coach keeps the lines of communication open.

ADRIENNE: HER "OPEN DOOR" POLICY

Adrienne is good at coaching, although the terms *manager* and *leader* are more often used to describe her strong points. Still, Adrienne is a coach, in that she meets weekly with her team of copywriters to discuss progress on marketing assignments and to share with her team compliments from her boss and others in the organization about the fine work they are doing. But Adrienne doesn't limit her communications with her staff to these group meetings.

Adrienne's staff members know that all they need do is knock on her door to discuss a work problem or even a personal problem. Adrienne will also often stop at people's desks to chat about some project or other they are completing. Her goal is to gather information about any problems they are encountering, either because of skill gaps they have or difficulties they encounter within the very political consumer products company in which they work.

Such information, then, can become the basis for her one-on-one monthly meetings with each of her staff members, in which she talks about concerns either she or the employee has about the work. Sometimes these sessions lead to registering the staff member in a training program to develop his skills; sometimes they call for a meeting among Adrienne, the staff member, and the product manager to be sure that the copywriting department and product management are united in their goals; and sometimes they simply enable Adrienne to tell an employee just how fine a job he or she is doing. Whatever the result, Adrienne considers the sessions valuable because they keep her in touch with her staff's needs (including the need for an occasional pat on the back)—something that might not otherwise happen, given the many distractions in the office, if these exchanges were less formal.

4. *Ability to Instruct Employees.* A good coach is able to train employees, either singly or in a group. Even before that, the coach is able to conduct a training-needs assessment to determine gaps in knowledge that must be filled. (For more on this subject, see Chapter 2).

5. *Ability to Give Feedback.* A good coach knows how important feedback is in improving the performance of any employee. There is no such thing as having too little time to praise someone for a job well done or to provide corrective feedback, including suggestions that tell the employee you believe he or she is capable of doing the work right. In short, a good coach doesn't allow today's lean organizational structure to provide an excuse for *not* offering positive reinforcement of good work or corrective feedback in a positive manner.

MIKE AND THE SELF-IMPORTANT SUBORDINATE

Many managers wait until the first performance review to coach a new employee, which can allow bad habits to develop. That's what happened to Mike, head of a new product division in a major high-tech firm. He supervises five business-development teams. His newest recruit is Cora, who formerly had her own business and could crow about five patents attached to her name.

Mike hadn't thought it was necessary to review proper business protocol with someone with Cora's background. But it became clear very soon that Cora, with her entrepreneurial experience, considered herself a privileged person. She would arrive several hours late and leave an equal number of hours early. There were long lunch dates with customers, reputedly for the purpose of discussing a product idea, and, supposedly to stay abreast of industry developments, equally long visits to customers of her former company. She was late and, worse, didn't attend meetings Mike held with his direct reports to discuss product and marketing plans. Mike tried to ignore the problem—until he heard complaints from Cora's product team and his own supervisor.

Cora's team members felt that they weren't getting any direction. Cora called meetings and then canceled them minutes beforehand. Assignments given weren't reviewed; often, they were forgotten or, worse, reassigned to others on the same team. Cora claimed that her distraction was due to some family problems, but her employees began to wonder. "Cora seems so out of it," Jeff said to Nellie, a colleague, unaware that Mike could hear their conversation. "She may be on something," Nellie replied. "She can't seem to focus for more than a few minutes on anything."

Overburdened with work, Mike would have ignored the situation if his own boss, Claire, hadn't talked to him. She pointed to a list of tasks that Cora was letting slide. So, less than a month after Cora joined the company, Mike met with her to discuss the state of affairs. Mike felt that Cora had to be reminded that she no longer was her own boss—she had obligations to the company and needed to focus on these.

The meeting seemed to go well. Cora pointed to a sick mother as the cause of her inattention to corporate issues, explained also that she had commuting problems, but offered to stay late to make up for her late arrivals and came up with a plan to work with an outside firm to catch up on missed deadlines on several projects.

Mike felt that he had succeeded in putting Cora on a narrow but straight road to success. And he put the problem out of his mind. This was a big mistake, as you will discover later in this book. But let me just say here that coaching is an ongoing responsibility, demanding regular meetings with staff members—regardless of their job performance—to demonstrate that their work is important to the organization.

When is feedback needed? The answer is all the time, not only when errors occur repeatedly in an employee's work or his or her performance doesn't meet expectations. While you should schedule regular coaching sessions with your employees to ensure that work meets—if not exceeds—goals, you want to meet and coach a staff member in particular when his or her work habits disturb you, when progress has been made on a work problem and acknowledgment is in order, when a problem unrelated to the employee's effort surfaces and the individual needs guidance, and when an employee asks you how he or she is doing. The last situation is especially important, since it suggests that you have failed to be clear to the employee about his or her job responsibilities or the quality of his or her work.

The Duties of a Coach

The term *coach* is associated with on-the-job training, but the *role* of coach involves more than training, although that is part of the coach's responsibility. Besides offering training, as coach you are responsible for:

- Acting as a role model for higher performance.
- Hiring the best employees.
- Creating a work culture in which employees have reason to be motivated.
- Clarifying expectations, both micro expectations associated with particular jobs and macro objectives tied to the organization's overall strategy and mission. Within a week of beginning a job, an employee should have met with you to agree on three to five (and no more than five) goals to work toward. Otherwise, the next duty is of little value.
- Providing regular feedback on your employees' behaviors that will put them on the right performance track and keep them there. Understand that this is a two-way communication process. You don't just

give feedback; you also ask for feedback from employees on how they are doing, any problems that have been encountered, and any confusions they have about the priorities that have been set.

•   Applying the performance-evaluation process not only as a measurement tool tied to raises but also as a developmental aid.

•   Providing the training and resources employees need to improve their performance.

•   Praising, praising, and praising some more to reinforce positive performance.

Let's look at these in greater depth.

Acting as a Role Model

Many managers see a coach solely in the sports context—as a Knute Rockne who calls the staff together and gives pep talks. Yes, this is part of being a coach, but there is much more. Certainly a managerial coach should be supportive and nurturing, ready with know-how to help employees succeed in their jobs and with recognition when they do. But managerial coaches, unlike their sports equivalents, perform many of the same tasks as team members from the start of the workday to its end, five days a week, role modeling work behavior for their employees.

You probably remember the expression "Do what I say, not what I do." As a managerial coach, you don't want your staff members to snicker and attribute such a phrase to you. For instance, you can't tell your employees that honesty is important in their reports to you yet you lie to senior management about your department's quarterly results. Or you might talk to your work team about the importance of customer service, inside and outside the organization, yet be known as the manager who never returns customer calls.

One employee told me about her manager who was forever ranting about the need for everyone to be at his or her desks by 9:00 A.M., yet the manager would too frequently stroll into the office after 9:30. She always had a reason, from transportation foul-ups to late nights working at home, and though her reasons might even have been legitimate, over time her behavior belied her words and her message about punctuality became an office joke. So, you have to recognize that when you are in the field (to continue with the sports metaphor), your staff will be watching your plays *and* emulating them. Be sure that they are plays that you would want to see emulated.

One other point: Don't make promises to employees if you don't plan to keep them. Be particularly wary of promises to maintain open and honest communications, to provide each employee with the opportunity to reach his or her potential, the chance for empowerment, and the offer of recognition and reward for excellence and outstanding performance. Your credibility is important to successful coaching, so be sure you can deliver on your promises.

Hiring the Best

Yes, in a sense, coaching begins even before the individual is on staff, as you select those people who have the job skills and experience and, maybe most important of all, the potential to move beyond the current job. In short, you want to hire for your department individuals who fit this profile:

- They are continually in search of more knowledge and are eager to develop new skills.
- They won't accept the current way of doing things. They have their own ideas and challenge existing practices.
- They want to know the whys and wherefores of things. In keeping with their desire to find more efficient or effective ways of doing their work, they won't accept anything without explanation.
- They are restless and dissatisfied if they don't have challenges. If they have finished their own work, they are the employees who offer a helping hand to co-workers or to their boss.

Creating the Right Climate

To be successful in your role as coach, you need to create a climate that reflects a free and open exchange of ideas and is seen as a learning environment. Your goal is to create an energizing atmosphere that stimulates employees' internal motivations to produce. You create such an environment by:

- *Keeping Threats, Even Implied Ones, Out of Your Conversations.* For instance, never say to an employee, "If you, Phil, want to succeed in this job, you had better. . . ." Or, worse, "Debbie, if you want to *keep* your job, you had better. . . ." Such comments are seen as implied or overt threats, and they will be met with denial, flight, or anger—all responses that can undermine the time and effort you spend training Phil or Debbie to use their full potential.

• *Building Rapport with Your Employees.* I'm not suggesting that you lunch daily with your employees or go for drinks after work. But you should demonstrate a caring attitude toward your employees, a willingness to put aside the stack of papers on your desk to discuss personal problems as well as work-related ones. A manager earns the trust of his or her employees by demonstrating an honest interest in them and fostering open and candid two-way communication. And a wise manager keeps the employees' problems confidential.

• *Developing a Flexible Management Style.* Just as you wouldn't use the same response style for every situation you confront, you should not use the same management style in working with the diverse members of your group. Employees are individuals with individual needs. As a manager, you should treat all your employees fairly but not necessarily the same. For instance, an employee who is new will need more direction than a more experienced employee. Likewise, a five-year veteran in the department who is taking on a new responsibility will need more direction than another five-year veteran who is doing the same work she has been doing for the past five years.

• *Supporting an Employee's Effort.* When you are discussing skill gaps or the need for additional training or other developmental work, you want to come across as a cheerleader, not as an evaluator. You want your remarks to be perceived as helpful feedback rather than as criticism. Keep in mind that the phrase *constructive criticism* is an oxymoron. Provide constructive feedback instead. Keep your remarks upbeat, pointing to both those things your employee has done right and to those things he or she did wrong. And end your comments with a statement that reassures the employee that you have confidence in his or her ability to do the task well or to complete the assignment on schedule or to learn how to use the newest software program.

• *Looking at Mistakes as Learning Opportunities.* You should point to a problem and tell the employee, "Okay, this isn't working. What can we learn from our approach here?" The message you send to the employee is that mistakes can be valuable for teaching, thus supporting your learning environment. The employee won't be frightened to test out his or her ideas because the individual will know that you recognize that not all efforts will be successful—in short, that there is failure associated with risk, but that mistakes do not mean that the risk taker is a failure.

•   *Separating the Behavior from the Person.* You want an employee to come away from the coaching with his or her self-esteem intact. Let's say that a member of your team dominates the discussion. In coaching him, you might tell the individual, "You often have good ideas, Sam, but we lose others' ideas when you monopolize the team discussions." Sam will leave the meeting with the feeling that you appreciate his effort but are aware that his behavior needs to be changed and that he should learn to listen as much as talk at staff meetings.

•   *Recognizing Improvement.* Just as you don't want to destroy an employee's self-esteem by criticizing some behavior or some work the individual has done, you also want to build up that person's self-esteem. When he or she has made an effort to improve performance, this staff member's self-esteem and further efforts to improve can be encouraged with your acknowledgment of those improvements. Even small improvements should be recognized since this feedback can stimulate the employee to work on greater changes.

•   *Building on Strengths and Assets.* You can energize employees by letting them know that you recognize their strengths. It doesn't matter if you know that Carol occasionally is careless, or comes in late, or has a hard time writing proposals. When Carol completes a vendor comparison and comes up with several ways to save the department money, it's important to tell her how much her efforts are appreciated. After this, Carol certainly will be more amenable to discussing her tardiness or carelessness and to taking your instruction on how to put together better proposals.

Clarifying Expectations and Providing Feedback

If there is one situation that can keep your department from attaining high performance, it is confusion among employees about your expectations. You need to be specific not only about the tasks that have to be done and the priorities for assignments but also about the game plan for the team. That game plan is made up of several elements:

•   *Department Mission and Operating Goals.* Ideally, these should have been developed with the group. But periodically you should remind the staff about them, perhaps in regular status reports, noting progress toward achieving them.

- *Corporate Strategy and Mission.* If you want to get the most from your employees, you need to let them know as much as possible about the bigger corporate picture. That includes information about the company's financial position. Whether news is good or bad, knowing the situation is better for employees than their speculating about it.

- *Corporate Values.* Your staff should know what initiatives senior management has identified to help the company achieve a competitive advantage. Don't just read the list as written by top management. Discuss with your team how these values translate to behaviors that are part of every member's job. When employees know these values and have a clear idea of their role in the drama at hand, they are better prepared to understand and accept the feedback you give them, even when negative. Here's how to make that feedback valuable:

- *Plan what you will say.* This ensures that you don't allow any personal frustration to creep into your remarks.

- *Be patient.* What may be very simple for you (because you have done this kind of work for many years) may not be so simple to someone doing it for the first time. In time, with your help, an employee may master the job and even find a more efficient way to do the same work.

- *Be specific, not general.* You want the individual to have enough details to be able to make specific changes in behavior. It's not enough, for instance, to tell an employee to "think more globally." Rather, you can suggest that he "stay in touch with co-workers in our European subsidiary—we need to be alert to synergistic opportunities. We missed out on signing a contract with that multinational because we didn't know that our European division had contacts with its British executive director." Or, rather than tell an employee to be "more customer-focused," you should say, "I was disappointed that we haven't done a customer focus group this quarter. If we are to stay abreast of our customers' needs, we need to hold these meetings at least quarterly."

- *Be descriptive, not evaluative.* You should be specific about a situation, not judgmental. Let's assume that one of your staff members did a poor job meeting and greeting some potential clients yesterday. Instead of telling him, "You really messed up yesterday," you should say, "You need to do your homework before clients visit. You didn't know. . . ."

- *Be sensitive to your feelings at the time.* You may destroy the rapport you have built with an employee if you give negative feedback when you are angry. The temptation to relieve your own frustrations by blaming this person may be great, but it's a temptation that you should resist. The short-term satisfaction you achieve doing this could have long-term repercussions as you destroy the relationship between you and this employee.

• *Use words, body language, and tone of voice to show that your intention is to help.* You want your employee to listen to your feedback, even if it is critical of performance. Your communication style will make a difference.

• *Focus on behavior that can be changed.* You will only frustrate your employees by identifying shortfalls over which they have no control. To keep from falling into this trap, never make assumptions about a situation. Begin any discussion about some work undone or finished behind schedule by asking "who," "what," "where," and "how." Note that I haven't suggested that you use "why" questions; they can easily put an individual on the defensive. "Why" questions are best saved for follow-up times, to get more insight after you have a clearer idea of the cause of a situation.

• *Show how the job should be done.* You don't only describe how the work was done wrong; where possible, also show how it should be done. For example, it isn't enough to tell an employee, "You goofed. Try again; maybe next time you'll get it right."

• *Listen to the employee's explanation.* Sometimes you will get an excuse. But there may also be plausible reasons for a problem to exist that you aren't aware of. If so, say, "Thank you."

• *Give your employee some extra time.* You know that you have to give constructive feedback, pointing up those aspects of an individual's work that were especially well done to ensure their repetition, as well as noting faults in a job done. But once you have given the feedback, don't just walk away. Give the employee a little personal time to explain why he did the job as it was done. Wouldn't you want some extra time to explain your reason for approaching work other than the way your boss wants?

Applying the Performance Appraisal as a Developmental Tool

Employee evaluations are perfect opportunities for you to put on your coaching hat and discuss ways in which your employees can improve their work. Many managers forget the developmental side of evaluations.

Good appraisals don't only assess employees' performance; they also identify opportunities for improvement.

Too often at the end of an appraisal year, managers talk only about the rating for the past year and its fiscal consequences. Instead, in your coaching role you should lay the groundwork for next year's performance appraisal; for instance, discuss an employee development plan that addresses the problem areas that kept the individual from achieving his or her outcomes in the past year. And such development plans are as important to your high performers as they are to your average or poor performers. If an employee has consistently exceeded standards and done so for several years, she is probably frustrated by the lack of opportunities for promotion or new challenges. This is the time, then, to discuss training programs that develop skills that could lead to advancement—in other words, to increasing her employability.

The end-of-year meeting isn't the only time you can address these issues. At every quarterly review, you might want to work out development programs with your employees to minimize any shortcomings that are likely to cause them to fall behind in the goals set for the year. In the next chapter, the role of appraisals in coaching will be discussed in greater detail, as one of two ways to add stretch to your employees' performance. The other way involves conducting training assessments. For both, the key is to create development plans for your employees.

Taking on Your Developmental Responsibilities

You help your employees to grow professionally by reviewing their job descriptions in order to define the core competencies of their jobs. With this information, you can then determine if each job holder possesses these competencies or not. A competency is a skill, ability, area of knowledge, set of experiences, or attitude; and it is a manager's responsibility, in his or her role as coach, to determine if members of the team lack any competencies. This assessment is done, first, by breaking down each competency into specific behaviors, then by observing staff members at work to see what they can and cannot do.

The findings then become the basis of developmental plans for staff members. Successful plans focus on no more than two or three areas for development and contain specific time frames for accomplishment. Of course, each skill or area of knowledge should be well defined. Within the plan, too, the means for developing that skill or knowledge area should be spelled out. It makes no sense, for instance, to create a development plan for an employee that has her attending night school to become more proficient in some new office technology when there are no funds to pay for the training.

The developmental plan need not involve off-site training. An employee can grow in his or her job with customized assignments, ranging from such simple ones as completing a self-development tape or acting as a buddy to a newcomer to more complex ones like being given a temporary lateral transfer or being asked to attend a conference, to those with great stretch like working with mergers, acquisitions, or new divisions that are growing to improve business results or with a cross-functional group at an offshore location.

Where a development plan calls for you to act as a trainer yourself, you should:

• *Present the big picture.* Your employees know their jobs, but they may not know how they contribute to the bigger corporate picture. Let them know their role's influence on the company's strategic direction if there is one.

• *Provide sufficient time for an employee to develop the new skill.* We all seem to have big workloads. You can't expect your employees to immediately learn new skills or acquire added capabilities overnight, so any training effort should provide enough time for employees to master the new material.

• *Start from where the employee currently is.* Don't overwhelm the employee in providing instruction, but also don't treat him or her as incompetent because of a need for training. Treat the person as a competent human being who has proved to be a successful learner in the past and can absorb this new training as well.

• *Present your instruction in the form of a problem to be solved.* This may actually be the case when the training is designed to fill a knowledge or skill gap. Let's say that you have an employee who does less than well in making a critical presentation to a client. If you don't want the incident to be repeated, you have to meet with the employee, provide constructive feedback about his or her performance, and together decide on how he or she is to perfect the capability, whether it is part of the employee's current job or represents an expansion of responsibilities and potential for advancement.

• *Find a place that is free from interruptions in which to do your training.* Set aside at least an hour, but no more than two hours, because employees can become too fatigued to absorb instructions over a longer time span.

• *Demonstrate the desired outcome.* The employee has to know why the work is to be done as you instruct. Taking him or her through the process to completion should help make that clear. While the employee may identify over time a more effective or efficient way to do the same work, initially you want your worker to follow your instructions carefully.

When you show someone how to perform a task, the training should approximate the conditions of the job. Use the actual equipment and, ideally, install the equipment in a space similar to that in which it will be located when he or she is working with the equipment. This will make the adjustment to the real thing easier.

• *Plan for follow-up.* As a part of your one-on-one training, you should come back several times to ensure that the individual is completing the task as you have instructed. In particular, you need to look out for shortcuts that may slip into the work and that could lead to quality problems or, worse, raise safety problems. For instance, in one plant, workers found that removing a safety shield on a die cutter increased productivity. Unfortunately, it also increased the likelihood of an employee's being severely injured. When supervisor Dick explained to his new hire how to use the machine, it never occurred to him to explain why there was a shield in place. So it was very fortunate that he followed up about an hour later. He found that Jim had removed the shield. Worse, the removal was a suggestion from another worker. The incident became the basis of a group coaching meeting to teach the staff safer operation of the plant's equipment.

• *Provide support.* Sometimes a buddy can be assigned to someone learning a new skill, provided you have tested the buddy to be sure that he or she knows how to complete the task correctly. But in addition to assigning a buddy, you might want to leave the trainee with written instructions. Type the instructions double-spaced or with large margins; give the trainee the sheet during training, and allow him or her to make notes in the margins.

Praising as a Means of Reinforcing Good Performance

Praise is included separately on the list of coaching duties to indicate its importance as well as to differentiate it from feedback. Feedback may be part of praise, but it also points to those aspects of an employee's work that were not done well, suggesting how future jobs should be handled.

Praise, on the other hand, is designed primarily to recognize an employee's outstanding performance and to motivate him or her to repeat such performance.

The problem with praise is that it is very rarely given. Most managers seem more inclined to give criticism than praise. One manager even told me, "I don't have the time to give praise." I know that this manager is extremely busy, but the employee deserved the praise and sought some confirmation that his extra effort was recognized. Because the praise was not forthcoming, to this day that employee goes out of his way to tell others on staff how much he dislikes his boss. Worse, he has gone from being a better-than-average employee to being a screw-up, which many co-workers believe is an effort to get his supervisor's attention. He seems to maintain an internal auditing system, and his calculations show that the boss still owes him one.

MARTA: WHEN "PRAISE" LOWERS MORALE

There is praise and then there is praise. Marta is well aware of the value of praise and would argue that she praises her employees, but she has yet to learn how to use praise effectively. Or, for that matter, what is good praise and what is bad praise. Let me share with you some typical situations in which Marta offered praise to staff members.

First, there was the time when Tim, one of her staff members, completed a research study a few days ahead of schedule. He had worked late several nights to get the report done and ready for her final review before she submitted it to the product manager. As he proudly presented it to Marta, she told him, "I'm so pleased that you completed the report a few days before it is due. Now I'll have some extra time to read it and check to be sure you haven't forgotten to include any critical information." Tim left wondering why he had put in the extra effort to complete the task ahead of time. Marta had used the occasion only to rub salt into wounds caused by earlier criticism of Tim's past reports.

Second, let's take the time that Harry's marketing campaign brought in 10 percent more sales than projected. Marta announced this fact to her staff at its Monday morning action meeting. Everyone was delighted when Marta announced that she had even bought doughnuts and would be providing coffee for all to celebrate the occasion. The staff shared in Harry's success and there were lots of compliments, but the group's enthusiasm quickly waned when Marta casually remarked to a staff member, "Harry's fortunate that he made those numbers.

His other campaigns haven't been as successful." She wondered why the party atmosphere suddenly died, but the reason clearly showed on Harry's face.

Third, Marta would be at a meeting and react enthusiastically to suggestions from staff members. The problem is that her responses were so ambiguous that the group had no clear idea what it was that Marta was so pleased about so that they could work beyond that. There were comments like, "Interesting remark," "Good," or "OK." Because Marta never elaborated, the puzzled group spent much time talking at these meetings and little time thereafter following through on the "Good" thoughts or "OK" suggestions.

But the worst example was the phony praise that often came from Marta. The staff knew that each day Marta would stop by her administrative assistant's desk to compliment the woman on her latest outfit. The phoniness of the daily remark was evident in her intonation and the minimum attention she gave the woman as she passed her cubicle on the way to her own office.

What, then, is good praise? It is sincere, concise, and specific. And it is delivered in a manner that communicates enthusiasm for the work done or appreciation of the extra effort expended by the employee. For example, "Jim, you really helped us achieve our goal on time by working last weekend." This compliment points up the importance of the employee's activity and, better yet, his contribution to the department's goal or mission. Whether by inflection or intonation, be sure there is no hidden message in good praise—for example, that Jim should have spent his weekend on the task or that you think that Jim had to work over the weekend because he goofs off most workdays.

As coach, you want your praise to encourage further efforts—in the same way as the climate you create in the department is positive and supports increased performance, or that your feedback is constructive and communicates your faith in employees' ability to learn new skills or realize their goals or meet the standards, or that you make the appraisal process a means of adding stretch to the goals your employees work to attain.

Your employees are your most appreciable asset. In the next chapter, you'll learn how to uncover that potential we all talk about our employees having but that they so seldom realize.

CHAPTER 2

Coaching as an Ongoing Responsibility

MANAGERS, SUPERVISORS, AND TEAM LEADERS know that people are their most appreciable asset. In coaching your employees or team members, your intent is to increase the worth of your organization's human capital. As a good coach, you are a watcher, using your observational skills to determine the gap between employee performance and potential and to close that gap by developing your employees' full capability. After all, you know that as these gaps are closed and your employees fully develop their abilities, they could assume some of your responsibilities, freeing you to work on more visionary projects. In today's lean organizations, managers who don't look for and coach their employees to their fullest capability will have a problem, too. Compare the coaching performance of Steve with that of Sid.

> STEVE AND SID: COACHING FROM FEAR VS. COACHING FOR
> EXCELLENCE
>
> Plenty of talented employees have worked on Steve's team, but he doesn't really want to coach them beyond their ability to do their current jobs well. Why? He's afraid that if he adds stretch to their jobs they might in time want his position—and possibly get it. Consequently, all his bright, promising employees have either moved on to greener pastures or are in search of them. When Steve is away on business or vacation or out ill, his crew's productivity suffers because there's no one able to give direction. Steve frequently complains that he has been in the same position for ten years, but actually he is fortunate that he

30

wasn't laid off during the last downsizing. Senior management had wanted to keep only those managers who get high performance from their crews. And Steve is not one of these.

The company's executives want managers like Sid, who is constantly developing his crew members and runs the top crew in the organization. Sid believes that when he has high performance expectations of his employees and communicates these, his crew will work to meet them. Yes, Sid's department has a problem keeping workers, but for only the best of reasons. As his employees have demonstrated their capability, they have moved on to head up crews of their own or to take on special projects or to assume higher positions within other departments. Does Sid mind? Their departure has caused short-term problems, but he has enjoyed seeing the individuals he has helped develop become recognized formally. Besides, as these crew members have grown, so has Sid's worth to the company.

How Sid Encourages Stretch

Sid doesn't just start with good employees. He helps develop his stars by:

- Conducting training-needs assessments as soon as his employees come on board. He carefully reviews résumés and meets the first day with new hires to identify gaps in information and knowledge, holes that he immediately fills to ensure that newcomers pull their weight as quickly as possible.
- Incorporating developmental planning in his quarterly and annual performance appraisals, adding stretch, but stretch within reach of his crew members.
- Communicating his belief in his employees' abilities.

Let's see how Sid makes his employees, like Brad, for example, believe they can do much more than they thought they could. When Brad first came aboard, he seldom spoke at team meetings, lacking confidence in his ideas. It was clear to Sid that Brad had tremendous technical ability but wasn't comfortable speaking in public. Sid worked with Brad from the outset to encourage him to share his insights with the group. He met with Brad privately and discussed Brad's ideas with him, noting how valuable they could be to the group as a whole.

Sid also found opportunities for Brad to demonstrate his creativity to himself so he would feel secure enough to prove it to his co-workers. At first, the pace of discussion during Sid's crew's weekly meetings was too fast for Brad. So Sid slowed the pace enough to give Brad the time to articulate his ideas. Eventually, the group would learn to slow itself

> down to hear Brad out. Sid also found other teams in the plant in which Brad could make a major contribution but where the pace was slower so that Brad would not be intimidated when speaking out.
>
> With Sid's encouragement and support, Brad's confidence increased until he assumed his fair share of the brainstorming in the department's problem-solving meetings.

As a coach, you can motivate, inspire, and encourage your fast-trackers, but you must also build the confidence of your more timid talents—people like Brad. Your efforts will be repaid time and time again as these individuals use their newly discovered and nurtured talents to become new team superstars.

How to Start

The process begins even before one of your employees comes on board, as you sit with potential candidates for a job opening. As you interview the applicants, you will note gaps in knowledge or experience. The individual you ultimately hire may even lack experience in some aspect of the work or be unfamiliar with your own organization's work processes or procedures.

As a coach, your first task in shortening the learning curve for the new staff member, and ultimately building a staff of superstars, is not to get so preoccupied with your own work as to forget the need to fill these learning gaps when your new hire finally arrives. Besides introducing the new recruit to his or her co-workers or getting the individual started on his or her first assignment, you need to sit down with your new hire to review the job description and any concerns you might have about the individual's ability to handle the work. Your goal is to discuss openly and honestly your assessment of the individual's training needs. Together, you and your new employee need to develop the first of what will be several development plans during the individual's time in your department.

Bringing New Employees Up to Speed

Some of the new hire's deficiencies may be handled by assigning a buddy; other skill gaps may require enrollment in a training program or a course at a community college; still others may take something as simple as giving the employee your company's procedures manual and asking him or her to read it carefully. If the latter is your action, however, then you will want to meet with the employee after a week or so to ensure that the individual has indeed become familiar with all the procedures and understands not only the work procedures but the reasons for them.

Assessing Training Needs

What about employees who are already on staff and perhaps have been with you for some time? Take a pencil and paper and draw up a list of all your employees. Which ones lack some skill that would make the difference between their being a mediocre or average performer and a super-performer? Which ones have potential ability that has not been developed because their current jobs don't call for using those strengths? (As you look over your list, you may also identify one or two employees who have performance problems that, in your opinion, require more than training. These persons may need counseling if they are failing to meet job standards because of their attitudes or a personal problem. For help with them, see Section II of this book.)

Once you have identified those staff members who could perform at higher levels with more training, your next step is to meet with each one to discuss your conclusions. Don't wait until the next round of quarterly performance reviews. As quickly as possible, schedule one-on-one meetings with those individuals you believe have the potential to do more. Keep in mind that time lost is productivity lost.

Some employees will welcome the opportunity to discuss their training needs, particularly if they see additional training as a means of increasing their employability. Others will be concerned that your assessment threatens their job security. In discussing your observations with this latter group, you can tell them that the assessment was designed to alert you to the competencies—the skills, abilities, and knowledge—all your employees need. Your intent is not to find fault but to identify opportunities to improve each staff member's performance.

JUAN: HOW TRAINING CAN BRING UNEXPECTED BENEFITS

This is how Juan handled Lucy's response to his assessment that she needed to become more adept at using the company's customer database. During his visits to the work area, he had seen that Lucy often asked Blanche for help in choosing mailing lists for her product mailings. Sales were good, but Juan knew that Lucy was one of his best market managers, as familiar with her product line's customers as the product manager. Consequently, Juan couldn't help but believe that if Lucy had a better working knowledge of the database, then sales would be much, much higher.

He wanted her to work with Bruce to learn how the database could be used more to target product customers. Bruce, a veteran with the company, had worked with the outside consultant to design the system and consequently knew its ins and outs better than any other marketing manager. Lucy knew how to use the database to market her products well, but she wasn't familiar enough with it to apply her knowledge to another product line.

"Are you telling me that I'm not doing a good job?" Lucy asked in an offended voice, ready to cite capture rates and sales figures in self-defense.

"Not at all," said Juan. "On the contrary, I think you *are* doing a good job. But I think you have knowledge about the market that you aren't applying because you need to know more about how to use our lists. You could do a much better job, and I want to give you that opportunity."

Presented in these terms, the idea of working with Bruce, one of the best marketers in the company, seemed a compliment to Lucy. So she willingly agreed to call Bruce to discuss getting together for some meetings in which he would share his know-how about the system. Juan had already alerted Bruce that he wanted him to train one of the marketing managers.

How did Bruce feel about his new responsibility? Like Lucy, he also saw this as a compliment. After twelve years with the same company, with a great marketing record but nowhere to go up within the organization, he had begun to wonder if it wasn't time to look for a job elsewhere. Juan's call meant that he recognized Bruce's worth, and that caused Bruce to rethink his future plans. In the end, Bruce never did leave because Juan had other plans for him besides training Lucy on the database.

Enriching Others' Jobs and Reviewing Your Own

Juan had been asked to take on leadership of several new product teams. But he couldn't take advantage of this opportunity unless he could find ways to reduce his own day-to-day workflow. His solution was to delegate many of his routine tasks to Bruce. Enriching Bruce's job would keep his level of performance as high or higher and also free Juan to bring marketing input into many of the new product efforts that up until then had been exclusively product-driven.

When Juan had called Bruce to alert him to his helping Lucy, Juan had also set up a future meeting with Bruce at which he planned to delegate much of the routine work to Bruce. In time, Juan thought, he could empower Bruce, sharing leadership of the group with him. Maybe he would even make him into another coach for the team since Juan's intent was to make each of his marketing people super-performers. Juan began the process of enriching Bruce's job by reviewing his own. He determined which of his tasks he could give Bruce, either delegate or empower him to handle, depending on the nature of the work. As a part of that process, Juan also considered training that Bruce might need to assume these new responsibilities.

Should you want to enrich an employee's job and thereby motivate and add stretch to his or her performance, you need to consider more than training to help those employees make good decisions, solve problems on their own, and otherwise work with little or no guidance from you. Your intent in training is to access intellectual capital—in other words, the ability to use knowledge or ideas gained from one experience and transfer them to another.

This is the less formal means of adding stretch through coaching. Let's look now at how performance appraisals can be the basis for developmental plans that can be used to increase your employees' contributions to the company.

The Developmental Side of Performance Appraisals

Each year, after the year-end appraisal, you should sit down with your employees to discuss their strengths and weaknesses. If an employee has encountered problems during the past year, your objectives for the coming year will include some developmental goals. But if you are appraising one of your better workers, then you might want to create goals that add greater stretch than you would ordinarily suggest for your average performers. These goals could be formalized and made a part of the documentation, or they could be part of a wish list that you and your stars agree to work toward but do not include in the evaluation process.

Let's assume, for instance, that you are creating stretch goals for someone like Bruce, an employee who has consistently met or exceeded his supervisor's expectations and is feeling frustrated by the lack of opportunities for promotion or new challenges. Bruce would welcome goals that represent a challenge and that involve increasing his employability through training in skills, not for today's work but for tomorrow's opportunities for advancement.

Certainly you would want to make an effort to empower employees like Bruce. You would want to train them in problem solving and critical thinking, familiarize them with the broad picture, and communicate department goals and other critical issues. That should prepare such employees to make good decisions on their jobs. To begin, you might set down on the appraisal form some new standards by which Bruce's work would be measured, such as his participation in the department budgeting process or in product management/marketing meetings or the firm's efforts to expand marketing beyond your country's borders.

On the other hand, you and Bruce might agree that Bruce will work with you on budgeting for the department, replace you at some product management/marketing meetings, and become involved in department global marketing efforts, but you might not include these new responsibilities on the form. Rather, you would provide copies for Bruce and yourself, and you would tell Bruce that these were efforts you wanted him to focus on during the upcoming year. Should he meet the standards for performance as indicated on the appraisal form, as well as realize some or all of the stretch goals, you would acknowledge in the next evaluation his involvement in these efforts and evaluate his performance accordingly.

In developing stretch goals that employees will work toward, you must:

- *Involve the employee.* This point should be a given, but there are still managers who don't realize that they won't get buy-in for any plan if they attempt to impose their thinking on their employees. Even if you make a goal's completion critical to next year's performance evaluation, and achievement of that goal could benefit the employee, you're unlikely to get the person's cooperation if you don't make him or her a part of the planning process.

- *Begin at the beginning and go on from there.* Your task may begin with convincing some top performers that they can achieve their goal, as was the case with Brad, who lacked the self-confidence to speak up at team meetings yet was one of the most creative technicians on Sid's crew.

To get employee support for the stretch goals you want to set, *together with your employees* look at opportunities for growth within the department and determine your stars' interests or aspirations to make the challenges in a re-engineered job more stimulating. If there is a project that the employee can lead, sparing you from this responsibility, discuss it with him or her, pointing to the learning experiences that such an assignment can offer.

• *Write down your development plan.* It doesn't matter whether the plan is included on the formal appraisal form or simply written on a piece of paper attached to the form that you keep filed in your desk and review at quarterly reviews and other meetings with employees. If your involvement is critical to the achievement of specific development goals, you need to note that in writing, too. It's as important for you to assess progress on development goals designed to add stretch to an employee's abilities as it is to review periodically the progress made on more traditional goals.

Setting Stretch Goals

If you are having a problem with an employee in identifying stretch goals, as a part of the discussion ask him or her, "What can we do to help you maximize your capability?" The purpose of the question is to expand the employee's self-confidence and get the individual to begin to think outside the box that is the job description.

You might want to work with this employee to set two operational goals, both of which will use the individual's ability beyond what the current job requires. Ideally, one such goal might help create higher productivity, whereas the other might improve operations. To build commitment to achieving these two goals, you will need to focus on why these goals are important, giving factual reasons that reflect business return, not just feel-good results. Point to the opportunities and challenges associated with the goal.

As coach, you should make it clear that the stretch goals will likely demand further development on your employee's part. We've talked about the skills your stars will need to learn, but there may be other skills that they will have to unlearn, and they will need patience as they work to achieve these stretch goals that over time will benefit not only their organization but also themselves.

Motivating the Employee

As part of the stretch-goal exercise, discuss with employees why achieving the goal is important not only to the organization but also for them. Here is where good coaches excel. They know that energizing the workplace through coaching can motivate employees, but they also realize that intrinsic motivation comes from the employees' need to achieve their dreams and aspirations. A good coach is able to help people identify their intrinsic motivators and use them to optimize their performance, to the benefit of both the organization and themselves.

Questions that can help you unearth these inner motivators include:

- What really matters to you?
- How do you think you can be more valuable to the organization?
- What would make you happy professionally? Personally?
- Do you think your professional goals are ambitious enough?
- If you had the choice of any career or position within the organization, including mine, what would you want?
- What accomplishments would build your self-confidence or make you feel better about yourself?

Speak with honesty and listen with empathy so as to better understand how you can support the employees in achieving their aspirations. But never make promises.

ANNA: MAKING THE GOAL A REALITY

While participation in cross-functional teams might seem laborious, inviting an employee to represent you in a high-visibility team could be a stretch goal for that individual. So Anna, the head of marketing for an online food store, discovered.

Anna had been given two assignments on top of an already heavy workload. One task was to complete a key business proposal; the other was to join a team in developing a process for putting content on the company's Web site in a controlled, well-considered manner rather than the helter-skelter style currently used by the IT staff. Both responsibilities were important, but Anna realized that she couldn't do both well and also complete her daily workload. Weighing both the importance of the two tasks and her own strengths, Anna felt that she could make a bigger and better contribution to her organization by writing the business proposal.

To work on the process team, she chose Joe from among her staff of copywriters. Joe was a good writer, but he also was logical and, more important, knowledgeable about the company's products and its Web site. As critical, maybe more so, he had a need for a responsibility that would re-energize him after working for well over a month on a mundane product catalog. Anna could have asked Joe to take her place on the team and then focus on her own work, but she didn't. Still, she realized that it was important for Joe to speak with her about his contribution to the effort and the team's progress. So she set up a series of weekly feedback (think *coaching*) sessions with him to stay abreast of developments. On one or two occasions, her advice proved helpful to Joe in completing his stretch assignment—and Anna gained a new perspective on Joe's product knowledge and ability to work on a team.

When the project was successfully completed, Anna met with Joe to review the whole effort. She also used the occasion to discuss his taking a course in project management. Joe had demonstrated a strong understanding of teamwork, even the capability to lead a team, but there were project-management skills that he lacked that would hold him back from fully utilizing that ability. As Joe's coach, Anna was determined that he have every opportunity to use his talents.

Making the Goal a Reality

Let's look at how Anna can handle Joe's need for project-management skills. Anna is right in assuming that such knowledge will increase Joe's worth to the organization. To see that Joe understands her plan, she will need to meet with him to do the following things:

1. *Clarify the nature of the training.* Anna needs to point out how good project management can increase the likelihood of a team's achieving its mission. If Joe is to participate on more projects—something that he enjoys based on his recent experience—he will need to have the same skills as other members of such teams.

2. *Identify the goals or outcomes to be reached.* Anna needs to clarify her expectations—both the skills, abilities, and knowledge Joe will acquire from the training and how he can use those competencies to help the marketing team work more effectively with peers and customers on projects to identify food products that are marketable online.

3. *Facilitate the task.* In this instance, *facilitation* is, as defined in *Merriam Webster's Collegiate Dictionary*, "the act of making something

easier." Toward that end, Anna needs to listen (think *listen actively*) as Joe, a single father, expresses his concern about a semester-long evening course in project management. She will need to identify other training options that are available, such as a series of seminars over time or an online learning program.

4. *Set limitations.* Anna wants Joe to take responsibility for developing the project-management skills. At the same time, she does not want this opportunity to interfere with his daily work. So she has to be clear about what impact she will allow this training to have on his obligations to the department. These are her boundaries.

5. *Empower the employee.* This step may be the most important action Anna can take in coaching Joe—that is, providing an opportunity for him to develop a whole new skill set. Anna has to be prepared for Joe to ask to participate on team projects both within and outside the department so long as they do not interfere with his regular work. She also needs to point out to Joe that many of the skills that he will acquire he can use in the work he is doing on his own.

6. *Backtrack.* Once Anna and Joe have come up with a training plan to fill this gap, they should review the reason behind the training initiative and how the results will benefit both Joe and the department. The best way for Anna to be sure that she and Joe are in agreement is to have him state, in his own words, what they both have settled on. She might say to Joe, "I think this training is important to you and your contribution to the marketing group. I'd like to be sure that we are in agreement about your willingness to take on this training and how you can apply it. Could you summarize what we have both committed ourselves to?"

7. *Follow up.* At subsequent meetings with Joe, Anna needs to discuss what he has learned and how he is applying it.

Empowerment

Empowering your employees may be one of the most effective ways you have to add stretch to your employees' performance. The *E* word may have become something of a cliché in recent years, but the concept has never been more important as more and more companies demand greater productivity from their leaner organizations. When we empower employees, we lower decision making to the level of those who report to us. In coaching, when we empower employees, we also demonstrate trust in their ability to make the right decisions based on the training (think *mind stretch*) they have been provided. And when they make a mistake, we communicate, by supportive response, an awareness that even the best employees can goof up on occasion.

Many efforts at empowerment fail because employees are not given the skills, abilities, and knowledge they need to succeed. That's not so likely to occur when empowerment is part of a coaching effort to boost individual and organizational effectiveness, since training and development are important elements in coaching. To ensure that you are successful in encouraging employee stretch through empowerment, be sure to do the following:

• *Train your employees for the opportunity.* If you don't train them properly, your employees won't be able to handle the work and, equally troublesome, their self-confidence will erode, which will make it more difficult to get them to attempt similar stretches in the future.

• *Believe in your employees' abilities.* Trust your employees to do the job well. You have to show that you have faith in their ability to make the right decisions. That means being patient when they make the wrong decisions.

• *Be clear about your expectations.* This is even more important when you empower employees than when you give them routine tasks. Your employees won't be successful if they have no clear idea of the results you expect. The results serve as a destination by which they can set their course.

• *Build on employees' strengths.* To ensure that coaching isn't the only time your employees feel empowered, focus on those occasions when they do things right. Yes, they will make mistakes and you will need to make note of such incidents. But you don't want these mistakes to discourage your talented employees. In most instances, the problems can be resolved via training or further coaching.

• *Share information.* Put the project, assignment, or task that employees are being empowered to do within the bigger picture. Without that broader perspective, they aren't likely to make the right decisions.

• *Encourage employees to believe in their potential and capabilities.* Help them before problem-solving meetings to see the opportunities there. Get them to look at problems as challenges and to generate creative ideas, then to pursue these ideas in an effort to solve the problems.

• *Recognize your employees' accomplishments.* If you can't provide financial rewards, look for more challenging assignments to give them further opportunities to demonstrate their abilities. Or, better yet, redesign their jobs to make fuller use of their newly discovered talents and capabilities.

Recognize that not all of your employees will be successful in their first efforts at empowerment. As their coach, it is your responsibility to help them learn from their mistakes so they can go back and do better the next time. But use your judgment. Some employees lack the aptitude to be empowered. If you suspect after several efforts that this is the situation, give the individual one last chance. If he or she still isn't successful, then you may want to look at the individual's daily work and identify ways to redesign the job so that it makes the most of his or her other strengths.

On the other hand, when your top performers are successful, they blaze a trail for their co-workers to follow—a trail that can lead to increased performance for the whole department. In fact, as coach, you may want to convert your top talent into assistant coaches, responsible for helping your new and average employees improve their performance.

Departmental Stretch

You build stretch within the entire department when you assign your top performers the task of teaching others how to do their jobs well, as Juan did with Bruce. The greater responsibility enriches their jobs. It also brings home the important role that their performance plays in the department. This in itself can stimulate even greater performance from them.

You can also train your new and average employees to reach these higher levels of performance by observing how your superstars work and comparing their performance with the average workers. By identifying the behaviors that set the former apart from the latter, you have a syllabus for a training program that will help those mediocre performers achieve star performance.

Once you know what makes your good performers as good as they are, hold group meetings during which you share these insights with the group. Not only will you increase the productivity of the department but you will also influence the performance of key personnel, as one star learns from another and your department benefits from the synergy.

The same coaching skill that you use to make your employees do their work better can be used when your group operates as a team or when you lead a cross-functional group. If you think about the last occasion you led a team, you should be able to identify comparable coaching responsibilities you had as team leader. For example, you ensured that the team had the right players, you created ground rules or guidelines with the group to ensure that it operated smoothly, you helped develop a shared sense of purpose and wrote a mission statement that translated the purpose into goals, and you identified the resources the group needed, including training in team skills. Most important, during the course of a meeting, as a facilitator, you coached the team effort to success. As facilitator, you ensured that the discussion ran smoothly, occasionally identifying and remedying behavior that impeded the team's performance.

Jay is a manager who is a great team coach. Jay stimulates discussion by asking his group a general question, and he cuts off discussions that go off the subject by asking the group to summarize the conclusions to date. He brings quiet participants into the discussion by asking them general questions, and he can get the attention of two participants involved in a side conversation by asking one of the two a specific question.

I have been on community teams with Jay, and I know he gets high marks as team coach. How did he develop his skill? Jay points to a manager for whom he worked once who—yes—coached him both in his job and on teams!

Let's look more closely now at coaching sessions—at the conversations that make them.

CHAPTER 3

Let's Talk:
"Should I Say That?"

I MENTIONED THAT MANAGERIAL COACHING actually begins the day you hire a new employee, even during the job interview. Sports coaches have the advantage of seeing prospective team players on the field before they offer them a place on their team. That isn't the case for managerial coaches. While you can and should contact references, they aren't always willing to tell the truth about a former employee or even to speak with you about an individual. Some companies will give only the dates of employment and departure, job title, and salary.

That situation makes the decision to hire or not to hire dependent on the information you gain during your interview with the prospective candidate. I won't discuss here how you should conduct an interview; there are numerous books on the topic. Let me say only that you should indicate on each prospect's résumé any shortcomings in experience or skills you discover during the interview. Once you make your hiring decision, this information will be important in your role as coach, which should begin officially on the individual's first day on the job.

The Start of a Work Relationship

Leslie is head of sales and customer service for Jewelry Line, an online jewelry company headquartered in the Midwest. She recently hired Gladys as a customer-service representative. Gladys had the basic computer skills but she lacked familiarity with one software program that the company used to maintain account information. She also knew little about the company's product line. Leslie thought that Gladys could master the software program and, in time, would become familiar with the firm's products. Her skill gaps were shortcomings but they were more than made up for by Gladys's enthusiasm and evident willingness to do a good job. Most important, in Leslie's opinion, Gladys had a warm and friendly manner that past experience showed was well received by the company's telephone customers.

On Gladys's first day on the job, Leslie met with her to welcome her to the organization. She had already arranged for her new hire's desk to have all necessary supplies. She could have introduced Gladys to her co-workers, walked her to her work station, and left her there, but Leslie also wanted to review with Gladys some important corporate *and* department policies and to explain her desire to meet regularly with staff members in the quiet of her office to discuss their progress with the work. In other words, Leslie wanted to introduce Gladys to the idea of regular coaching sessions.

The meeting with Gladys began with a discussion of Jewelry Line's vision and mission and its place in the industry, including the names of some competitive firms—both stores and online sites like Jewelry Line. She suggested that Gladys spend some personal time familiarizing herself with the company's Web site, but she also recommended that her new hire visit the competition, including bigger outlets like the Home Shopping Network, to familiarize herself with their offerings.

Next, Leslie talked about her own management style. For instance, Leslie preferred one-on-one conversations with staff members rather than conversations via e-mail. She felt that knowing her staff members helped her to supervise them; interpersonal communications gave her more opportunity to find out about her customer-service reps. She shared with Gladys her own experience as a customer rep with the company, her rise to management, and her goals for the department.

Then, Leslie discussed some of the rules she expected staff to follow. Most important, there was the need to have phones covered at all times. Even a visit to the ladies room demanded that a colleague be alerted at busy times so calls weren't tied up. No caller was to be kept waiting for more than three minutes, Leslie explained. The staff of five customer reps needed always to be ready to answer a colleague's phone in the individual's absence. Staff also had specific time to take lunch—60 minutes, no more, from noon to 1 or 1 to 2. The company maintained a cafeteria, and staff members could buy their food or bring their own. There was a lounge to warm TV dinners or reheat food cooked at home.

Extended lunch was not permitted except with supervisory approval and arrangements for phone coverage had to be made in advance.

Tardiness and absenteeism were also issues mentioned by Leslie. "We offer 24/7 service to our customers. We have operators abroad who handle evening orders," she explained. "But staff here must be at their work stations by 8:00 A.M. and stay until 6:00 P.M., at which point calls are transferred to our overseas service.

"I understand that transportation and family problems can occur that can delay arrival to the office," Leslie continued. "Certainly we can all come down with a cold or other illness. But I expect staff to contact me as soon as they know they will be late or won't be in the office so I can arrange for coverage of the phones."

As Leslie spoke, Gladys kept nodding her head. She thought that Leslie had the right to be concerned about these issues, and she knew that she would do her best to comply with these requirements. Since she had been a full-time mother for over ten years, she had worried that she would not be trusted to juggle her family commitments with her work responsibilities. The decision to hire her had surprised and pleased her. "Leslie trusts me," Gladys thought.

But Leslie's next remarks made her wonder just how trusted she was. Leslie told her that she would want to meet with Gladys for an hour every second week to discuss her progress on the job. "Why would she want to meet with me?" Gladys asked herself.

"Leslie," she said, "please don't worry about me. I appreciate your giving me this job, and I'll make it a point to abide by your rules." As Leslie listened to Gladys, she could hear both timidity and worry. A supervisor for over ten years, Leslie recognized that Gladys wasn't concerned about her ability to do the job or her compliance with the rules. Gladys was worried about the prospect of meeting regularly—specifically, why.

Leslie asked, "You sound uneasy. Did I say anything that upset you?"

Gladys replied, "Yes. When you hired me, I thought you felt I was qualified for the job. Now you are telling me that you plan to check on me regularly to see if I fit in." Leslie smiled. "Gladys, you misunderstand. I meet with all my customer-service representatives. It enables me to find out how I can help them do their job better. And it gives you and your co-workers the opportunity to let me know what you think we can do better to accomplish our goals."

Leslie continued, "The new software program you'll have to learn came about from one such meeting with your predecessor, Irene. She loves working with computers and she had learned about the program from a computer geek she knew. Irene suggested we look into its use here. After some study, I agreed with her that it made tremendous sense—it allowed for faster information entry. Irene isn't with us in this office because she's abroad teaching our overseas service how to utilize the system. When she's done, she'll be working with IT full time."

Gladys looked up. "So you want my ideas about how to run the department?" she asked.

"Yes. It's a little early for that but, in time, as you become familiar with how we operate, yes, I'd like to hear any thoughts you might have about how we can be more efficient or effective in our work. That's one reason I'd like you to check competitive Web sites. Most of our customers are homemakers like you were, and I hope you can make some suggestions about how we can upgrade our Web site to appeal to that market." As Leslie finished, she saw Gladys's smile return. "Now," said Leslie, "let's talk about how we can get you working on our software program. What do you think about . . . ?"

Leslie's first coaching session with Gladys was very effective. She reviewed with her some of the information that they had discussed during the job interview that Gladys would need to know now that she had the job—like the department's mission, her style of management, and the requirements of the job. Leslie knew how stressful a job interview can be and how likely it is for a candidate to focus on leaving a good impression with the interviewer and not hear, let alone recall, all that is said during the meeting.

After the fact, Leslie also felt that she had made a good hiring decision. Gladys wanted to do a good job—which experience told Leslie increased the likelihood by 50 percent that she would do just that. Leslie also recognized that Gladys could be sensitive and she made a mental note to herself to use her future coaching meetings with Gladys to reassure her that her time as a full-time mother, away from the workplace, wouldn't be held against her.

She also addressed a problem that sometimes arises when a manager decides to meet regularly with staff members for the purpose of coaching. Even if all goes well with the meeting, given the uncertainty associated with job security today, many employees worry that their manager is either unhappy with their work or—worse—looking for reason to justify layoff or termination, particularly if the company has an employment-at-will policy. So it's important for a manager to explain the importance of coaching to the employee. Of course, that is much easier if the individual is new. But if you plan to coach current staff, you will have to offer some reassurance during the first meeting with employees. So Mariella, another manager, discovered.

Introducing Coaching to Staff Members

Leo was the first employee scheduled to meet with Mariella, his supervisor. She had announced at the operational meeting the week before that she planned to meet bi-weekly with each member to discuss his or her work so as to monitor progress against goals set at the start of the year and to identify opportunities for operational improvements. She suspected that one or two of her workers needed more direction—in particular, how to prioritize their tasks—to ensure that they completed their work on schedule. So Mariella planned to discuss that as well—in particular with two of her employees, Laura and Pat.

By meeting regularly with staff members, Mariella fervently hoped that everything in the department would run more smoothly—or, at least, as well as it can in today's leaner organizations. It seemed that crisis management was the order of her workday. This meant that she didn't have the opportunity she always wanted to tell staff members when they had done a good job. Mariella hadn't said so at the operational meeting, but she hoped that the coaching sessions would give her an opportunity to praise some of her staff members for their hard work.

Mariella realized that her own busy schedule kept her from acknowledging the fine job some of her staff did. "At least, these regularly scheduled coaching meetings will ensure that every one of my seven employees will get my full attention for one hour every two weeks." In talking to a peer, Mariella had said just that. Her colleague, Ralph, had laughed, but he had to admit that Mariella had a point. The pressures of the workday gave managers little one-on-one time with staff members. "I'm ashamed to admit it but I don't spend much time with my staff. Mariella, you may have an idea there. Let me know how it works out. I might try it with my six workers," he said.

Mariella hadn't expected her staff members to be concerned about these meetings, but her meeting with Leo, admittedly someone who was a worry wart, suggested how uneasy her staff might be about her plan. As soon as Leo sat down, he asked Mariella in a belligerent tone, "So, what's the problem?"

Mariella was surprised. "There's no problem—at least, I don't think so," she replied. "Is there some problem I should know about?" she asked, concerned with Leo's reaction.

"Not really," he said. "I'm swamped with a load of marketing jobs on my desk, but that's not unusual." He seemed eager to leave and started to stand up.

"Wait," said Mariella. "Is there something I can do about the situation?"

"Sure," said Leo. "Hire clerical support for the department so we aren't buried under all the paperwork that goes with the assignments we get. I know that's out of the question, so there's no point in talking about it."

Mariella wasn't so sure. Before discussing the idea that Leo had suggested, she decided to continue her discussion about Leo's assignments. "Will you be able to complete all the marketing jobs on time?" she asked.

"I might miss a deadline here or there by a day, but that's also not unusual." Feeling on the defensive, Leo decided to ask Mariella the question he had been holding in since he first heard about these meetings. "Okay, Mariella, what's the deal here? If you're looking for an excuse to downsize the department, you won't find it based on these meetings—we're doing more work, not less. But I know that won't matter to senior management."

On the defensive herself now, Mariella replied, "Admittedly, in the past it hasn't mattered to some members of management. But it has always mattered to me. I know how hard this department works, and we can't spare a single employee. My intention in holding coaching sessions is to find ways to help you. Tell me a little more about the jobs that may not be finished in time."

Leo described three projects. One had been delayed owing to the product manager's failure to get all the information to him on time. The second job needed little work but kept being put aside as new work came into the office. Mariella wasn't too concerned about these two jobs, but she was very upset when she learned that the third project involved market copy for a new product to be introduced at an industry conference two months away.

"I know that it should get immediate attention, but I just can't seem to get to it," said Leo. "I start to work on it and then someone comes to me with a rush job. I finish that and begin on the copy for the product introduction and suddenly I'm called into a product meeting or given another rush job. I seem to spend most of my time firefighting. I figured that I'd come into the office this weekend and get caught up. My mother promised to stay with the kids on Saturday. I can't stay late during the week because I have to be home when the kids finish school."

Mariella recognized that Leo was a single father with two young children, and she could understand why he couldn't stay late or work at home in the evening with an eight-year-old and a five-year-old to care for. A mother, Mariella had little time for work once she got home—and working late into the night only tired her the next day.

"Leo, I'm glad we talked. I hadn't realized how heavy your workload was. I'm particularly concerned about the new product market campaign. Unless you object, I'd like to reassign some of your work to one of the department's staffers. Worst case, I'll bring in a creative temp to help us to make sure that you finish that job on time. I don't like any staff member having to rearrange their life to work weekends here in the office. What do you think?"

Leo was delighted but a little uneasy about her suggestion. "If it won't be seen as my trying to get out of work, that would be great," he said. "Could you really do it?"

"We have the money in the budget to do it," said Mariella. "From what you said, I have another idea. I can't justify hiring a staff member to provide clerical support but we could hire a marketing temp for the entire department. The person could take on some of the smaller jobs, assist with some of the crises around here, and even process some of the paperwork. What do you think?"

"I think it's a great idea. So will the rest of the department. I expected bad news from this meeting, not such good news. We should have talked about my work situation earlier."

"That's the reason for these coaching sessions. My intention is to learn more about the work you're doing and to identify ways to help you—from reassigning work to identifying training opportunities, to stepping in to find ways to ensure that you continue to do good work. Which reminds me," said Mariella, "I've been so busy that I didn't have the chance to tell you how well your e-marketing campaign did. Several people in the organization have complimented me on it."

Not all of Mariella's coaching sessions were as productive as that with Leo. She did suggest to Pat that she was unnecessarily spending time rewriting marketing campaigns that required nothing more than quick updates and Laura and she spoke about Laura's need to better organize her work day—in fact, Mariella recommended that Laura look into a time-management course. All in all, Mariella felt that the six or so hours she had devoted to coaching was time well spent. When she shared her experience with Ralph, he agreed—and told her he planned to try the idea himself. Mariella planned to continue her sessions with her staff members.

Needless to say, Mariella implemented the plan she described to Leo, which made him a spokesperson for coaching sessions both within his own department and in the organization as a whole. He saw it as a means to get his boss's full attention for at least 60 minutes, and he subsequently planned what he would want to cover during his coaching meetings with Mariella, including any problems he had, progress on various campaigns, and—yes—some of the marketing campaigns he was especially proud of and ideas he had for better controlling incoming assignments. All in all, the sessions proved helpful for everyone once they became familiar with the idea.

The Coaching Interview

The purpose of the coaching interview is to exchange information. Ideally, feedback will be positive on both sides. The manager, in his or her role as coach, will have nothing but good things to say about the employee. The situation is likewise for the employee. If your staff member has encountered a problem in his or her work, given your experience and position, you should be able to come up with an action plan to address the situation.

The goal of coaching sessions is to address the problem before it becomes a serious performance problem that necessitates a counseling session.

Let's start with this simple situation. Nancy, a correspondence writer in the sales department, was complaining about her workload. Jacques, her manager, couldn't understand the problem. Nancy's predecessor had no problem with the number of letters that she handled. Jacques asked how many letters she did weekly, and the number was no larger than that of Margie. So Jacques asked to see the letters. Let's take the conversation from there.

> Jacques: You are doing a conscientious job, Nancy, but if you don't mind I have a suggestion to offer.
>
> Nancy [uptight]: No, I guess not. What's wrong?
>
> Jacques [holding three- and four-page letters in his hands]: Nothing is really wrong. You have all the facts right, and your ideas

are good. But these letters are too long and wordy. Let me see if I can find a letter from one of your peers. It was in reply to a similar billing complaint but he took only a page and a half to address the issue. Do you see what I'm saying?

Nancy: Yes. I am doing a lot of extra work unnecessarily.

Jacques: Yes, but it is more than that. You are asking consumers to get to the point of the issue in more time than would seem necessary. That can be annoying.

Nancy [nervous, feeling threatened about her job]: What do you want me to do?

Jacques: Nancy, I know you want to be thorough but I believe that you can write more concisely. To begin with, compare your letters with replies to similar problems done by your predecessor. Next, let's you and I sit down and I'll give you some tips on how to make your correspondence shorter and more effective. Your sentences should be succinct, not long. If you need further help, I'll sign you up for a business writing course.

So, Jacques assumed the training role of a coach.

Lending a Helping Hand

An executive can also be a coach to one of his managers. Lou, vice-president of shipping, was concerned because work on an important project was delayed. He decided to bring it up during his coaching meeting with Terry. In previous coaching sessions, Terry had talked about problems in getting commitment to the effort from members of the group. Lou wanted to find out if the problem was continuing. After complimenting Terry on a business plan she had completed for a new business relationship, Lou asked Terry how the team's effort at identifying candidates for strategic alliances was going.

"I guess that it is going as well as can be expected," Terry replied. "I can't seem to interest the group in the project. Since our mission is only to identify prospective candidates, not to initiate any contacts or contract projects with companies, members of the group drag their feet in doing research on the companies we identify."

"That's unfortunate," said Lou. "What do you think could be done to motivate the team?"

Terry thought for a moment and then said, "If our authority can't be expanded to allow us to make contact with prospective strategic partners, maybe we should reassign the work to someone with the authority to do more than visit one Web site after another."

Lou realized that Terry's team members weren't the only ones who needed to be re-motivated about the project. "Were we wrong to set up a team to investigate prospective corporate partners?"

"Yes, I think that you and others in senior management would have been better to keep the work to yourself. I guess that I agree with the other managers on the team that we have more than enough work than to sit around and come up with ideas that no one will want."

"I disagree. I know Jed, our CEO, and the top team, including me, think that you are the right people to bring prospective candidates to our attention. After some serious thought, including hiring a consultant to submit suggestions, we realized that you and your peers were closer to the kinds of operational issues that could be the basis for increased sales or reduced costs through joint ventures and other partnerships for our company. I still think that's true. But clearly we haven't sold the idea to you and the other members of the cross-functional team. How can we do that?"

Terry thought for a moment. "It would help if Jed sat in on a meeting to show us that he cared about the work we are doing," she said. "We have also submitted several recommendations to top management yet have heard nothing. Maybe a status report would demonstrate that our ideas aren't just being gobbled up into a big black hole."

Lou replied, "Terry, I guess that we haven't really supported the team as well as we could have. I'll talk to Jed to see if he can attend the next meeting. I'll also get an update on the suggestions your team has made to date. I seem to recall that one of the four ideas is being explored by marketing. We can get back to you on that. And . . ."

Terry interrupted, "Let us know, too, why ideas were rejected. It would help us with future work."

Lou then paused. "Terry, I think that you have a great idea there. Your team may need further direction from senior management. What do you think about bringing your team together with members of top management and, maybe, having an authority on strategic alliances present to teach us all a thing or two about the idea?"

"That would be great, Lou," Terry said. "I've read that strategic alliances can be the basis for competitive advantage. We're nothing like Cisco, Starbucks, or the other companies that use them, but we could learn from them. Do you think we could invite someone from one of these companies to visit?"

Lou thought for a moment. "I can't promise that, but I can see if there's someone from a firm with experience in strategic alliances who could visit the team, even run a full-day workshop to teach us all about how to do this a little better."

• • •

Note that the feedback during this coaching session was two-way. The conclusions reached weren't solely related to Terry's effort to lead the team: they had corporate implications. Lou learned that there was more that senior management had to do to make the team effort a success. Unfortunately, the team's lack of enthusiasm was due to failure by top management to communicate just how important its work was. And the idea of training—for both top management and the team—made a lot of sense. Indeed, as Lou thought about it, maybe the company should consider a more structured program, with a dotted-line relationship to the CEO office.

As you can see, once managers and employees become familiar with the idea of coaching sessions, they can see the benefit of meeting with their supervisor and sharing face time to discuss work, ideas they have, problems they are encountering, and even the reasons behind decisions made that can influence their work. Coaches can recognize good work, identify opportunities for training, brainstorm more effective ways to get the work done, and otherwise improve the performance of their employees. At the very least, coaching sessions prevent work problems from escalating by making managers aware of difficulties and, with the employee, coming up with solutions.

As you will experience, a coach will encounter a variety of situations. The secret is to approach this meeting so that your staff member sees it as an exchange of feedback and an opportunity to come up with solutions to problems he or she is experiencing. And, most important, you perfect the knack of phrasing information-gathering questions so that you get the information you need to help your employee do his or her job well. And, maybe like Lou, you can even identify a corporate competitive advantage.

Coaching Traps and Problems

WELL DONE, COACHING CAN BOOST individual and organizational effectiveness. Poorly done, it can alienate employees and undermine performance. Let's look at the most frequent traps coaches fall into and how to avoid them.

Hiring the Wrong People

Professional coaches hire the best. Managerial coaches should do likewise, yet too often managers/coaches settle for less. For example, many coaches wait until they have someone on board before they worry about job performance, rather than begin the coaching process even before someone is hired in order to make sure that they get the very best person for the job. Sloppy hiring procedures may leave a coach with a problem performer, somebody he might never have hired if he had known then what he now knows about the individual.

Often, all it takes to identify people with the potential to do good to outstanding work is to hold lengthier interviews, ask more targeted questions to learn about job skills and attitudes, and schedule follow-up interviews either with you or, better yet, with other interviewers. Multiple interviewers generally increase the range of questions as well as provide a variety of perspectives for consideration of applicants. For instance, Barbara may find out some things about the applicant that Casey didn't, but Casey may learn some things that Barbara didn't. And Doreen may discover some interesting things about the candidate that neither Casey nor Barbara did.

BRAD AND NORMAN: THE RIGHT OUTCOME FOR TWO MR. WRONGS

Two managers had interviewed a young man for an opening in the accounting department; the two managers would have to share the employee because they had budget enough only for one new hire, although there was sufficient work for two assistants. Norman was favored over another man, Brad, who was less articulate but brought to the job similar experience and skills. Both Thérèse and Mark still weren't sure; although they both liked Norman, there seemed something wrong, so they asked Fannie to meet with him and Brad to get a third opinion.

Fannie spent an hour with each applicant, then met with her colleagues to share her opinions. She agreed that Norman was extremely articulate, but she pointed to something that neither of her peers had noticed: he had never held a job for more than a year over a seven-year period. When questioned by Fannie, Norman had offered numerous explanations for leaving the jobs; in one instance, he admitted that he had been fired. He explained that he disliked high-pressure situations and he had been fired when he was insubordinate to his boss. Fannie admitted that Norman made a great first impression, but as she sarcastically added, he should. "He has had lots of practice interviewing for jobs." And, she added, "I don't know if he will stick around here. He has unrealistic expectations about how quickly he can move up in an organization. When he discovers that he can't be CEO after a month with the company, he will likely get wanderlust again."

Brad didn't fare any better. Fannie had asked him questions designed to get some sense of his flexibility, which is critical when someone is working for two managers. "Brad has a better job record than Norman," Fannie said, "but I think he would have a hard time in the kind of unstructured work situation the job you have entails."

Fannie suggested that the two managers pass on both candidates and take a little longer in their search. Mark was willing to try to make do with Brad, working around his deficiencies, but Fannie made a good point: "The best way to prevent having to spend considerable coaching time with an employee, let alone deal with a problem employee, which could occur with Brad, is to select someone with every reason for succeeding on the job." To do otherwise would ensure that both of her colleagues had headaches down the road.

Allowing Disorientation to Continue

Coaches who neglect to orient an employee or postpone the orientation may find themselves with a potentially effective employee whose work starts to flounder. Such employees are off track because no one has taken the time to put them on the right track; they could have done this by clarifying the performance level expected of them or filling skill gaps first identified during recruitment but neglected in the hurry to get them to work.

Aware of a new hire's shortcomings during interviewing, managers often plan to close that gap with training—either off-site or on-the-job—once the individual is at work. Unfortunately, by the time this person arrives on board, the situation has gotten so needy that the manager's first thought is to get the individual started working. Managers don't undertake a training-needs assessment or develop a training plan for the individual to ensure that his or her performance is up to standard, let alone review with the employee the job description and discuss specific expectations for performance.

Employees shouldn't be forced to fill the gaps in either expectations or skills by trial and error. The likelihood is too great that they will make mistakes, injure their self-confidence, get reputations as poor performers, and become subjects not for coaching but for counseling.

Making Implied Promises

Many managers make the mistake in coaching of suggesting that added effort on an employee's part could land a promotion or a high rating and big raise. It's unwise to use such promises as an incentive unless you can truly deliver on them. A broken promise can undo any improvements in the performance of the employee, as well as cause you to lose your credibility with both your staff and the new employee, who will tell others how he or she was fooled by you.

Sometimes, in order to leave an employee with no misunderstanding, you may even have to raise the issue just to squash it. That is what Neil had to do with Jenny.

> ### NEIL: MAKE NO PROMISES UNLESS YOU CAN KEEP THEM
>
> Neil wanted Jenny, a bright and talented new hire, to take a course in marketing for nonmarketing personnel. As head of marketing, Neil had

found that it always helped if his assistant had an appreciation of the discipline and an understanding of the jargon. But Jenny saw much more in his request. She had told him during her interview that she wanted to move into marketing, and she believed that Neil had decided to put her on a fast track to marketing assistant. Fortunately, however, Neil was aware of her wishful thinking. He didn't discourage Jenny from pursuing her career goal, but he did disabuse her of the belief that a promotion to marketing assistant would directly follow completion of the course.

Changing Management Styles When Coaching Doesn't Work

Good managers, like good coaches, practice *situational management*, adapting the degree of direction they provide employees to their experience and self-confidence and to the nature and importance of the task assigned. But there are some general guidelines in coaching that remain pretty much the same regardless of employee or circumstance: the need for open, honest communications; mutual respect; recognition for excellence and outstanding performance; and shared responsibility for decisions and implementation. These aspects of coaching aren't capes you put on when it is convenient but discard and replace with more autocratic overcoats when things don't go as smoothly as the textbooks suggest. If you do that, you will find it difficult, if not impossible, to reestablish the positive relationship that you had as coach. Trust between you and your staff goes out the window.

What could cause you to lose faith in coaching as a managerial approach to employee performance? Let's assume that you've been put on the spot. Plant management is installing new production equipment, and it wants your crew to install the equipment and be prepared to go onstream with it in a month, six weeks at maximum. You tell management that you can't get it done in that time period unless it allows for overtime and extra staff during the transition. Management agrees. Now you have to tell your staff.

You have spent considerable time building rapport with your staff. You know that the changeover will come as a surprise to them, but you believe that your crew members trust you enough to know that you wouldn't commit them to such a tight deadline unless it was imperative to their continued employment or unless you believed that the deadline was feasible—both of which were the case in this instance. So you are more than shocked when the employees you have nurtured, trained, and empowered oppose the plan. Rather than calmly discuss the reasons for your staff's resistance, and make an effort either to convert your employees to your course of action or achieve some compromise, you tell them that they have no choice; you even threaten retribution if they don't work hard, including putting in overtime, to make that deadline. The next case study illustrates this situation:

HAL: THE COACH WHO LOST HIS COOL

Hal, a manager in a southwestern electronics plant, found himself in a tight situation. Hal felt that he and his staff had reached a higher level of communication and that his employees would acquiesce in any request he made of them. So their opposition to his announcement that the staff had one month to install and go on-stream with new production equipment left him annoyed. The greater the opposition, the more he lost control of his temper.

"How could you commit us to something like this?" Doris asked stridently. "We need at least two months to master use of the equipment." Doris was informal leader in the group, and after she spoke, the doubt among crew members developed into outright opposition. Hal found that his efforts to tell the group how it would be possible to implement the plan were drowned out by vociferous team-member resistance. Rather than try to restore order and discuss his plan coolly, he raised his voice and angrily told the employees to shut up. "You have no choice," he said. "The equipment will be installed in March. You will have it on-stream by April 1."

"Sure," Doris said, "April Fool's Day. Which is exactly what Hal is if he thinks we will do what he wants."

Hal overheard. Later in the day, he had words with Doris about her attitude, which only further solidified opposition to the plan. There was talk in the department about going over Hal's head to discuss the plan with the plant's manager.

Hal's Basic Mistakes

Changes in an organization never come easily, and this was a major one at the plant. Hal wrongly assumed that his time spent as coach made it unnecessary to consider how best to tell his team about the change, which as a manager faced with a major operational change, he should have done. Coaching is not a panacea, a cure-all that will make all management situations you encounter a breeze. But Hal's bigger mistake was to revert to a dictatorial manner when his group questioned his judgment. He violated some key responsibilities of a coach, from listening to staff members' opinions to involving them in the decision and its implementation.

While Hal had made a commitment to senior management, after explaining to his staff the reasons for having done so, he could have asked the group for its ideas about how the changeover might be handled in the tight time frame given them. As a manager as well as a coach, Hal should have thought through the announcement. As with getting support for any changeover, he should have considered the kind of opposition he might run into and should have tried to build support even before the announcement.

From his coaching, Hal knew his employees well and he could have used this knowledge to predict each member's reaction to the news. He should certainly have talked to Doris, who, as informal team leader, could have helped him get buy-in to the plan. As coach, he could have made her project leader; since the position represented a growth opportunity, Doris would then have had more reason to give vocal support to the plan. At the very least, a conversation with Doris would have clued Hal into the kinds of responses he could expect. This would have allowed him to anticipate what to say in response to the resistance. He could even have practiced his responses before the staff meeting to ensure a calm reaction to the employees.

In this instance, he could have told his team why the equipment changeover was so important to the plant. Once his employees understood its importance to their work and, more germane, the capacity of the plant and consequently its continued operation, their attitudes very likely would have changed dramatically. He should also have considered what answers to give to questions that the group might have had, for example: (1) What steps would be taken to acquaint the crew with the new equipment? (2) What would be done during the interim to ensure that work on the old system continued until the changeover? (3) What team rewards, if any, would be associated with a successful changeover? Even recognition by plant management would have been a persuasive factor in building support for the idea.

Hal got the changeover completed in a month, but it took him a lot more time to repair the rift in his relationship with his crew that his angry reaction to its response had created.

And One More Mistake

Hal hadn't considered how his crew would respond and he lost his cool, but he also made another mistake. He began to talk *at* them, not *to* them, about the change. He said, "I want this done," and "I expect you to make it a reality," and "I promised you would do it, and you will do it." He even went so far as to practice a little fear management, implying that failure to achieve the transition in the time allotted might force management to make some reassignments of crew members in order to place on the crew those who would be quicker learners. Instead of this heavy-handed response, Hal could have shifted pronouns and adjectives from *I* and *you* to *we* or *our*, thereby reinforcing the sense of team that likely would have made even the one-month deadline less threatening to the crew.

Undermining Employees' Self-Esteem

I have mentioned the importance of the pronouns you use. The same is true of adverbs. When giving feedback, beware of correcting behavior using words like *always* or *never*, or other adverbs that could undermine a worker's self-esteem, suggesting that he or she *never* does anything well. For instance, you shouldn't say, "You are always late," or "You never complete work on deadline," or "You try all the time to get out of work." Instead, be specific: "Marie, on September 4, you were late by a half hour. What was the problem?" Or, "Michael, while you were traveling on business, I expected you to call. Why didn't we hear from you?"

Focusing on Attitudes

Just as feedback that makes use of exaggerated adverbs isn't constructive (think, instead, *destructive*), so too is judgmental attitudinal feedback. Suggesting that someone is lazy or argumentative or uninterested in her work is demoralizing, more likely to decrease the individual's level of performance than otherwise. After all, attitudinal feedback gives employees little direction to help them improve performance; it suggests no specific actions they can take to do so. Besides, such feedback is not legally defensible if it shows up on the employee's evaluation and is used to make a decision about a raise, a promotion, or, worst of all, continued employment.

Rather than tell an employee that she is "lazy," better feedback might be, "You don't lend a hand to other workers and, instead, have been frequently seen reading a novel or the newspaper, even though your co-workers would welcome your help." Rather than tell an employee that you think he has no interest in advancement, you might note how he has turned down several training opportunities or refused to participate in some high-visibility projects. Or if a customer service rep is short-tempered, particularly when customers ask lots of questions, rather than accuse her of being argumentative, you might tell her, "Mildred, customers complain that it is very hard to get product information from you. As a result, some customers have confided that they are going to competitors."

Failing to Follow Up

Some feedback is better than no feedback. Managers who don't assess their employees beyond the quarterly or trimester appraisal reviews aren't giving their employees sufficient information to help them increase their performance. But feedback is as important, maybe more so, when you delegate an assignment to an employee or when you train one of your staff to master a new skill, and even more important when you empower him or her to do something. Feedback at these crucial junctures may make it unnecessary for you to give negative feedback at the quarterly reviews or end-of-year evaluation. Consider the following scenario:

SOPHIE: THE IMPACT OF FOLLOW-UP FAILURE

The product line for which Sophie, a marketing manager, was responsible had had a tough year. Part of the problem was that the home-improvement tools she marketed had been on the market so long that there didn't seem much more that she could do to interest potential buyers. Consequently, when she and the product manager came up with the idea to market the tools in grocery stores to housewives who had small repairs to do, Sophie looked forward to the planning meeting at which she would present the idea to senior management, including the potential sales figures.

Busy numbers-crunching for the meeting, Sophie asked Irma to use the demographics she had developed to prepare graphics to go with her presentation, which would be on Monday at 10:00 A.M. Because the presentation was a full week away, Irma, Sophie's assistant, had plenty of time to do the work. In the interim, Sophie was busy with numerous chores herself, in and out of meetings and knee-deep in paperwork for what was called by marketing managers "hell week" (or "planning," as senior management called it). Sophie didn't think to ask Irma about her progress on the graphics. She had hoped to check with her on Friday afternoon, but a last-minute meeting with sales distracted her.

Need I tell you what happened on Monday? First thing that morning, Sophie went to Irma and asked her for the graphics. Irma looked at her and said, "I forgot." She pointed to the stacks of paper all around her workstation as explanation, became upset as she saw the grim look on Sophie's face, and began to cry. Sophie just stared at her. Without the graphics, she would have a much harder time getting the money she would need to position the product line in a whole new marketplace.

Who was to blame? Sophie, of course. As Irma's coach and supervisor, she didn't do what she should have done: follow up. Even before that, she should have clarified priorities when she gave Irma the assignment. By making it clear that this wasn't just another clerical assignment, Sophie could have minimized the chance of such a situation happening. If Sophie had told Irma that the graphics were crucial to her presentation, it is possible that Irma, aware of their importance, would have put aside all the rest of her work to do the best job she could on the graphics. At the time, all Irma knew was that Sophie needed some graphics prepared on the basis of a bunch of numbers she had given her; there was no reason to suspect that the job was more important than the correspondence and other tasks she had to do.

But Sophie could have ensured that the work was done on time by following up during the week to see what progress had been made on the assignment. She could even have told Irma that she would need to see black and white proofs by Wednesday. By Thursday, she would want to look at the color proofs with any revisions. "By Friday," she could have said, "the final charts should be done."

Follow-up is equally important when training an employee in a new skill or procedure. Once you have shown the employee how to do the task, then had the individual explain the steps in the task in his or her own words, then asked the person to do the work to show you comprehension of it, and left the employee with some written instructions to remind him or her about each step, you have only taken the first steps in ensuring that this employee performs the new skill correctly.

You haven't finished with training unless you come back about an hour later to see if the employee is doing the work as you instructed. If the individual isn't, then you point to those steps in the process he or she is doing correctly before noting the mistakes being made. Otherwise, you will destroy the individual's self-confidence in his or her ability to learn how to do the task. Then you and the employee go through the training process once again: you do the task, you ask the employee to explain how the job is done, then you watch the employee as he or she does the task correctly.

Done? Not quite. You should visit later in the day—say, a few hours later—to check again to see if the work is being done correctly. At the end of the day, you might also stop by to see the employee's progress with the work. If all looks well, you can tell the employee so and recognize his or her accomplishment. If there are still problems, you should discuss calmly and quietly the nature of the problem.

Let's assume that all is well. Done? Not yet. Stop by the following week to be sure that all the steps in the process are being followed as they should be. If it is imperative that each step be done as instructed, then you want to make that point clear to the employee and make sure that he or she hasn't developed some shortcuts that erode the quality of the final work. If there continues to be a problem, you want to discover why.

Placing the Blame

The first response most of us give when an employee is having trouble completing a single task (or performing the job as a whole) is to assume that this person knows the nature of the problem and is capable of solving it. Often this isn't the case. Further, when managers hold this view, they can build up resentment toward the employee whom they begin to think is just doing the work wrong to make everyone look bad or to get out of a task or to get even for some slight.

It is usually better to begin with the assumption that the communications on our part as managers were somehow inadequate. We didn't make clear how important the work is, how this work is to be done, or how important this work is in relation to the other tasks to be done. Repetition of the instructions may help to clarify the cause of the problem.

Let's get back to the employee who doesn't seem to be learning how to complete a task and whom we have instructed twice about the work. If the employee is to do the task correctly, you have to find out the cause of her confusion. If English is a second language, that may be behind the problem. If she lacks some basic information essential to doing the task, then you should go through these fundamentals before going over the steps in the task again. Another source of problems can be the employee's own desire to do more; she may have introduced shortcuts in the process to impress you, but these may actually undermine the quality or quantity of the work. In plants, as we have seen, such good intentions on the part of new workers can even create conditions that make accidents more likely.

Ignoring the Problem

Managers have so much work to do and so little time in which to get it done that it's easy to take the course of least resistance and become blind to staff shortcuts or other less-than-perfect efforts. Unfortunately, when managers ignore these small problems, they can grow to the point that they are no longer coaching problems but are now issues for counseling, as shown in the next case study.

Lynn: A "Small" Problem That Mushroomed

Lynn, head of systems, had come up with the idea for a monthly department report that would be distributed to department heads and other senior managers in the company. The report's purpose was to ensure financial and management support by making these individuals familiar with past accomplishments and future opportunities through use of the new technology. Copy was provided by systems engineers and users and given to Roxanne, Lynn's assistant, who was responsible for producing the final pages using in-house desktop equipment. The report was printed off-site.

The latest issue came out, and as Lynn quickly looked through its pages, she noticed lots of typographical errors. Roxanne was responsible not only for keyboarding the content and logistics but also for editing and proofreading the report. Lynn had seen a few errors in the past, but she hadn't talked to Roxanne about them; she knew that Roxanne had been busy assisting in the development of some technological updates and follow-up training, and Lynn didn't want to come down on her after such a hard week. Besides, Lynn had to admit to herself, she had enough on her own plate; she didn't have the time to deal with something like a few typos in the "constituency" report. But their number had continued to increase. Lynn knew that she had to talk to Roxanne about the situation. Very likely she would have postponed her conversation once again if she hadn't overheard a conversation between Roxanne and another assistant, Marilyn.

Marilyn had noticed the typos, too, and had asked Roxanne if she wanted another pair of eyes to help proofread the report. "No," Roxanne replied. "It really doesn't matter. Most readers won't notice."

As Lynn listened, she was appalled. "Of course, it matters," Lynn thought to herself. "This report went to senior management, and its purpose was to send a message to top management about the department's commitment to excellence—*in everything*." She called Roxanne into her office.

"Roxanne," Lynn began, "I looked over the report. There are some really great items in this month's issue, but I also noticed several typographical errors. I like to issue this report because it reflects the very best work done by the team. These typos, small as they are, diminish that image."

"Oh, come on," Roxanne said. "They aren't that noticeable. If they were, I would have stayed late to fix them before I sent the pages to the printer. But we've had errors before and no one has said a word. Even you," Roxanne finished.

"I noticed before," Lynn admitted. "I should have spoken to you about them earlier," she continued. "Would it help if we asked several of the other assistants in the department to read copy, too?" she asked, moving the conversation from a criticism of the work to development of an action plan to prevent the problem's recurrence.

Was Lynn to blame for the few errors growing into many more? Yes. Like Sophie, who didn't make clear to Irma the importance of having the graphics in time for a presentation she was making to senior management, Lynn had not made clear to Roxanne how important it was to produce a "perfect report" for distribution to senior management. By her failure to say anything, Lynn had given Roxanne the impression that she could get away with not always doing her very best. But it was the last time she let any member of her team think so.

Not Recognizing Improvement

Acknowledging good performance doesn't have to mean big dollars. Recognition for a positive change in behavior can come in the form of praise and other positive reinforcements. Unless you acknowledge performance improvements, no matter how small they may be, however, these small improvements aren't likely to be permanent. Nor are they likely to be followed by bigger improvements over time.

Your time commitment to getting people motivated and keeping them motivated doesn't have to be much. About ten to twenty minutes in a meeting with staff each week, on Friday afternoons, to review what the group has accomplished, should be sufficient. Such a meeting would allow you not only to celebrate staff accomplishments but also to acknowledge what individual members of the team have done—to name these staff members and be specific about their accomplishments so all can join with you in recognizing them.

Failing to Give Direction

Too often, you know your department's mission or goals, but you fail to share them with your staff. Or you might tell your employees the department's goals but then fail to keep them informed of progress toward those goals. Either kind of inaction can diminish employee motivation. Without information on department goals, your staff won't have a focus. And without any indication that they are closing in on the short-term goals and that overtime can accomplish the long-term goals, they will grow weary.

When you share your group's goals with members or, better yet, when you set them with your team as a group, you should also discuss the bigger picture: how the department's goals align with corporate goals. And at that point you also want to discuss with the group how you can keep team goals in front of members daily, like hanging progress charts that are updated daily or having a department newsletter (like Lynn's) or Monday morning meetings with coffee and Danish courtesy of the company.

Making Unrealistic Demands

You believe that you know your organization well enough to come up with a realistic solution to an employee's problem. What happens, however, if you, in your role of coach, prescribe a simplistic solution to a complex problem facing your employee or advocate a stretch goal demanding that the employee spearhead change in an organizational area in which he or she will face only opposition? Similarly, what will occur if you give an employee a responsibility with a deadline that is totally unrealistic because your organization expects quick results? In each instance, you will lose credibility as a coach in the eyes of your employee. How do you overcome these problems?

For instance, as a manager, it might be simple for you to get Project A completed, but your employee likely doesn't have the same collegial network to do the same. When such is the case, you may have to involve yourself in the action plan to achieve the results expected. To avoid the problem entirely, each time you assign work to an employee, you need to consider the obstacles that the individual might encounter and which problems can be hurtled by the employee and those that may require you to give the employee a little push over. In such instances, that extra hand should be a part of the action plan between you and your staff member. If, in a similar vein, an effort has a very tight deadline, you need to offer your employee the needed resources to make the schedule.

If, after serious consideration, you have to admit that the task is even beyond *your* ability, then it would be totally unfair to give the responsibility to a staff member. Likewise, a goal requiring change about which the employee will face nothing but opposition. In such a circumstance, too, you might be wiser to retain that task yourself rather than demoralize someone by passing it on to him or her.

Being Impatient

Finally, coaches can easily fall into the traps of sharing their opinion too early in the feedback session or, worse, losing their patience after having explained the same task for the tenth time, learning about a stupid mistake that will cause a project setback, or reading a simple memo that needs editing.

Premature feedback may indicate to an employee that you aren't listening (remember, the 80/20 rule in which you should be listening 80 percent of the time and talking 20 percent) or, alternatively, that you have a bag full of trite answers regardless of the problem. In both instances, the solution is simple: shut up and learn to really listen.

Coaches who fail to exhibit patience send a message to their employees that they "can't believe just how stupid they are." Patience sends a very different message; it tells employees that the coach recognizes that they are human beings and, as such, they have human fallibility, yet that is no reason to quit. Employees see their boss's patience as evidence that they believe that their staff members can succeed in their work. So they should *try again*.

• • •

As I review the many situations I've described in this section of the book, it occurs to me that I may have given you, the reader, the wrong impression about coaching; that is, that you only coach when there's a problem. If you coach only to address a performance problem in the making, you're wasting a valuable management technique. That's because your staff members will regard meetings with you as always negative. Rather, they should come to regard coaching sessions as meetings for the purpose of growth, not punishment. Don't assume that your employees know that they are doing a good job. Use your coaching meetings as often to recognize outstanding performance as to advise an employee on how to handle a difficult situation or avoid a problem in the making.

Counseling

CHAPTER 5

Why Counsel Troublesome People?

BASED ON YOUR COACHING, you can boost both individual and department or division performance. But that hard work can be undone by just one staff member who doesn't carry his or her weight. The individual's work output may be poor or below standard. Due dates may be missed, affecting the work of others down the line. The employee may lack initiative and seem uninterested in the job, behaving as if every workday were a blue Monday. Or he or she may be continually late or absent, *by coincidence,* almost every Friday.

Managers should begin to counsel the employee to turn around his or her performance, but increasingly many move swiftly to termination without any effort to change work behavior. Why does this happen? These managers work for companies with an at-will employment policy, and they mistakenly believe that their employees consequently have no due-process rights. They don't realize that not providing documented warnings and a reason for firing an employee can cause the individual to assume that he or she is being fired for an unlawful reason. Disgruntled, such an employee will seek out a lawyer unless offered a severance package or other reason for not charging some form of discrimination. Consequently, even managers with reason to fire employees can lose in court if the employee makes a good enough case.

Even in companies with an at-will policy, managers are wiser to intervene in the event of problem behavior, hold well-documented counseling meetings, and make an effort to turn around the situation—if, for no other reason, than to justify subsequent termination in the event that there is no change in performance.

There is another reason for intervention as soon as a performance problem is evident. Poor performance can affect others' work within the department or the work of the group as a whole. And there are still other reasons that managers should immediately act to improve job performance; these include:

- *Lost Productivity.* A poor performer produces only about one-third the work of average workers.

- *Lost Business.* Problem performers aren't likely to extend themselves to get or keep an account or to handle difficult customers tactfully.

- *Lost Time.* Poor performers take up a disproportionate amount of supervisory time, as much as 50 percent. This means that there isn't much time left for the rest of the staff, including time to coach them.

- *Lost Talent.* Many of your best workers, as they lose respect for you and begin to doubt the fairness of your evaluations, will job-hunt; your less productive workers will stay, but as they are no longer afraid of you, they may try to get away with the same stuff as your troublesome employees.

- *Lost Self-Esteem—Yours.* As you firefight to make up for shortfalls in the problem performer's work, you may become angry and frustrated and burnt out. In time, you may lose your self-confidence. This could affect your own job performance and others' perception of you.

And lastly, consider this: a problem employee may in fact have much to offer—if good counseling helps the individual turn around his or her performance. That's talent saved, not lost!

Failure to Take Action

Given these consequences, you have to wonder why managers don't take action before a performance problem escalates to these serious levels. Numerous explanations are given, besides a misunderstanding of at-will. They range from overidentification with the employee's feelings to lack of faith in the human resources department to support the manager's actions, to reluctance to play judge and jury over another's career. Let's look here at three key reasons why:

Fear

Managers worry that they will lose control of the discussion as the employee cries or gets angry, that the effort will end in the employee being fired, and that ultimately they will find themselves in court, defending their actions. Such fear is understandable. Articles in the press citing six-figure awards to plaintiffs in lawsuits about unfair discharge are more than enough to scare a manager with a problem performer, particularly if that individual is a member of a protected work group. It's a lot easier to engage in wishful thinking that the performance problem will resolve itself; either the problem will disappear or the employee will leave on his or her own. But neither happens very often.

If it helps you as a manager to confront a long-term employee about a performance problem, and counsel the individual to turn his or her work around, think of what you must do as a version of tough love—what I call "tough-love supervision." Tough love is a nationwide program designed to aid troubled teens and their parents. It's a program that encourages young people to take responsibility for their behavior. And three of tough love's ground rules can be adapted to counseling:

1. The goal is to remedy poor performance, not to demean a person. Annoyance is directed at the work and not at the employee.

2. It is based on a genuine desire to see the individual do better. If you keep this positive attitude in mind, you won't feel as if you are destroying another person's career by bringing up performance faults. You are actually helping the individual.

3. It seeks to achieve agreement with the problem performer and help you build together an action plan to turn the employee's performance around.

Crisis Management

Another reason performance problems aren't addressed has to do with today's leaner organizations. With so much to do and so little time in which to get it done, managers can become so accustomed to crisis management that they aren't as aware as they might otherwise be of everything happening around them. Problems that they should notice go unnoticed—until someone or some incident brings it starkly to their attention. Even then, however, they may do nothing. They make the mistake of not doing anything because they see counseling as too time-intensive. They think it is easier to fill the performance gap themselves, although, given their schedules and the importance of their organization's strategic intent, it is a terrible waste of their time to do the undone work of one of their employees.

Lack of Training

Although training in counseling skills would enable a manager to resolve individual performance problems that diminish the productivity of the entire department, few companies give new supervisors or managers or team leaders the instruction they need to help them with troubling or troubled employees. This is unfortunate because counseling is a responsibility and, like most managerial responsibilities, can be mastered with training and experience.

A Definition of Counseling

The semantics associated with counseling may actually be more complex than the process itself. Some describe counseling as an ongoing process for development, and they describe coaching as a means of addressing specific performance problems. There are others who consider counseling as one element of coaching (they throw mentoring into the coaching pot, too).

Does it really matter what we call one process or the other? Not really. But it is important that you be clear about the purpose of each process as you use it. When we talk about counseling, we are referring to a nonpunitive disciplinary process, the most important step of which is one-on-one meetings with the problem employee in which your purpose is to get the employee to acknowledge the difference between actual performance and expected performance; identify the source of the problem; and develop an action plan to bring performance up to minimum expectations, if not higher. The secret to good counseling is in the communication process, and that entails the following three practices:

1. *Communicate openly, directly, and honestly.* Don't be ambivalent about telling an employee that he isn't doing the job that you want done. If you hem and haw about a performance problem, talking around the topic rather than being clear about its nature and seriousness, you leave the employee with the mistaken notion that you aren't really concerned about the situation and that there is no need to change his behavior. At

the least you leave the employee confused, at worst you leave yourself open later to a lawsuit based on your failure to make absolutely clear to the employee the problem with his performance and the implications of a continuation of that behavior.

You need to make clear that you're talking not only about the effect on work itself and the standards by which the individual's performance is being measured (your expectations of the employee) but also the consequences of continuing poor performance, like being denied a raise or, worse, the start of progressive disciplinary action, which ends in termination if the problem continues.

2. *Practice active listening.* In particular, you want to learn how to use silence to encourage the employee to talk about what is happening in the workplace, the problems she is having, and what she will do to achieve the results you want. Certainly, you don't want to dominate the conversation, lecturing the individual about her performance problems. Rather, you want to create a dialogue in which you speak only about one-fifth of the time, thereby practicing the 20/80 rule. Setting a conversational tone also minimizes the likelihood of the discussion turning into a confrontation while increasing the likelihood that you and the problem employee, together, will come up with a workable action plan for turning her performance around.

3. *Probe and question.* The key to one-on-one counseling is, first, to ask open-ended questions that will identify possible causes of the problem performance, then to ask more pointed questions to determine the specific cause. You can then follow up with a closed-ended question to confirm your conclusion: "Although you say you have a clear idea of your responsibilities, isn't it true that you have a hard time prioritizing your assignments?"

If you consider these three skills, it should be evident why all three are so important to counseling: they enable you to make clear to a problem performer that she is accountable for a certain level of performance, that you are not receiving that level of performance, and that you expect that improvement. When you practice all three at once, you create a supportive environment in which a problem performer feels free to open up to you and discuss what is behind his or her misbehavior or performance deficiencies. Then, together, without demoralizing the employee, you can both define areas for improvement and agree on an action plan for achieving that improvement.

If your communication style already is a combination of assertiveness, active listening, and probing, then you are fortunate. But if you aren't there yet, don't worry. Developing a counseling style is something that can easily be learned. Listening and probing skills come with practice; and assertiveness comes with self-confidence, with practice, and with documentation that supports your comments about the employee's performance.

The Need for Counseling

If you are fortunate, you won't have to apply your counseling skills frequently. After all, many shortfalls in performance can be handled during the performance-appraisal process, at one of the three or four meetings you hold during the year. If you've planned your appraisal reviews correctly, you've set aside an hour or more for each of your employees and therefore have sufficient time not only to identify their accomplishments but also to discuss failures in their performance and create action plans to ensure that they will reach the standards for their job or meet their goals by the end of the year.

Generally, in appraisal interviews you will be discussing situations like an employee's failure to follow up with a vendor on an order (an oversight), a staff member's reluctance to fully utilize the new office technology (need for additional training), or an employee's failure to complete a market research report on schedule (work overload, need for a temp). Unless these problems are part of a pattern, they usually can be remedied through some coaching in the form of training or redirection.

Performance problems that demand counseling include continuing poor work quality or quantity, frequently missed deadlines, disorganization, chronic tardiness or absenteeism, frequent and lengthy disappearances from the workstation, lack of initiative or even a total lack of interest, with the employee seemingly wishing to be anywhere other than at work, lack of cooperation, and even insubordination.

Some of these problems will be found to stem from skill deficiencies, others from repetitive or dull jobs, still others from post-downsizing depression or grief, or burnout, or frustration about being asked to do the impossible without the equipment, funds, or time to get the assignment done, a condition in many of today's downsized companies. Other performance problems—like making disparaging remarks about the company, the boss, or work to others within and, worse, outside the organization, like customers; refusal to follow instructions; minimum output but maximum complaints about department policies or procedures; or sulkiness or uncooperativeness—may stem from an attitude problem rooted in a conflict with you, a peer, or corporate policies or procedures.

Finally, many performance problems can be traced to personal problems in the employee's life, from financial difficulties to divorce, to a chronically ill child or parent, to an emotional problem, to substance abuse. A study by the National Institute on Drug Abuse found that substance abusers are late three times more often than the average worker, sixteen times more likely to be absent, four times more likely to have workplace accidents, and three times more likely to use health-care benefits.

Let's look at a situation in which there was a need for counseling, but the manager was unaware of it until it was brought to his attention—by staff, peers, and his boss through a 360-degree feedback program.

CHARLIE: HOW 360-DEGREE FEEDBACK OPENED HIS EYES

Charlie is the manager of an office supplies warehouse on the East Coast. In an organization that had severely downsized the year before, he was so busy fighting fires that he was blind to the existence of a problem others saw, a situation not unique in today's fast-paced companies. Charlie got the first inklings of a problem after his company instituted a 360-degree feedback program in which managers get feedback from various individuals, from their boss to their staff members to peers to customers. His boss, staff members, and even some peers gave him low marks for developing his employees.

A 360-degree feedback program has various purposes. At Charlie's company, it was designed for developmental purposes. Consequently, managers were encouraged to go to those who gave them feedback to get a better understanding of the conclusions and create self-improvement plans to increase their management skills. When Charlie met with some of his peers, he found them reluctant to explain why he had received such poor ratings as someone who helped to train and develop his workers. Charlie felt that he had done a "pretty good job": two of his employees had even been chosen by these very peers for jobs in their departments. Depressed by the loud silence with which his query had been greeted, he asked his best friend, Pete, why he had gotten 2s and 3s, on a scale of 1 (worst) to 5 (outstanding), from his managerial buddies.

Summing Up Gloria

Pete wasn't so reticent with Charlie: "It's Gloria," he said. "Everyone else in the plant is working himself or herself to death, yet Gloria sits outside your office and reads romance novels or the newspaper in the morning, runs around spreading rumors, refuses to help others because she says she's too 'busy,' and complains about the organization to anyone who will listen, from colleagues to customers, yet we all know that you haven't done anything about it. You probably don't know what's happening because you keep your door closed all day."

Charlie didn't know how to answer. He kept his door closed because the noise outside his small office made it hard to concentrate otherwise. But each time he stepped out and saw Gloria, she seemed very busy. "Gloria has worked for me for ten years," he explained. "She has her peculiarities, but I can count on her when the chips are down," he answered.

"I don't know," Pete replied. "You asked, and I told you."

As Charlie drove away from the office that night, he thought about Pete's comments. Clearly, Pete wasn't aware of Gloria's strengths. Yes, he concluded, Pete was wrong. He'd ask his staff members the next day what they thought of his assistant to prove that Pete was mistaken.

Reinforcing Pete's Assessment

That is exactly what Charlie did. When Gloria went to lunch, he brought Michael, Richard, Joe, and Barbara into his office and asked them about the 360-degree feedback they had given him. They all had nice things to say about Charlie until it came to the question of developing employees.

"We all think you are great," said Barbara.

"Yeah," Michael agreed. "Sure," said Richard. Joe, a longtime member of Charlie's department, didn't speak.

"Okay, Joe," Charlie said. "I've never known you to be speechless. So what's wrong?"

At first Joe denied any problem, but under Charlie's prompting Joe finally told him, "It's Gloria, Charlie. I've known Gloria as long as you have, but her attitude bothers me. And your failure to notice it bothers me even more."

When Charlie looked at the faces of his other staff members, he could see that they were in agreement. At that point, he had to leave his crew to meet with his own boss about his evaluation. Ed had been Charlie's boss for less than a year, and the two had often come to blows initially as Ed, a tough, task-oriented manager, adjusted to Charlie's more people-oriented work style.

Charlie expected lots of feedback from Ed, but actually Ed had only one complaint. Yes, you guessed it—Gloria. It seemed that Gloria had been rude on the phone to one of the firm's biggest clients. "I know that it's important to you to be liked by your people," Ed said, "and I might not be as concerned about how my people feel about me so long as I know I have their respect. But I can't understand your support for Gloria. There have been some meetings in which she has spoken out in a very disrespectful manner toward you. How can you put up with her?"

"I spoke to her . . ." Charlie started to say, then stopped. It suddenly occurred to him that he had spoken many times to Gloria about her behavior and attitude, and over the short term there had been improvements. And then the problems began again. Because he had worked with her so long, knew her husband and kids, and even went to ball games with the family in the summer, he no longer had an objective eye on the problem.

Asking the Tough, Self-Analytical Questions

As the case study shows, it was time for Charlie to ask himself some tough questions about Gloria (questions that you should be asking about the members of your staff):

- *Am I making allowances?* In Charlie's case, it was true that Gloria knew how he operated and often anticipated his needs, but it also was true that she had to be told to do some things more than once, refused to take on new responsibilities as the department became more electronic and the work had to be given to other secretaries as overtime, and would testily let him and anyone else who called Monday mornings know that she wasn't happy to have to work for a living.

- *Do I feel angry?* As Charlie watched Gloria slip away from her desk to gossip with the new temp, although she knew he needed the report she was retyping by 3:00 P.M., had several pages to go, and it was already 2:30 P.M., he had to admit that he was angry. If the report was to be done on time, he would have to take some of the pages and type them himself.

"It wasn't the first time," Charlie thought. Suddenly he realized that he was being taken advantage of. "No wonder I go home frustrated because I haven't done as much as I could—I'm doing some of Gloria's work," he realized.

- *Have I used my own busy schedule as an excuse to avoid confronting the problem?* While Charlie certainly didn't deliberately use his workload as an excuse not to sit down with Gloria and discuss some incident or other when she was out of line or didn't perform as she should, he had postponed meeting with her time and time again. He would tell himself that he would bring up the matter during the next appraisal review, but at the review he would either touch only lightly on the matter or ignore it in his rush to complete the review.

- *Am I acting more like a father or mother or a personal counselor than a boss?* Relationship-oriented managers like Charlie establish a rapport with employees that is part of what makes them effective. However, in a close relationship, employees may share personal problems with a manager that sometimes encourage the manager to offer personal advice that could aggravate the employment dilemma. In these circumstances, it is better that the individual see a professional counselor (think psychologist, psychiatrist, family counselor, or financial counselor) who can help the employee get to the true nature of his dilemma. The manager may listen and express concern, but he shouldn't let the circumstances inhibit him from his primary responsibility: improving the employee's performance at work.

As he considered his behavior with Gloria, Charlie had to admit that his chats with Gloria had made him aware that her husband, Jerry, was having work problems, and this had most likely made him go a little easier on her than he would otherwise have done. He certainly had said nothing about her frequent phone calls to Jerry or her long conversations on the phone. Like a father, he had gruffly reminded her of the costs, but he hadn't said anything about their effect on Gloria's productivity or the ability of customers to get through to the sales department or, most important, her work performance as a whole.

- *Are staff members angry or jealous?* Charlie didn't have to think hard about this question. While Joe alone had spoken up, and then only after some prodding from Charlie, Charlie knew that Michael, Richard, and Barbara, as well as Joe, were annoyed. Over lunch, they probably asked each other, "How come good old Charlie lets Gloria goof off but runs us ragged?"

- *Is the situation becoming the topic of conversation?* Unfortunately, Charlie didn't have to think too hard to answer this question, either. It was yes. His 360-degree rating made that evident. If he didn't correct Gloria's performance, he would be judged poorly not only by his staff members but by his peers as well. Even his boss had grown tired of hearing Charlie defend Gloria.

Once Charlie accepted the existence of a problem, his next step was to visit Human Resources to discuss what he would have to do to turn around Gloria's performance.

Understanding Counseling

When we think about counseling, we usually think of the one-on-one meetings with employees regarding their performance shortcomings. Actually, counseling involves more than that. Counseling is a process, and that process is a part of most corporate performance management efforts.

Most organizations have two counseling tracks: one for performance problems, another for rule violations and other misconduct. The existence of two tracks reflects the fact that rule violations are a more serious issue than job-performance shortcomings; besides, poor job performance is not necessarily a deliberate act by the employee and can often be corrected with either training or positive reinforcement. Since the purpose of this book is to help you boost the performance of your employees, counseling for improving job performance and increasing individual and organizational effectiveness is the focus of this section of the book. Before we continue with that discussion, however, let's take a brief look at the procedure companies often use for handling rule violations or other misconduct.

Counseling Misconduct Cases

Counseling for rule violations or other misconduct differs from performance counseling in that it begins immediately with a verbal warning. This is followed by a written warning if the violation or other offense is repeated. Depending on the nature of the offense, the employee may be suspended without pay for a specific period to rethink his or her behavior. A repetition of the rule violation thereafter is followed immediately by termination.

Specifically, as the following list indicates, disciplinary counseling is at most a five-step process. The actual number of steps depends on the seriousness of the conduct, the work history of the employee, and how the employee responds to the initial steps, or warnings.

The Five-Step Disciplinary Process

Step 1. Issue a verbal warning. The verbal warning is usually used when the misconduct is minor or it is the employee's first offense. It lets the employee know that you are aware of what she has done and that you expect her not to repeat the offense.

Step 2. Issue a written warning. If the verbal warning isn't heeded and the employee repeats the violation, or if the offense demands more than a verbal warning but not a reprimand, then you might want to issue a written warning in memo form. A copy is given to the employee and one is placed in his personnel file.

Step 3. Reprimand the employee. Often this reprimand won't be given by you but rather by your own boss or someone in your firm's Human Resources Department. The message here is clear: another repeat of the incident, and the employee will be suspended or terminated, depending on the nature of the offense.

Step 4. Suspend the employee. This action is taken in the event of repeated misconduct or a serious offense. Sometimes the employee is paid while he is away from work, sometimes he is not—the nature of the situation often determines that. The employee is expected to use the time away from work to do some soul searching about his desire to stay with the firm and, as an integral part of that, his future conduct.

Step 5. Terminate the employee. If the problem still continues, then the employee is terminated. Generally no thought is given to a demotion since the assumption is that the employee is at fault, as opposed to the case of a poor performer who has tried to turn her job performance around but can't quite do it. Depending on the misconduct, termination may actually be the first step and not the last step in disciplining a problem performer—for instance, in cases like extreme violation of safety rules or theft.

A serious violation of corporate policy demands immediate firing. All that is needed is that you have the right person and credible evidence that he or she has done something in violation of policy or state or federal law, like theft, fraud, falsifying documents, and assault. Violation of any of the provisions of the Sarbanes-Oxley Act (SARBOX) of 2001 may not be foremost in your mind when we talk about termination for fraud, but deliberate discrepancies in expense or income reports are covered by SARBOX and consequently cause for immediate action not only to protect you but also your organization. Whatever the violation, it is essential that you work with the human resources director to obtain all the facts and make an informed decision. As a manager, it is vital that you investigate any illegal matters immediately.

The Four-Step Performance Counseling Process

Performance-improvement counseling involves four steps: verbal counseling, a written warning, demotion or transfer, and termination.

Step 1. Verbal Counseling

Most often, counseling takes the form of sit-down meetings with employees over a period of time, but it can also consist of a simple, spontaneous remark to an employee, such as, "Hope, you should be at your desk now, shouldn't you?" or "Sam, I thought we agreed that you would have that report on my desk by noon?" Frequent informal remarks can also signal the need for a sit-down meeting.

Both informal and formal counseling should be documented. That notation would include your observation and remark and the date and time of the incident. There is no question that documentation is critical not only in counseling but also in any efforts to boost employee performance. In the case of counseling, your notations can suggest the beginnings of a pattern of poor performance. Reviewed prior to an appraisal meeting, they may even enable you to avoid counseling entirely by nipping a potential problem in the bud, before it blossoms.

If you need to counsel an employee, you are better positioned, with the documentation you have kept, to prove to the employee that there is, indeed, a problem despite the employee's arguments to the contrary. And arguments you will hear can range from "I used to be that way but I've recently improved," to "You don't understand how hard I have to work," to my favorite, "You are right about my strengths but totally wrong about these problems."

Step 2. A Written Warning

Most corporate progressive-discipline programs demand that employees be issued a warning before they are moved to more severe discipline, like a demotion or termination, if the counseling sessions aren't working. The warning is usually presented in a written memo. Upon the employee's receipt of the memo, you and he would meet again to review the employee's plans to improve his or her performance. This meeting with the employee would be documented and, along with a copy of the warning, the description of the meeting would be placed in the employee's personnel file. At this point, it should be made as clear as possible to the troubled or troubling employee that a continuation of the problem could mean separation from the company.

Step 3. Demotion or Transfer

A demotion or transfer is not a cop-out in instances when the employee's performance isn't his or her fault and, for whatever reason, training or extra direction from you will have no effect. Here's a case in point:

> ### MITCH: HANDLING A NON-TEAM PLAYER
>
> Mitch was hired as a marketing researcher before his department reorganized into teams. Over time, it became evident that Mitch wasn't a team player and was much more productive working on his own than in a group setting. He would try but invariably he would become frustrated by the time spent as a part of the product group. He would go off by himself and complete the team's project on his own. His efforts were excellent, but frequently their implementation went poorly because of a lack of buy-in from the team's members, who resented being left out of the problem solving.

Mitch was fortunate because his boss was able to transfer him to a position, at his current salary and level, in which Mitch could work pretty much alone, analyzing others' research on prospective joint ventures before consideration by senior management. But often transferring an employee who doesn't perform as required is not a viable option for a boss. If, for example, an opportunity for a transfer to another job or another department doesn't exist, then a manager may have no option but to demote the employee or to terminate him.

When the situation allows for a decrease in the person's responsibilities and subsequent lowering of grade level and pay, then you may want to demote the staff member rather than terminate if corporate policy gives you such an option. Even though a lower grade can be demoralizing to the individual over the short term, it is better than being terminated. Termination is really your only other option because retaining an employee despite a failure to fully do the job is unfair to other staff members with the same job who must meet the higher standards.

Step 4. Termination

The numerous wrongful termination lawsuits and multimillion-dollar judgments may worry you so much that you would rather tolerate poor performance than fire the staff member, but one of your responsibilities as a manager is to identify employees who are not working up to standard and correct their performance shortcomings. If an employee continues to make repeated mistakes or fails to satisfy department goals or standards, or to act as if he or she would prefer to work elsewhere, then you are justified in letting that individual go.

Keeping on the employee will only create further management headaches for you, as the efficiency and effectiveness of the group are pulled down by the poor performance or attitude of the unrepentant subperformer. In terminating the employee, just be sure that you have documented your attempts to turn the employee's performance around. It will also help you if you stay in touch with Human Resources during the counseling process to ensure that you don't fall into any legal pitfalls (see Chapter 8).

Preparing for a Counseling Interview

Let's return now to Charlie, whom we left as he was on his way to the Human Resources Department to discuss his problems with Gloria.

CHARLIE: HE SETS UP A COUNSELING INTERVIEW

After meeting with Human Resources to understand better the company's policies and procedures for counseling a poor performer, Charlie called Gloria into his office to discuss with her the client's complaint about her and other problems with her performance. He didn't blame the need to counsel her on his boss or anyone else. He was up front with her, taking responsibility not only for his failure to act sooner but also for the decision to meet with her to develop an action plan to overcome whatever performance problems existed. She was resistant but agreed to discuss the matter further with him. So he scheduled a counseling interview with her. And thus Charlie began the counseling process with Gloria. (Counseling worked with Gloria, for those who would like to know. But, as Charlie admitted, it wasn't easy.)

Contrary to the impression that management textbooks seem to give, counseling interviews aren't a cinch. These one-on-one meetings have five goals, which are listed below (and reiterated and expanded in Chapter 6, where they form the core of the chapter), and they aren't successful unless all five are achieved.

1. Win the employee's agreement that there is a need for change.

2. Identify the cause of the problem.

3. Agree on the specific actions that the employee will take to improve his or her performance.

4. Follow up regularly with the employee to ensure that he or she is reaching the goals you both have set.

5. Recognize the employee's accomplishments to reinforce continued correct behavior.

During your interviews, there is a sixth issue that you should address as well. It isn't frequently mentioned, but it is important. You must make a determination as to whether the effort is really worth it. Not only should you consider the problem employee's track record with your company, his or her motivation and willingness to change, and worth to the organization (the talents the individual could bring to the department if he or she worked to standard or beyond), but also the worth of your time spent counseling the individual.

If the problem with the employee is so deeply rooted that you honestly doubt you will succeed, or if counseling will demand more effort than you have the time to give and you know you are unlikely to follow through to see if the employee does make an effort to turn around his or her performance, then it may be better to consider your two other options before investing too much time in one-on-one counseling: either transferring the employee to another area within your organization where this person can perform more effectively, or terminating him or her. At the very least, you may want to shorten the amount of time you give to counseling—from, say, two months to one month. And if there is no improvement, then you may terminate the individual.

Most companies don't specify the amount of counseling required before a warning is issued or the employee is terminated. The option is usually yours, although you should discuss the person's background and any actions you would like to take with Human Resources to be sure that you are on safe legal grounds (in particular, have the documentation to justify your decision). Think of it this way: You don't want to spend so much time on a lost cause that you won't have counseling time to give to other sub-performers with greater potential for improvement or, for that matter, enough coaching time to provide to those average employees who could become outstanding performers. Furthermore, you don't want to distract yourself from projects that are of bottom-line importance to the department. Remember, counseling does not always work to bring around the employee; see the following case study.

LEN: WHEN COUNSELING FAILS

When Len took over the circulation department of a major magazine publisher, he found that he had inherited a major performance problem in the person of a forty-nine-year-old, ten-year veteran with the department, Phyllis. He also had to reorganize the department to handle work associated with the firm's decision to publish a major new magazine. Len had to ask himself if he could turn Phyllis's performance around after two other managers had failed to do so and still give the restructuring all the attention it would need to ensure good customer service to the magazine's charter subscribers.

Corporate historians reported that a problem with Phyllis's performance had been evident after she had been with the company only six months. Her then-supervisor, Bert, had done little about her missed deadlines, poor paperwork, and other work shortcomings. Bert "didn't like to make waves," which meant, among other things, that everyone in the department got the same rating, a 3, meaning that all met standard, which Phyllis's performance certainly did not. After five years with the company, Bert moved on to another job in another company.

After working with Phyllis for a few weeks, Bert's successor, Todd, decided to do something about her performance. Keeping careful documentation of her performance, Todd was able to demonstrate to Phyllis that she did not deserve a rating higher than a 2. That was the rating Todd gave her the first year the two worked together. Phyllis promised

Todd that she would improve, and together they set intermediate standards as a first step toward Phyllis's performing at the same level as everyone else in the department.

The effort seemed to work. In six months, Phyllis had met the intermediate standards. Renewal mailings went out on schedule. Invoices didn't have errors on them. Phyllis came in bright and eager each morning and stayed until after 5:00 P.M. to be sure that the paperwork was in order. When the firm had a special supplement to mail, Phyllis even worked through lunch for several weeks to help, something previously unheard of. Todd was pleased with Phyllis's performance. While her performance wasn't at the same level as that of her co-workers, the change in her attitude was so dramatic that Todd decided to give her a 4 to continue to motivate her the second year the two worked together.

Resuming Old, Bad Habits

Immediately thereafter, Phyllis's performance began to decline. She always had an excuse, but Todd knew the truth: Phyllis had slipped back into her old habits. He was about to begin counseling again, and was even considering putting Phyllis on warning, when he was offered a new position in the magazine's New York office. Before Todd left, he had an opportunity to talk to Woody, his replacement; Woody promised to put an end to her cavalier attitude toward her work while the rest of the department worked itself to exhaustion. And Woody did try—at first.

Woody began meeting with Phyllis once every two weeks to check on her work, and once again she responded positively. But as the department's workload increased, Woody had less time for Phyllis. Once again, this led to a decline in her performance. Woody recognized what was happening. As long as someone kept at her, Phyllis would do the work as she should. But if you turned your back for even a few days, her performance declined.

Woody knew that he should begin the counseling process with the intent of terminating her if there was no significant, long-term improvement, but he felt that he didn't have sufficient time to hold the counseling sessions, document the meetings, issue the warning memo, and so forth. He worried about Phyllis going to court over a decision to terminate her after she had been with the company seven years and had received 3s and even a 4 most of that time. In the end, Woody chose to give Phyllis a 2 each year, which, according to the firm's appraisal program, meant that she "met some standards but not all." Since a 2 still meant a raise, albeit a very small one, Phyllis did virtually nothing in the three years before Len replaced Woody as head of the department.

Len Lowers the Boom

When Len looked at Woody's evaluations, he couldn't understand why Phyllis hadn't been terminated sooner. He knew the department would be assuming even more work in the near future, and everyone would have to pull his or her weight to get the work done. Phyllis would drag down the group's effectiveness and efficiency, and Len decided to act immediately. With the support of Human Resources, he met with Phyllis and told her that the department's role in the company's expansion made it imperative that everyone do his or her full share. He placed her on warning, which was justifiable on the basis of past appraisals submitted by Woody. No one in the department was allowed to perform at a 2 and stay, he said. Phyllis had one month to meet the work standards by which her peers were measured. Further, if her performance declined at any point thereafter, she would be terminated immediately.

This happened two months later. Phyllis had tried to play the same game with Len that she had played with Todd and Woody, but Len wouldn't have it. He knew that he would have had to keep meeting indefinitely with Phyllis to get a full day's work from her. And he didn't have the time. No manager with a problem performer has that kind of time.

After reviewing Phyllis's history with the company, Len had answered the question all managers must ask themselves before they begin counseling a problem performer: Is it worth the effort? In Phyllis's case, the answer was no. What about any problem performers on your staff? Keep in mind that time is a very important asset today, as important as your best performers. You can't become such a nurturing manager that you fail your first responsibility: to get the job done.

CHAPTER 6

How to Turn Around Problem Employees and Employees with Problems

THERE ARE FIVE OBJECTIVES that you will need to accomplish when counseling problem performers:

1. Win the employee's agreement that there is a need for a performance change.
2. Identify the cause of the problem.
3. Agree on the specific actions that the employee will take to improve his or her performance.
4. Follow up regularly with the employee to ensure that he is reaching the goals you both have set.
5. Recognize the employee's accomplishments so as to reinforce continued correct behavior.

These five goals are important whether you are counseling an employee with a work-related problem or one with a personal problem that is influencing job performance. Before we look at how each of these goals can be achieved, it is important to remember that just as you may act as a team coach in the role of group leader, you may also have to serve as its counselor. Consider each of the goals above and change the word *employee* to *team* to appreciate the similarity between counseling a team and an individual.

Consider the roles of a team member. Members of high-performing teams should be committed to their team's mission and operating guidelines. They should complete their assignments on schedule, as promised. They should be open-minded about other members' ideas, not antagonistic. They should be sensitive to their co-workers' needs and feelings, and they shouldn't allow differences in opinion to influence the respect they show their colleagues. They can confront issues, but they should do so without being offensive; they may question another's ideas, but they shouldn't allow themselves to question another's professionalism or personal worth simply because this person holds an opinion different from their own. Finally, they should keep their differences of opinion within the meeting room.

When team members fail in any of these areas, they require counseling. That being the case, how should you begin? With goals such as these in mind:

Goal 1: Win Agreement

Let's consider, first, that you need to address a problem with the performance of one of your employees. To put the individual at ease at the start of the meeting, you can open the session with a variant of the following: "Jennifer, there's something that's concerning me and I need to talk to you about it," or "Michael, there's something bothering me and I need to see if I can get your help in getting it taken care of."

Once you have the employee's attention, you can then move on to the nature of the employee's problem behavior by describing what was expected and how she is failing to meet that expectation. Of course, your employee may disagree with your perception of the situation. You may see a gap, whereas the employee may not or may acknowledge a gap but blame it on others or on a lack of critical resources or on some other factors beyond her control.

MARVIN: COACHING TURNS TO COUNSELING

In Chapter 1, I mentioned Cora, the former head of a high-tech firm who was having adjustment problems working for others. Unfortunately, coaching didn't help her very much. She continued to come into the office late and had an assortment of excuses for her tardiness and sudden departures from the office, from dental problems to car trouble to leaks in her bathroom. Worse, deadlines weren't met. Her staff grew increasingly disenchanted with her as their team leader, so much so that two went over her head to complain to the Human Resources Department about the situation.

Human Resources heard the grumbling from the tenth floor and contacted Cora's former supervisor, Marvin, who had been promoted. Marvin knew about Cora's past adjustment problems, but he had been working with a team in another locale and did not know how badly the situation had deteriorated. Indeed, in Marvin's absence, Greg, the HR director, had had to go over to Marvin's office. When he came back to the office, there was his supervisor, Effie, in his office, demanding that Marvin put an end to the situation *immediately*. Actually, given the tone of her voice, it was IMMEDIATELY!

Marvin decided to use his regular progress meeting with Cora to discuss her performance difficulties. Marvin isn't well regarded himself by the operation, but staff respects him as a leader and manager—they just see him as insensitive to people, more a number-cruncher than a caring human being. Cora heard him out and she agreed to be in at 9:00 A.M., take only an hour for lunch, and leave no earlier than 5:00 P.M. But she refused to accept the criticism of herself as a team leader and manager. Later, she even brought it to the attention of the project team she oversaw. "How could Marvin tell me that I'm a poor manager and leader? He doesn't know what that entails?" All that members of the group could do was to look at each other in astonishment. Cora seemed to be close to postal, so no one dared speak up. What happened? Marvin reported to Effie that he had met with Cora and that he thought the problem had been handled. She knew that she had to change her style of management and work, and that was that.

Unfortunately, Cora never did change. If anything, her work performance got worse at the same time. Cora seemed to go out of her way to demonstrate to senior management that she was more than qualified for her position, using the time of team members for unnecessary presentations and work projects designed to get Cora credit for her entrepreneurial skills. She continued to be a lousy leader and manager, and the team continued to carry her by doing much of her work, unbeknownst to Marvin. At weekly progress meetings, Cora gave every impression that every accomplishment of her team was due to her own know-how and ability. When Marvin discovered the truth—and he did discover the truth eventually—Cora was fired.

Most textbooks make counseling seem so easy, but for the process to work, first and foremost the employee must agree that a problem exists, that he or she is responsible, and that his or her supervisor is justifiable in bringing the problem up. What does that mean?

If you were the manager preparing for a counseling session, you would have done your homework. This includes knowing how often the problem occurs and the consequences of the problem on the person's work or on the performance of co-workers or the department as a whole. More important, you have to have documented your observations. After you have raised the issue, you have to be ready to listen to the employee's explanation. To prompt her, you might say, "Tell me about it," or ask, "Is my understanding accurate?" or "Is there more I should know about what happened?"

Of course, there is the possibility of a misunderstanding, and the employee may be in the right. So listen with an open mind to the explanation. If you believe the employee, then the matter is over. If you have doubts about the employee's view of the situation, then you can tell her that you will look further into the matter, then get back to her. (Parenthetically, if the employee is lying, the knowledge that you will follow up with other parties to confirm her story will prompt her to 'fess up.)

How would this play out if you had a problem within your team? If the individual were a member of your staff, then the discussion would be very much the same as that with a problem performer. A more informal conversation might be called for if the problem member were a peer or, worse, a superior on the organization chain of command. In the latter case, you might want to invite the person to have coffee in your office or, better yet, take him or her to lunch to talk about the team's progress and discuss how your peer could help the team achieve its mission. Don't emphasize the individual's failure to pull his or her weight. Rather, talk about the ways that the individual could contribute *more* to the overall effort.

Probe gently to determine if a problem exists. Perhaps the team member isn't really supportive of the mission, or it may be a matter of workload and too little time to commit to the team effort. In the former case, if you can't convince the individual about the worth of the effort, then you might want to suggest that the person drop out of the group. If it is the latter case—interest in the project but too much else to juggle to give the effort his or her full attention—then you might want to discuss with the member an action plan that might keep him or her informed of team progress but not involved in an active way—perhaps he or she could assign a staff member to participate in his or her place.

If the colleague doesn't "get it"—that is, that there is a need for more effort on his or her part—you may have to more directly confront the issue. To appreciate how that is done, let me share with you a situation faced by my friend Charlie, a warehouse manager (see Chapter 5).

CHARLIE: CONFRONTING GLORIA WITH THE FACTS

For Gloria, Charlie's assistant, there was actually a letter from a client who was annoyed enough by Gloria's brusque manner to write to the plant manager, Charlie's boss. There were also several other incidents that Charlie could cite based on the observations of other managers, such as the occasion when Gloria was seen reading a Danielle Steele novel while the other assistants in the plant were rushing about to complete a last-minute order, or the occasion when Gloria refused to help a co-worker process an order while this other assistant completed an important report due out that morning.

Because Charlie had been blind to the existence of a problem until it was brought to his attention by the results of a 360-degree feedback, he did not have a lot of supportive documentation. Still, he had enough evidence so that the issues he raised with Gloria were not subject to interpretation or argument. Further, since he had set standards with Gloria at the start of the year as a part of the company's evaluation process, he could point to how the undesirable behavior represented a major discrepancy with the work standards to which she had agreed.

Gloria continued to deny the existence of any problem for much of the meeting. She had been reading a book because she had "a terrific headache and needed to take a break" from a major project she was doing for Charlie at the time. She might have said no to the co-worker who asked for help, but, Gloria told Charlie, she had her own work to do. "Can't I stop for a minute to catch my breath," she asked, "before someone with much less to do tries to pass her undone work on to me?"

Gloria then began to list the many tasks she was responsible for. Charlie had never complained about her performance before, and Gloria felt she could convince him that the complaints he had heard about her work were unfounded. Charlie sat silently and listened without interrupting her. Charlie knew that listening to her comments in response to his description of the undesirable behavior was important to the success of the counseling process, especially in the earlier stages. It would not only demonstrate to Gloria that he wanted to hear her side of the story but would also give him insights into the problems in her performance.

He didn't want the meeting to turn into a confrontation; rather, he wanted a conversation in which he would play the smaller part—the 20/80 rule. He hoped that his silence would encourage Gloria to tell him about what was happening in the workplace, the problems she had, and why she was behaving as she did.

When Gloria had explained each of the incidents to her satisfaction, Charlie paused for about five seconds and then said, "I didn't realize that you were so busy. I can understand why you occasionally ask for help from some of the other assistants." Then he paused again, using silence to get Gloria to add more information.

"Well, it is true that occasionally one of the assistants lends me a hand," she acknowledged. "Work can stack up."

"I'm sure," Charlie answered.

"Are you telling me that I should be helping out if I have the time?" Gloria asked.

"What do you think?" Charlie asked. "Should you?"

"I guess I should," Gloria admitted. "But there are times when I just can't."

"Looking back," Charlie asked, "do you think those instances I mentioned earlier were times when you couldn't help because of critical work that had to be done?"

"No," she admitted. "I had work to do, but I could have put it aside to lend Linda a hand."

By asking questions and listening carefully to the replies—demonstrating his interest in her comments both by his remarks and by body movements, such as leaning toward Gloria and nodding his head—Charlie had begun to achieve his first goal: to get Gloria to accept the existence of problems in her performance. As they talked, he was also able to communicate to Gloria the implications of her behavior both for the department and for her. The department was short-staffed, and everyone had to pull together if client firms were to get their orders as promised. Those members of the staff who acted as if they were above the team and didn't cooperate wouldn't get a raise, might even be placed on warning, and could be terminated.

Note how important the standards for performance set with Gloria were to Charlie in his confronting Gloria about her performance. Likewise, as a team leader, to strengthen your words of concern, you can rely on the ground rules you and the team should have set when you first assembled. If a member's behavior violates the team's guidelines, you can point that out, thereby strengthening your argument for a change in the person's behavior. Likewise, you can address those who lose team focus by reviewing the importance of the team's mission.

If you are familiar enough with your team members to know what matters most to them (think *motivator*), then you can use these as drivers, as well, to get them to behave more productively for the team's sake. Finally, you can utilize peer pressure, giving the individual insight into how his or her teammates might be responding to the situation and how this could affect future relationships with these individuals.

Getting an individual to admit to the existence of a problem is critical, whether you are counseling a peer on your team or a staff member. Once the person acknowledges there may be a problem, he or she is ready to discuss the reason behind the performance problem.

Goal 2: Identify the Problem's Cause

Often the source of the performance problem isn't clear, as turned out to be the case with Gloria. She believed that, because she was Charlie's assistant and he was warehouse manager, her work took priority over everyone else's. In her mind, this meant that she shouldn't be bothered with "nuisance phone calls from customers who didn't know what they wanted" or with requests for help from the assistants of those who reported to Charlie.

Charlie had not had much documentation to use to help him identify the source of the problem with Gloria. He had to use his first meeting with her to get her to acknowledge that a problem existed and to find its cause. But sometimes, despite much documentation of a problem in performance, it doesn't reveal the cause of the problem. Or a manager may assume that he or she knows the cause of the performance problem, but after probing beneath the surface, the manager may uncover an entirely different picture from what at first seemed to be the truth. Consider what happened to George:

GEORGE GETTING INPUT FROM COLLEAGUES

The head of purchasing for a print house, George had decided to keep Lisa on when the company downsized his department. Now, six months

later, he wondered if he had made the right decision about which individual to let go. George carefully documented his employee's performance, and his records showed that Lisa took anything he said as a
reprimand and became argumentative in response. She had also been
in arguments with co-workers and other managers. Her behavior had
become disruptive to the department, so he scheduled a counseling
session with her to discuss the problem and try to come up with some
solution.

Over lunch, he met with Micki and Chrissy, two other supervisors at the
Atlanta-based printing company. Since Micki had once supervised Lisa,
George decided to use this meeting to ask Micki if she had any advice
on how to open the discussion with Lisa. He would be meeting with
her that afternoon for the first in a series of "unproductive counseling
sessions," in his opinion, if he didn't get a better fix on the nature of
the problem.

When George mentioned the situation he was facing, he found that
Micki and Chrissy were in similar binds: Micki was already counseling
Simon but to no avail, and Chrissy would begin counseling Bill next
week. Simon was a workaholic, Micki explained, and he put a great
deal of effort into his job. But he got too involved in minute details. He
got so wrapped up in them that on two occasions major print jobs were
completed behind schedule. Bill presented a different management
challenge. He didn't care about deadlines, frequently came to work
late, produced sloppy paperwork, and didn't care how he or his office
looked. The following conversation ensued:

> Chrissy: How do I tell an employee to bathe regularly? [George and
>   Micki laugh.] No, I'm serious. When he came to the company,
>   he was dressed in a suit and was at work a half hour ahead of
>   schedule. Now I'm lucky if he's only a half hour late. And he
>   seems to have one shirt and one pair of pants and to wear
>   them each and every day.
> George: I think I know what's wrong with Bill. His wife left him
>   about six months ago. It could be that the poor guy is so devas-
>   tated that he just doesn't care about anything anymore, in-
>   cluding his work.
> Chrissy: Do you think that's the problem? When I meet with Bill
>   next week, I'll ask him if he's had any personal problems that
>   could be behind his performance problems. If you're right,
>   counseling may be worth the time. I thought I would just be
>   going through the motions and would ultimately have to termi-
>   nate him.

George: Well, ladies, what about Lisa? Do you have any idea why she is always on the defensive?

Micki: I would be frightened if I worked in a department that had just undergone layoffs. Say, that could explain her defensiveness. At least it's one issue that you can raise with her.

George: I will. Micki, I wish I could help you with Simon, but I don't know anything about him.

Chrissy had no inside information about Simon either, but she had a suggestion: "Review his job with him." Chrissy explained how at her former job she had had problems because she had no clear idea of her job priorities. "I thought I was doing a super job, then I found myself in counseling and nearly terminated," she recalled. "Could that be Simon's problem?"

"It shouldn't be," Micki said, "but I'll make sure at my next session to go over the job description and make clear the priorities. Thanks for the input." The three supervisors were able to help each other. During their lunch, they came up with three likely reasons that would enable them to better direct their counseling efforts.

Situations That Create Problems

Among the situations that can create problem performers, and that you should consider when you have to counsel an employee, are the following:

• *Stress.* Sometimes the stress comes from the demands of the workplace. Sometimes it can come from factors outside the workplace.

• *Unclear Priorities.* Where this is the problem, the responsibility is more the manager's than the employee's. While the employee should verify his assumptions about what demands priority, the manager should make clear from the first day the individual is on the job which tasks take precedence.

• *Poor time or task management.* Some employees are more skilled at organizing their work than others. Those who lack the ability can easily become overwhelmed in today's leaner organizations in which they get multiple assignments, each of equal importance. Often, though, all these individuals need is some training in setting priorities, planning, and organizing their time.

- *Oversupervision or Undersupervision.* Oversupervision can make an employee, particularly a creative one, feel thwarted, unable to pursue her ideas without first clearing them with her supervisor. In economic downturns, oversupervision can also make some employees feel that their bosses are just looking for justification for terminating them. If the problem is undersupervision, the employee may not know how to get done what she has to finish.

- *Interpersonal Conflicts.* Conflicts may be between employees on the same level or between the employee and you. The resolution is mediation, either by you or, if you are a party to the conflict, by a third, objective person.

- *Breach of Promise.* Dissatisfaction with the job and company may begin right after an employee is hired if, during the interviewing process, the employee has been led to believe that the job he is being considered for is one with more responsibility or promotion opportunities than it really has. Maybe the promises were well intended, but circumstances beyond the manager's control now prevent him from making good on them. The cause doesn't matter, but the end result is a dissatisfied employee who takes his dissatisfaction out on co-workers and customers and by doing a second-rate job.

- *Personal Problems.* It's difficult to do any job as we should when our personal life is a mess. The personal problems of a problem performer may be of the employee's own making or they may result from a problem of someone close to him. Regardless of the cause, it distracts her; at worst, it makes the employee unproductive, argumentative, and uncooperative. Where the personal problem involves substance abuse, it could cause chronic tardiness, absenteeism, high accident and injury rates, or mood swings that make it difficult to know this person's emotional state on any one day.

These problems can cause poor effort from a team member in the same way that they can interfere with general job performance. Getting to the source of the problem, like getting acknowledgment of the existence of a problem, involves gentle probing and active listening by a team leader or a manager.

Most management textbooks leave the impression that counseling interviews are brief. You tell the employee she has a problem. She agrees. She comes up with a perfect solution, and you set up a follow-up interview. All done? Not so! A manager has to take it slow and easy with some employees. For instance, George was right about Bill—his wife had filed for divorce and the breakup had so devastated him that he was now seeing a psychologist—but it took lots of questions to get Bill to admit the nature of the problem.

CHRISSY: COUNSELING BILL

During her counseling session with Bill, Chrissy had no difficulty getting Bill to acknowledge the existence of a problem, but he hedged about the source of the problem. He just kept telling her that he was "taking care of it. Just let me have some time." Chrissy knew better than to blurt out questions about Bill's personal life, but what Bill left unsaid convinced her that George was right about a personal problem being behind the work problem. So Chrissy told him, "Bill, when I first hired you, you were extremely conscientious, concerned about exhibiting a professional image, and eager to take on more work to move up. I know you aren't happy with your appearance and the state of your work, and you are serious in promising to turn the situation around, but I need more than a promise that the situation will improve. What specifically will you do?"

That's when Bill admitted to seeing a psychologist to help him handle a personal problem in his life. Chrissy was silent, which prompted Bill to elaborate. He told her that he had started staying out late and drinking with some guys he had met at a neighborhood bar. He didn't like what was happening, but getting his license suspended for driving while intoxicated was the impetus for him to seek professional counseling.

Had Bill not been seeing a professional counselor, Chrissy likely would have advised him to consult the firm's employee-assistance program or to seek outside counseling. Even so, as was necessary, Chrissy pointed out to Bill that while she sympathized with his personal problems, she could not allow them to affect his work or grooming since he worked in an area visited by customers. "If the problems continue, particularly your tardiness," she said, "I'll have to put you on warning."

Bill asked if he could review the status of several projects on his desk and come back with an action plan that would ensure completion of the work as scheduled. He promised no more late nights, and he would be in promptly at 9:00 A.M. thereafter. Chrissy agreed to his offer, and she and Bill scheduled a meeting for Friday, three days off, to discuss the matter further.

MICKI AND GEORGE: COUNSELING SIMON AND LISA

Simon's problem turned out to be confusion about work priorities, and Micki was able in one meeting to address this by reviewing the standards by which his work would be measured. They were able to move quickly on to develop an action plan that would reassure Micki that Simon was clear about his work responsibilities and get him back to focusing not just on the details—the trees—but also considering the forest, or department mission, that was represented in his work.

Lisa wasn't as easy a performance problem to get a handle on. From the moment she entered George's cubicle, she was uptight. George knew he would have a hard time with her. Normally taciturn, she did not stop chattering about her work from the moment she entered. George suspected that Lisa knew that he was unhappy about her relationship with him and other staff members, who were also targets of her sarcasm and defensiveness, and that she was trying to avoid discussing them by distracting him with talk about every job on her desk at that moment.

Finally, in the middle of a story about a requisition form Lisa needed to complete updating her computer's software, George interrupted. Apologizing, he said, "That's all very interesting, Lisa. You obviously have your hands full. The layoffs didn't help," he commented.

"No," she said, now with a silence that was unnerving.

"It's been a tough period for all of us," George continued. "I wanted to discuss the impact it seems to have had on our relationship and your relationships with others in the department," George said, pulling out a log of his conversations with Lisa as he spoke. "I am concerned that you . . . ."

He hadn't even finished his sentence when the old Lisa returned. "You're always picking on my work," she said. "You are only doing it to get out of the promise you made me when you hired me," she continued.

Flummoxed, George asked, "What promise?"

"An upgrading and raise after six months if I did the job well," she replied.

"I don't think I made any promises," he replied. Controlling his own defensiveness, he continued, "During our interview, you said you wanted a job with promotability and I told you stories about two employees who had been upgraded after only six months with us. But,

Lisa," he continued "we also discussed the fact that the job you were taking would involve stretch. After four months, we also downsized."

"You promised," Lisa replied, a grim expression on her face.

"Even if your work merited an upgrading, which it doesn't," George said, his calm retained only with difficulty, "there is no place for advancement. And I am very concerned about your behavior. You become so defensive when you talk with others about your work that several people have asked that I assign someone else to work with them instead of you. I have to agree with their complaints. You make it very hard for people to work with you."

George was again preparing to pull out the workbook in which he kept a record of his employees' performance, when she jumped up and told him, "OK, OK. I get it." George wanted to move toward achieving the next goal in one-on-one counseling, but it was evident to him that he would get nowhere with Lisa until she had had a chance to think about what he had said. So he asked her to come to his office two days later to discuss how they could address her performance problems.

Goal 3: Agree on Specific Employee Actions

The third goal in one-on-one counseling interviews is to reach agreement on the specific actions the employee will take to improve performance. Here, the example of Bill, Simon, and Lisa continues.

MICKI, CHRISSY, AND GEORGE: GETTING TO AGREEMENT

Micki's single discussion with Simon had gone as described in management textbooks. Micki had said Simon wasn't doing the job she expected of him, he agreed, and they identified the cause as confusion about job priorities, and they were able to agree on what he should do in the future. He signed an action plan that clarified his responsibilities. Problem solved.

On the surface, Chrissy also had done well. Bill acknowledged his poor performance, Chrissy learned the reason, and she and Bill agreed on an action plan. Except that Bill didn't live up to the action plan he signed off on. The very next day, he was late again to work. This time he was hung over. Instead of her session with him giving Bill reason to get back on track, he seemed to think that his disclosure of the problem meant she would let him get away with an "occasional night out with the boys while his divorce went through."

Chrissy knew another meeting was called for, and scheduled one with Bill that afternoon. George also had arranged for another meeting with Lisa. George's purpose was to reach agreement with Lisa on the steps she would take to make her work relationship with him and others better, whereas Chrissy's purpose was to formalize the actions she expected from Bill to ensure that he arrived on time each day, continued counseling, and caught up on his backed-up assignments. She also had to make clearer to him the consequences if he continued to come to work late and allowed his work to fall behind.

Lastly, Lisa seemed more positive when she came into George's office. And with good cause. She considered the various opportunities in George's area and she proposed that he put her in charge of vendor quality assurance, which would guarantee her an upgrading, if not a salary increase. She attributed her performance problems to his failure to keep his promise, and said that the upgrading would put an end to the problem since she would be working with clients, not envious co-workers or tradition-bound managers (which, based on her expression, included him).

George was shocked. While he could transfer her to another department with a vacancy—and get her an upgrading in the process—he knew he would only be passing along the problem to another manager. So he repeated his previous statement that there were no opportunities for advancement in the department, that she was not qualified yet for promotion in the department even if there were one, and that her behavior with others inside and outside the organization had to improve or he would have to put her on warning. To win some cooperation from her, he offered to provide learning opportunities for her by sending her to a course on purchasing if her interpersonal relations with others improved over the next six months.

Lisa was clearly annoyed, but this time she did not run off. She listened and grudgingly signed off on the action plan that called for her to be more responsive to others' suggestions, work more collaboratively with co-workers, and work to build bridges she had burned with others in the organization. They agreed to get together in two weeks provided another incident involving him, a colleague, or client did not occur in the interim.

George took a deep breath when Lisa left. He suspected that further problems might occur, but he also expected that she would begin job hunting. Given her attitude, and that attitude's impact on her behavior, he decided to call Human Resources to find out if he could put her on warning if another situation occurred.

Chrissy was more sanguine about her meeting with Bill. She laid down the rules to Bill—and much more firmly than she had in her earlier meeting. She made clear to him that he would be put on warning if he was late again, which was one step short of termination. She would do this, she told him, if he didn't get his act together. She made clear that his personal problem did not give him an excuse to pull down the productivity of the rest of the department.

Before going on to the next goal, let me add one point about achieving this goal. Don't fall for the "I'll try" game, a game Bill was very good at. When Chrissy asked him to correct his behavior, he kept saying, "Sure, Chrissy, I'll try."

When an employee says, "I'll try," he has agreed to the action plan but only to the extent of trying to achieve it. And *trying doesn't count.* If you are ready to close the meeting, and the employee keeps saying, "I'll try . . . I'll try . . ." you may want to move beyond that imprecise promise to get the employee to actually state what he will do to make the action plan a reality.

Goal 4: Follow Up

You want to be sure that the employee is making the goals you both set. It's usually done at a follow-up meeting scheduled during the first meeting. Let's return to our example.

CHRISSY, GEORGE, AND MICKI: THE FOLLOW-UP MEETINGS

Chrissy and George had both set up follow-up meetings in two weeks, whereas Micki had agreed to meet with Simon in a month. Surprisingly, it was Micki who had to get together with Simon before the scheduled time. Rather than delegate to the department assistant some work for a proposal to produce a major publisher's new magazine, Simon had done the work himself, lost time in completing the proposal as a consequence, missed the deadline for submitting the proposal, and lost the client for the firm.

Since the agreed-on action plan between Simon and Micki called for Simon to delegate as much detail work as he could in order to complete bids and other proposals on time, his failure to complete the project on schedule was cause for a meeting between the two. Although he had acknowledged a problem at the start of counseling, this incident, more than the earlier discussion, brought home to him how important it was for him to delegate the details to others. He promised that there would be no repetition of such an incident, and Micki felt that he meant it. But she made clear to him that, given the importance of his work, a repetition would put him on warning.

A few days later, Chrissy met with Bill to discuss his progress. Since their second meeting, Bill had not been late. She also learned then that Bill had caught up on almost all his work. After their second meeting, Bill had provided Chrissy with a report on the status of his work. At this follow-up meeting, he showed Chrissy that, except for one major task, all other tasks had been completed. He had done so by putting in hours at the office after others had left. Bill also informed Chrissy that the divorce papers had all been signed, and he and his psychologist had agreed that he did not need further professional counseling. Chrissy reminded him that he was still in performance counseling, but she also told him how pleased she was about his efforts.

George continued to have it harder than Chrissy and Micki. He had to put Lisa on warning for losing her temper with one of her co-workers who had moved some files. Once again, Lisa blamed George for the circumstances in which she found herself. He had seen the Human Resources Department, and received its assurance that so long as he documented each of his meetings with Lisa, he would be within his rights to terminate her if another such incident occurred. The warning memo that Lisa left with made that very clear. It stated that on several occasions she had been rude to co-workers and clients and had made it difficult for others to work with her. It noted that she had met twice with George and had agreed to change her behavior, as evidenced by her signature on the agreed-upon action plan, but the problem continued. The circumstances that warranted the warning were also described.

Goal 5: Reinforce Improved Performance

You have to acknowledge improvements in an employee's performance to sustain that improvement. Toward that end, you might even want to reward the employee with a special assignment or opportunity for special training, as was the case with our example.

Gray Issues

Counseling can become much more complex than dealing with good or poor performance. Sometimes there are factors beyond the employee's willingness and efforts to change performance that will influence the decision about how much time the individual is given to improve. For instance, you might find yourself being pressured by your boss or others in the organization to transfer, demote, or even terminate an employee with a remediable job problem because he lacks the skills to handle some new office technology. The assumption is that it is more efficient for you to hire someone better skilled than it is to spend time training the problem employee. But is this true, or fair?

Sometimes the pressure is due to such an amorphous situation as senior management's belief that the problem performer just "doesn't fit in." That's what happened to Mel.

MEL: HIS DILEMMA IS DONNA

A manager in a consulting firm based in a small town in New York State, Mel had an assistant named Donna. When Donna moved out of her family home and got her own apartment, she started to come in late despite the nearness of her new residence to work. In addition, she began to take extended lunch hours. Mel tried to be understanding, but after a month of this behavior he decided to talk to her about her late arrivals and long lunches. She wasn't that late for work or after lunch, but she wasn't there to pick up the phone and the company did not like its customers' calls answered by voice mail. Like most managers, Mel spent much of his time in meetings with colleagues or clients.

Mel's Boss: A Complicating Factor

Mel felt that all he would have to do would be to remind Donna of her responsibility to be on time for work and after lunch, and the problem would be solved. But Mel's boss, Sid, wasn't so happy about this solution. Truth was, Sid didn't like Donna. Her funky clothes and bright-orange hair didn't fit his image of an administrative assistant for Mel, one of the firm's top, and most highly paid, consultants. Sid's own assistant had a sister, and he suggested that Mel use the chronic tardiness and long lunches as a way to rid himself of Donna and get someone like his secretary's sister, someone who looked and dressed the part of an assistant to a high-priced consultant.

Mel felt himself caught between a rock and a hard place when he learned that Donna might need to go on flextime and take extended lunch breaks for a few more weeks, if not months. She had a new puppy, and she was having problems housebreaking him. Mel explained the situation to Sid, but it carried little weight. "Tell her she has to get in on time," he said, "even if she has to get rid of the pooch." Obviously, he hoped that Donna would choose the dog over her job.

Mel had no intention of suggesting to Donna that she get rid of her new dog. Nor did he want to lose Donna, who had worked for him for several years, knew him and the firm's work well, could anticipate the needs of clients when they called, and, maybe most important, was very organized, making up for his own disorganization. On the other hand, Sid kept pressing for Donna's dismissal.

A Showdown with Sid

Finally, Mel had it out with Sid. He admitted that there was a problem; he also believed that there were some problems with Donna's professional image. He would discuss all this with her, and they would try to reach some compromise, but he would not insist that Donna wear only business suits or recolor her hair to a less vibrant hue. About her lateness, Donna had arranged to have a co-worker at a nearby workstation pick up the phone on those days that she was late for work. She would make up for her tardiness by taking work home. As far as her extended lunch hours to check on the pup were concerned, she had talked a neighbor into doing this and walking the dog if need be. Most important, Mel pointed out the cost to the company of losing Donna, not only in terms of her knowledge but in real dollars spent for the high-priced temp who would be necessary until a full-time replacement could be found, for a recruitment firm to find a suitable candidate, and for the higher salary the company would have to pay a newcomer who would demand far more than Donna was currently earning. Mel made a strong case for helping Donna work out her problems. And his arguments were all valid.

Before giving in to pressures—whether from an increasing workload or from clients, colleagues, or even your boss—you should weigh the time you will have to invest in finding a suitable replacement for the job and the cost of recruitment, including training time and the lowered morale of staff members who will mourn the loss of their co-worker, against the return on counseling, which could include not only improved employee performance but also increased employee loyalty and commitment and growing managerial respectability among staff members. Remember, too, that there is no guarantee that the new hire will not have some performance flaws.

Summing Up

What do the experiences of managers Charlie, George, Micki, Chrissy, and even Mel tell us about the counseling process?

- You can't get far in counseling unless the employee accepts the existence of a problem.
- You should be clear about the purpose of the meeting.
- You need to describe clearly the undesirable behavior and to be able to show, through documentation, the discrepancy between the standard or desired behavior and the current level of performance.
- You should be prepared for the employee to try to distract you or otherwise try to control the meeting rather than address the need for counseling.
- You need to probe the answers given in order to get a clearer idea of the cause of the problem.
- You should ask open-ended questions to get the employee to share his or her feelings.
- You should paraphrase the remarks of the employee to show that you are truly listening to what he is saying.
- If you must, you may want to prepare a list of questions in advance to ensure that your conversation is focused.

- You should encourage the employee to identify several alternative solutions to the problem and to share his or her feelings about the consequences of each of these alternatives before settling on a single plan.
- You should learn how to use silence to get an employee to fill in the silence with the critical information you want.
- You should give the employee the chance to tell his or her story without interruption.
- You must be sure that the employee knows both the effect of his or her behavior on workflow and on co-workers' performance and the consequences of a continuation of the problem.
- You need to be clear about the kind of behavior or level of performance you want from employees. Make sure that you ask for behavior-related change, not attitudinal change.
- Don't reprimand. The more at ease the employee is, the more responsive he or she will be during counseling.
- You want more than a signature on an action plan as evidence of a commitment to change; the only commitment that counts is the actions of the employee.
- Don't make judgments about employees, like calling them lazy, difficult to work with, or losers.
- You should show confidence in the employee's ability to turn around his or her performance.
- Be prepared with information about the company's policies and procedures (or ready to get such information) to help the employee come up with an action plan.
- Refer the employee to the employee-assistance program or Human Resources Department if the problem is beyond your scope.
- If the source of the problem is a personal problem, while referring the employee to others, aim for agreement on actions he or she will take to turn around performance.
- Recognize that there may be factors beyond the individual's performance to include in any equation concerned with salvaging the employee.

If you are to turn around a problem performer and get good to outstanding performance from the individual, you have to demonstrate that the employee can't just go through the motions when in counseling. And the only way you can do this is to prove by your actions that you are prepared to move up to the next step in the counseling process—through the warning stage to termination—if the employee doesn't improve in very specific ways. So, after that first meeting, monitor the behavior, praising even minor improvements as an incentive for the person to make greater efforts.

If there is no change by the end of the agreed-upon time, you need to find out from the employee why he or she thinks the problem continues. Consider new options, such as additional training or more frequent monitoring in critical areas, to help the person overcome difficulties. Get a commitment to the new plan and set up a new date for evaluation. If the employee's performance rises to a satisfactory level by then, praise the individual, and if you think it is justified, consider some positive reinforcement, like a desirable assignment or a new responsibility to show your faith. But if the employee's performance doesn't improve significantly within a reasonable amount of time, it's time to talk warning, demotion, or termination.

So long as you can answer yes to each of the following questions, you can feel comfortable about your role in the counseling process.

1. Did I give the employee the opportunity to share with me all the information about the situation?

2. Was I clear about the specific behavior that needed to be corrected?

3. Did I ask open-ended questions followed by closed-ended ones to get to the heart of the situation?

4. Did I explain both the reasons the behavior change was necessary and the consequences if no change occurred?

5. Did I offer to help to ensure the change?

6. Was I clear that I expected the individual to meet minimum standards, regardless of his or her potential?

7. Was I ready to provide positive reinforcement if there was a change in performance?

8. Was I as fair as I could reasonably be to the employee, not allowing external factors to influence my assessment of his or her performance?

Let's Talk:
Specific Counseling Sessions

THROUGHOUT YOUR CAREER, you will encounter numerous situations involving problem employees and employees with problems. Managers tell me that they don't have a problem holding a counseling session, but they do have difficulty coming up with a realistic action plan—particularly for troubled employees. Consequently, we'll offer here some specific action plans to help you as well.

Counseling Peers on a Cross-Functional Team

Just as most management books provide a simplistic picture of employee counseling, books on team management talk in general terms about team counseling. The truth is, without positional power over your colleagues, counseling team members about their behavior is tantamount to your saying to the colleague, "I'm right and you're wrong."

So, when counseling peers, you need to make a point of not sounding self-righteous. This would only alienate them when what you want to do is to get their cooperation, their appreciation of the consequences to the team's mission of their continued misbehavior, and their agreement to an action plan that will change the situation. If they accept your assessment of their behavior and readily agree to your recommendation, you're home free. You've done your counseling job. But it isn't always as easy as that. Not all your team members will be team players, willing to cooperate and accept and act on the feedback from someone who is *just* a peer. As an example, let's look at how one team member's lack of punctuality affected the rest of the team, and how a manager handled the situation. When Jekyll Apparel formed a new product team, Jill, its leader, worked with the group to set operating ground rules, including the need for members to be punctual for the start of each meeting. Still, Ted never seemed to be able to get to sessions on time.

Jill didn't let that cause her to delay the start of the meetings, which began on schedule. She knew how busy Ted was, so she never said any-thing, even though his late arrivals—usually fifteen to twenty minutes after the scheduled meeting started—tended to disrupt the group's dis-cussion. Ted was responsible for developing the numbers for any business plans the group submitted, and he usually came loaded down with paper-work. While he got seated, and arranged his documentation on the table or on a nearby chair, discussion seemed to stall.

Was Jill right not to talk to Ted about his chronic lateness and its effect on the team? If the problem had been short-lived, maybe. But after a month, by which time Ted's workload had lessened, he continued to arrive at meetings late. On one or two occasions, he also came empty-handed, his assignments unfinished. Jill saw also that Ted's indifference to being punctual, along with his laxity about his team assignments, was infecting other members of the team. Betty, Ken, and Marian, three other group members, also began to arrive late.

Jill was upset but not as much as members of the group who contin-ued to take the operating guidelines seriously. Jill had seen some fac-tiousness between the tardy and prompt members, but she had assumed it had to do with the proposals on the table; it had never occurred to her, until Franny spoke up, that those who had made a point of arriving on time were furious with the late arrivals, and that it was being reflected in the group's discussions.

"Do you know, Jill," Franny said, "over the last two months I figure I have spent about seven hours or a day's worth of my time waiting for Ted and his cohorts to arrive for these meetings? Why can't we just start without them?"

"Ted is bringing some key data today," Jill replied. "We need it to move beyond our earlier discussion of new overseas markets."

"You're assuming that he has done the work," Zoë said. Beside her, Julio nodded his head. Julio then rose. "I'll be in my office, Jill. I have some correspondence to get to. Let me know when you want to get down to work."

Jill realized that she had a serious problem on her hands as Zoë and Bill followed Julio out of the room. When Ted, Betty, Ken, and Marian arrived, they were surprised to find only Jill present. She called Julio, Zoë, and Franny into the room and the group got down to work. Fortunately, for Jill—and for Ted's reputation among his peers—he had completed his expected number crunching. But that didn't let him off the hook, in Jill's opinion. Nor were Betty, Ken, and Marian innocent bystanders because they had begun to emulate Ted's behavior.

Confronting the Culprits

Before the next meeting, Jill met with each of the late arrivers. As you can imagine, Betty, Ken, and Marian all used Jill's failure to do anything about Ted's chronic tardiness and undone assignments to excuse their own behavior.

"You're right, I should have talked to Ted about coming late to meetings," Jill admitted to Marian when she went to see her colleague. "But that isn't justification for your pattern of lateness over the last few meetings. You also promised to have demographics for the team for both the London and Southampton markets. You're late with the information."

"Ted has been late, too, in the past, and you haven't said anything about it," Marian said in defense.

"Yes, I know. But we're talking about your commitment to the team, not Ted's," Jill continued.

"I . . ." Marian stammered.

"I know how busy you are," Jill said. "But the team needs your knowledge and support." Jill knew how important it was for Marian to be respected by her peers and it became her ace. Pulling it out, she said, "Your fellow team members will admire your contribution to the effort."

Marian started to defend her past behavior once again, then abruptly stopped. "Maybe you're right," she conceded. "I have been too cavalier about my participation in the new products group. I will be on time in the future. And, Jill," she added, "I'll have those demographics for you by tomorrow. We can distribute them ahead of the meeting, so everyone will have a chance to study them before the session."

"Great," said Jill. Jill also spoke to Ken and Betty. In Jill's discussion with Ken, she used the importance of the team's mission to his product line to get his agreement to change his behavior. Peer pressure worked with Betty, who was reminded of how angry she had been with a colleague who had never arrived on time in another team situation. "I can imagine how others on the team must have felt about my actions," she told Jill. "I've got a new computer program and I can use it to program my computer to buzz me when I'm due at a meeting. I'll be there next week on time," she promised. "Now for Ted," Jill began. She found him in his office working on his computer, and came right to the point.

> Jill: Ted, I'm concerned about whether you have sufficient time to continue on the new product team.
>
> Ted: Why do you say that?
>
> Jill: You've missed several assignment dates and been late for almost every meeting.
>
> Ted: Hey, what are you doing? Keeping records? Who do you think you are, anyway? My boss?
>
> Jill: Not at all. But when you joined the team, you agreed to the ground rules that we all wrote. When you are continually late and don't complete team assignments on time, you're not meeting the commitment you made to the group when you helped us set those ground rules.
>
> Ted: Others have been late.
>
> Jill: Yes, I'm afraid that's because no one said anything; they thought it was acceptable. It isn't. We all agreed we would make an effort to be on time, be prepared, and attend all the meetings. As team leader, I should have said something to you. But I knew you were so busy with other tasks at the start of the project that I turned a blind eye to what was occurring. Now I have to ask you: Can you make our meetings on time? Otherwise, I will have to look for someone else to do your job. I don't want to do that if I don't have to—you're too valuable to the team effort—but I will have to find a replacement if you can't carry out your responsibilities to the group.

Ted stared at Jill for a moment. The two had been at loggerheads during several sessions of the team, but he had to admit that punctuality had been among the ground rules. He doubted that Jill would replace him on the team, but he didn't want to risk losing his presence in this high-visibility group. "All right," he said. "It'll actually help me to better prepare for the meetings. I can review my handouts in the meeting room just before the session starts to be better prepared to explain the assumptions on which they are based."

Jill's Only Mistake

Jill made one mistake in handling this situation: She waited much too long before acting on Ted's tardiness. Consequently, the problem spread to others. But once she faced the need to address the problem, she handled it well. She didn't use her position as team leader to demand that her peers change their behavior, with the implication that her role on the team would allow her to go to their boss or even the team's sponsor and complain. Rather, she used her knowledge of her colleagues and the ground rules set at the start of the project; she also reminded each of the problem team participants about how he or she would be regarded by colleagues if they continued to violate the very ground rules they had agreed to support.

Counseling Marginal Performers

Let's look at more traditional counseling situations, like helping marginal employees turn around their performance. For instance, Margo showed little or no interest in her work. Her manager, Lois, was frustrated each morning as she walked into the department. Margo would be at her desk fixing her nails or adjusting her hair. It seemed to take her forever to complete the letters that needed to be written and copied and then inserted into envelopes. Her in-box had numerous letters that hadn't yet been retrieved, but they were nothing compared to the stack of opened customer letters on her desk that had to be filed.

Lois had hoped that Margo would stop dawdling and really get to work once the company entered into its busy season, but that hadn't been the case. Margo simply wasn't doing the work as quickly as she should. Lois hadn't ignored the problem. She had discussed the situation with Margo during coaching sessions. She had said, "Work is piling up on your desk and you need to do it to ensure office productivity. Are you having a problem?" Margo had assured her that all was well, and everything was getting done on schedule. Lois couldn't complain about any errors Margo was making—there were no problems in her handling of customer accounts. Still, Lois couldn't allow Margo to plod through her work assignments while other clerks in the department seemed to be working on overdrive. After several months, Lois decided that a more serious talk was called for, and she called Lois into the office for counseling.

Lois: Margo, I guess I haven't been as clear as I should have been. You are taking too long to complete your work. You are more experienced than many of your peers, and you should be able to work faster, but you just let the work pile up.

Margo [annoyed]: It gets done, doesn't it?

Lois: Yes, it does, but if you focused on your job more, you could finish more work during the day. I can't ask your peers to take on any added work—they lack the know-how that you have— and are just managing to juggle their work assignments. . .

Margo [interrupting]: I see no reason for me to assume more work than the others. We're all paid the same!

Lois: Yes, Margo, that's true. And you aren't likely to move beyond your current job and salary if you don't demonstrate that you are capable of doing more than you are. Your current job performance is holding you back from consideration for more than a cost-of-living salary increase and even advancement.

Margo: I'd like a decent raise, that's for sure. Can you promise me a 10 percent raise if I took on more work?

Lois: No, I can't promise that. But I can certainly promise that I would acknowledge your improvement in job performance in your appraisal at the end of the year.

Margo: Lois, I'd like the raise. But, to be truthful, I am bored with what I do day after day. I wouldn't mind taking on more work but I don't really want to do more of the same. Aren't there other tasks I could be assigned to do?

Lois: Would you be willing to take on new duties and responsibilities, in addition to your current workload?

Margo: Yes, I would—what do you have in mind? [a little wary of where the conversation was heading].

Lois: I've been asked to conduct some customer surveys, and I will need one of the clerks to help me. I had been putting off the work because your colleagues seem overburdened, and I didn't think you would want to help. But this work is just right for you to do. Your familiarity with the company will help tremendously.

Lois then went on to discuss the project and Margo's role. Margo seemed genuinely interested—for the first time in over six months. And the new tasks she was assigned seemed to energize her. During a follow-up counseling meeting, Lois could tell Margo how pleased she was in the flow of customer replies off Margo's desk, her handling of incoming mail, and cleaner desk. "The work is being done faster yet still efficiently," she told Margo. "As important, I am delighted with the work you are doing on the customer surveys."

Margo still began the day by checking her nails and hair, but as soon as she was at her desk, she was all business. Lois had no reason to fault her job performance, and Margo soon was off counseling. But Lois continued to provide Margo with feedback—both on her regular work and her work on the surveys.

Think about how Lois handled this situation. She solved the performance problem, but likely she could have done so much sooner—even in coaching—had she probed further than she did. Margo could have bypassed her boredom, assumed more work, and increased the flow of work for which she was responsible. However, in her counseling session with Margo, Lois did do as she should; that is, she objectively described the situation, including why it could not continue, and she identified the impact Margo's productivity was having on the group's performance as a whole—less experienced workers were being overburdened because Margo was not taking on the level of work her job experience allowed her to handle. More important, Lois listened to Margo about why she didn't just want to be stuck with more of the same routine tasks she currently did. Finally, Lois came up with a realistic solution to the problem, one that would re-motivate Margo and also help Lois complete an assignment that senior management was anxious to have done.

• • •

Clearly, the matter between Margo and Lois was about job performance. Not all counseling sessions are directly related to that. Take the session between Gordon and Jane, his ambitious but disgruntled assistant. Jane felt that she was inadequately compensated for her work and used sarcasm and snide remarks to express her dissatisfaction with her job. Gordon had had a good working relationship with Jane until one day she returned from lunch with some old friends with whom she had worked at another company. The camaraderie that existed between Gordon and Jane disappeared from then, replaced by angry retorts and slamming file drawers.

Unlike Lois, Gordon didn't wait. He called Jane into his office and asked her what was wrong.

Jane: Gordon, I think I'm overdue for an increase.

Gordon: Jane, I wish I could put you up for one, but we have pay policies that prevent that.

Jane [whining]: My friends have jobs similar to mine, are employed by companies in the area, and they earn at least 20 to 30 percent more than I do. I don't think that's fair.

Gordon: Every situation is different. Also, there's more than one kind of compensation.

Jane [sarcasm rearing its ugly head]: Maybe, but I'll take the cash.

Gordon [grimacing]: All right, then, let's consider this from a purely financial standpoint. We know that you're ambitious. I don't know anything about your friends' companies, but I know that this firm's policy is to promote from within. Since you're one of the most valuable people in this department, you have already received some excellent performance assessments, ones that you aren't going to keep if you behave the way you have. You might be thinking that you would make more money if you left here and found another job. Maybe, but keep in mind that you would be losing the respect you already have here. And you might not get the kind of money you are currently getting if you made a fresh start elsewhere.

Jane: Maybe . . .

Gordon: Also, I can't think of any company as committed as ours to training staff. You're smart enough to know that the opportunity we offer you to take various training programs is money in the bank.

Jane: Still . . .

Gordon: Another thing. Most assistants at other organizations don't enjoy the unique status that admins do here. You attend sales meetings, you are a member of project teams, you have cubicles and mini-offices in which to work. And you are less regimented than other employees, with flexible work hours, lunch periods, and the like.

Jane: Still . . .

Gordon: Wait a minute—let me finish. I think I am a pretty good supervisor as supervisors go, too. I'm patient and caring and concerned about your professional advancement. I wouldn't be

> sitting here with you talking about your recent attitude if I didn't care about your position with the organization.
>
> Jane: I guess I have been difficult to work with lately.
>
> Gordon: Yes, you have. I hope that you can think about the things I've discussed and demonstrate the professional attitude I expect from a staff member. Unless the problem reappears, I don't think we need to talk about the situation again. I do have to keep a written record of our discussion, but I believe that you understand our current situation and will be patient. Your time will come if you give it a chance.

Note that Gordon didn't promise Jane a huge raise to change her attitudinal behavior. Bribery, which is what that would have been, isn't a lasting solution to any problem. Gordon appreciated how Jane might feel after comparing compensation with former colleagues and how she might be looking for greener pastures. While Gordon might not be personally responsible for the situation, she was taking her predicament out on him. Rather than lose his temper, he preferred to save a talented worker and chose to use the counseling session to persuade her to look to the blessings from her job, not focus on its shortcomings.

Behavior similar to Jane's can be due, too, to feelings that work isn't appreciated, to a perceived lack of status, and to a demand for more opportunities for visibility and involvement in problem solving and decision making.

Counseling for Violations of the Rules

Counseling sessions are very similar in the need to (1) identify the nature of the problem, (2) gain acceptance that a problem exists, (3) discuss the impact that the behavior is having on the individual's performance or that of the entire workforce, and (4) come up with an action plan to resolve the problem and a schedule of future meetings to discuss progress in addressing the behavioral problem. Let's look at how these four steps play out in a discussion between Steve and Ben over Ben's tardiness and absenteeism, both of which have been going from bad to worse. Steve calls Ben into his office.

> Steve: Ben, I've been looking over your personnel folder. This is the fourth year you have been with the company and the third

department you've worked in. You did a terrific job in Finance and were moved to Credit Management as a reward for your top performance. Your work there earned you a second transfer to Accounts Receivable. However, your work was poor. You asked for a transfer and you were moved to Accounts Payable. Since you have been in my department, your performance has been barely acceptable. Worse, both your attendance and arrival times to work have become serious problems.

Ben: Steve, I think I'm doing an acceptable job. As far as my absenteeism and tardiness, I explained that I have had some car problems, which are responsible for both.

Steve: Obviously, the car problems are new. When you were in Finance, your record for promptness and attendance were commendatory. While in Credit Management, you weren't absent a single day, and you were never late. When you were in Accounts Receivable, you were out sick often—usually Mondays or Fridays. You came into the office as late as 10:00 A.M. In my department—well—the record is even worse—it's unacceptable. And I question your explanation that you are having car problems.

Ben: I told you my car is a wreck, and I can't afford a new one.

Steve: That may be a part of the problem, but I think there is more to it. Your record proves that you can do superior work and maintain a record of good attendance and timeliness. I also find it interesting that your absenteeism is often around the weekend. As a manager, I've found that behavior like yours is usually attributable to either lack of ability, which I don't think is the problem, or a problem with your supervisor or co-workers. If either of those situations is causing you a problem, I wish you would discuss it with me.

Ben: Oh, no. I like the people I work with, and I think that you're a fair supervisor.

Steve: Thank you. What about the work itself?

Ben [hesitating]: I guess it's okay.

Steve: You guess. You did outstanding work in Finance and later in Credit Management.

Ben: I really liked my jobs in those departments. The work was interesting.

Steve: What about the work in Accounts Receivable?

Ben: I hated it!

Steve: And Accounts Payable, my department?

Ben: Well . . . [hesitating].

Steve: You're not that interested in it, right?

Ben: It's boring. I spend the day at a computer keyboard entering figures. It's as bad as Accounts Receivable, maybe even worse.

Steve: You clearly are good with number-crunching. Suppose I changed your responsibilities. Instead of posting numbers, I assigned you to analyzing the financials as they are reported. Would that interest you?

Ben: Definitely!!!

Steve: All right, let's try it. I'm guessing that your excessive absences and lateness were tied to your feelings about your job. If you do well with your new responsibilities and your attendance improves, then we'll both be happier. If there's no improvement, then, I'm sorry to tell you, Ben, that I would have to let you go.

Ben: Yes.

Steve: Let's set up a time tomorrow to review your new responsibilities. I also want to set up a time in thirty days to review both your job performance and attendance. I assume by then that you will also have addressed any problems you might have with your car. I'll be looking for signs of improvement to show that we're on the right track. But, even with an improvement during the next four weeks, I'll be checking your attendance records regularly to be sure that the problem has been solved.

Steve didn't deny Ben's explanation, but he did have documentation to demonstrate that the problem seemed to be tied to the change in responsibility as Ben moved from one department to another. Ben could not deny the documentation that showed that a problem existed. As far as the cause of the problem, Steve probed gently to help Ben admit the nature of the problem. Once he understood the problem, he could recommend a solution. Ideally, a better approach might have been to ask Ben how the job might be made more interesting, but the nature of Ben's performance problem really required that Steve take the lead in recommending a solution.

Observe how Steve made it clear to Ben that termination might be the only choice left if Ben's absenteeism and tardiness continued with the change in responsibilities. If Ben continues to be out and late, Steve will need to act on his statement and fire Ben. Steve's department cannot operate with someone on whom the supervisor and staff can't rely.

Does the situation end happily? In most instances, if the problem is attributable to the nature of the work, then the change in assignment should have worked. But let's assume that it doesn't work, that Ben's behavior is due to an attitude problem. He's been moved from one department to another and it has made him angry. He has been punishing the company by being late and even not going into work, hoping that his absence will disrupt workflow and make the company aware of how important he is. So, one month later, Steve meets again with Ben.

> Steve: Sit down, Ben. I've been looking over your attendance record. There has been little improvement. You also continue to be late. Your change in work assignment seems to be going smoothly, but the problem that justified the need for counseling hasn't been solved. Under these circumstances, I'm sorry to say that I will have to terminate you.

> Ben: You have no right to do that. My work here has improved. I know the company, and I make a solid contribution to the department. So I was late a few days during the month. I was only out three days.

> Steve: While that is less than in the past, it is a continuation of the previous pattern. Each absence enabled you to take a long weekend. In one instance, you told me, "I didn't sleep well and didn't feel up to coming to work." On the second occasion, you complained that you had had a headache. On the last occasion, you told me, "I just didn't feel good." I'm sorry but those aren't sufficient cause for your continued absences.

> Ben: Steve, this company has treated me shabbily, moving me from one department to another, never concerned about how happy I was in Finance. You all have been unfair.

> Steve: I tried to find more interesting work within my department for you, but your absences continued. I'm truly unhappy to see you leave but your problem is affecting department productivity and that can't continue.

Ben [shocked]: Steve, I promise that I'll . . .

Steve: Ben, I can understand how you feel. I wish you the best of luck with your next employer. The Human Resources Department has been notified about the situation, and Sam, from HR, will be here to take you upstairs to discuss any compensation for unused vacation time, the continuation of health and life insurance benefits, and the like.

Ben: Please, Steve, reconsider.

Steve: The decision is final.

Since Ben was clearly upset, Steve excused himself to give Ben time to regain his composure.

Did you notice that Steve never said, "I'm sorry"? It would have implied that he or the company had done something wrong to Ben. Steve accepted that he would be the bearer of bad news, and did his job as a manager in letting Ben know that he was being fired for his shoddy attendance record.

After Ben went off to the human resources department with the HR manager, Steve recorded the meeting with Ben.

Ben falls into two categories of employee for counseling: he was a rule violator, playing free and loose with the company's attendance rules, and also someone with an attitude problem. The latter came out only after his supervisor had made an effort to turn around the situation. More often, the problem is noticeable from the start.

Counseling for Attitude Problems

Often employees with attitude problems do good work. Their problem is a matter of attitude, not ability. For instance, taking orders—no matter how respectfully and politely they are given—can be very difficult for some people, and they become surly and uncooperative. You can't ignore behavior like this or other examples of negative attitudes.

As a manager, you will likely encounter one or more of these individuals with attitude problems during your career. The secret in counseling them is not to talk about their attitudes but rather to focus on the behaviors that result. Not only is it easier to resolve such problems but it is also easier to make a case for dismissal based on behavior associated with the attitude problem. Think about the case with Ben. Steve couldn't argue that Ben had a grudge against the company for the many times it disrupted his work life, but he could point to attendance and lateness issues.

Steve was also able to document those specific instances in which Ben's behavior interfered with or disrupted work. Clearly, you can't tell someone with an attitude problem, "Your attitude has got to change." It wouldn't accomplish anything. However, if you can have a serious discussion about how the employee's behavior has caused several problematic situations, you are apt to get the employee's attention and have him or her admit that a problem does exist. Although the problem may not be one of performance, you still must make clear to the employee that his or her future with the organization is uncertain at best if the behavior continues. Termination—in spite of the good work performance—will become a distinct possibility. If you consider the kinds of performance problems that attitudinal issues can cause, you can appreciate why termination may be a consequence if no change is forthcoming.

Malicious Disobedience

You've met Ben earlier in this chapter. Phil is another individual with an attitude problem. Asked to send out warning letters to a list of customers with delinquent accounts, Phil did so. Although he had been told by another employee that there had been a mix-up with a number of the accounts and that a revised list of customers was being put together, he still sent out the letters to the old list. Phil's firm received considerable calls from upset customers as a result of his act. Some customers were so upset that they threatened to change suppliers.

Phil did it because he had been *ordered* to complete the mailing. Malicious disobedience—that is, following instructions to the letter regardless of the consequences—is often the way he responds to being told what to do. As his manager, you would have a tough time placing blame, particularly if you had been the individual who had instructed him to send off the letters. You would have only had the word of the other worker that Phil knew better than to use the original list.

What should you do? Since disciplinary action would be very hard to take in this instance, you need to meet with Phil to determine why he behaved in this manner. Usually the reason for malicious disobedience can be found in a grudge against either you or the company. You need to put yourself in Phil's place and try to remember anything that has happened that could cause such resentment. Was Phil passed up for a promotion? Is the person's raise overdue? Does the company generally maintain a rank-conscious attitude toward staff and he is at the bottom of the hierarchy and treated accordingly? Do you treat him that way?

The goal of counseling here is to get to the reason behind the behavior. Treating the symptoms will not cure the disease. The root of the problem must be uncovered. If it is found to be in the relationship between you and Phil, then half of your battle is won, provided you can improve the relationship and create an environment more conducive to a positive work situation.

Passive Aggression

Let's look at another attitudinal type. Passive-aggressives deal with feelings of anger and frustration by eliciting these feelings in others, thereby appearing to be the victim of the other's irrational behavior. They hear only what they want to hear and purposefully forget what you need them to remember. If you ask them to come over or to complete a task quickly, they will deliberately take their time. If you don't nag them regularly, they won't get their work done.

Passive aggression is one of the toughest attitudinal problems to counsel. These people seem responsive to your advice. They may even improve in performance over the short term. But unless you watch them like a hawk, they will exhibit previous misbehavior or fall back to their lower level of performance. Let's look at how you need to counsel these individuals.

As mentioned, your first step is to document the behavior of the person with an attitude problem. Narrow the issue to the specific problem or concern. Write down the specific verbal and physical behaviors and actions that concern you. Check, too, the frequency of such misconduct and its impact on workflow and colleagues' performance. When you meet with the employee, discuss the situation. Determine whether the individual has a logical reason for the behavior. If you can't get to the cause of the problem, don't think you can't resolve the problem. Describe the behaviors you don't want and tell the employee clearly and succinctly to stop doing what he or she is doing. Follow this up with a description of the preferred behavior—like cooperation, helpfulness, and courteousness.

Let's look at each of these steps more closely.

1. *Narrow the issue to the specific problem or concern.* Identify the specific type of behavior that the attitude leads to, like careless-

ness or inattention to work, or insensitivity to others, or rudeness.

2. *Note in writing the specific verbal and physical behaviors and actions that have triggered counseling.* Don't forget to record nonverbal behaviors like the rolling of eyes, the clenching of fists, the staring into space, and so forth. See yourself as a movie camera or a tape recorder as you report exactly the behavior of the employee.

3. *Indicate the frequency of the behavior.* Know how often the various behaviors that concern you arise.

4. *Report the impact.* Make a list of the good business reasons that the behavior must end; that is, how it is impacting the performance of the individual or productivity of the entire work team.

5. *Meet with the employee to discuss the situation.* Be sure that the employee understands how the behavior is causing a problem.

6. *Hear out the employee.* He or she may be unaware of what is happening. It may also turn out that the attitude problem you've identified is a symptom of some more serious problem that needs a referral to the employee assistance program.

7. *Be clear that you want the behavior to stop.* Too often, managers don't do this. But you must specifically tell the person to stop doing whatever it is he or she is doing.

8. *Explain the kind of behavior you want instead.* This is a step that many managers ignore. They assume that they must live with what the employee is doing. Not so. Managers have too much stress on them already. Every organization and manager has the right to demand that everyone who is on the staff behave in a courteous, cooperative, and helpful manner. If the employee refuses, be clear about the consequences of continuation of their poor behavior.

Other Attitude Problems

We've considered some of the attitudinal problems you may encounter. But, unfortunately, there are many others that you may have to address as a manager, like:

• *Naysayers.* These staff members can be toxic to any creative thinking in your group. Unless they are kept on a tight leash (or excluded from brainstorming sessions), you can count on them to ignore the pluses and point out the minuses every time someone in the group suggests an operational improvement.

- *Worrywarts.* These employees are in their glory when they can walk about the department prophesizing doom and gloom.
- *Jokesters.* There are jokes and good-natured laughter, and then there is barbed humor that wounds co-workers and members of management, including you. Out of control, a steady barrage of ill-timed humor can derail a team's train of thought, diminish the importance of a critical decision, or destroy team camaraderie.
- *Know-It-Alls.* These opinionated, outspoken staff members think they have all the answers. They may be valuable staff members, but their huge egos make them irritating and counterproductive co-workers.
- *"No" People.* These workers see no good in anything that is done. And, unfortunately, they seem to have the uncanny ability to extinguish positive thinking in others and smother creative ideas before they catch fire.
- *Whiners.* These staff members wallow in their woes and carry the weight of the world on their shoulders. Their behavior would be tolerable if they complained for the purpose of drawing attention to problems and if they offered solutions along with their complaints. Their behavior would even be acceptable if it were therapeutic, designed to help them cope with their frustrations. But these whiners' wallowing goes on and on and has no purpose.

Many managers tell me that they don't really know what kinds of action steps they can take with each of the individuals described here—from the naysayers to the jokesters to the worrywarts. Here are some suggestions.

- If you have a *naysayer* on staff, learn to disregard his or her negative comments. Become deaf to those remarks. Better yet, challenge your naysayer before his or her peers to come up with a solution to the problem, not simply criticize your action plan.
- If you have a *worrywart* on staff, minimize the opportunities that he or she has to react to bad news by delivering bad news with a positive spin. If you see one building fear in others, hold a staff meeting to address openly and honestly staff members' fears.
- Say Carl is the *jokester* on your staff. He doesn't just joke with co-workers, he finds cause to laugh at others' expense. Don't follow your

subordinates' example. Rather, set a good example yourself and not laugh. More important, sit down with Carl and describe situations and subjects that are off-limits to humor, regardless of the intent. Don't argue the case—instead, emphasize the negative consequences of the alleged humor and leave it at that. Make clear that continuation of such behavior will lead to Carl's dismissal.

• *Know-it-alls* are another case altogether. Actually, they can be helpful so long as they don't try to take over. Minimize their participation if you expect them to drown out everyone's creativity. If they come up with good ideas, look for ways to combine theirs with the ideas of other members of the team.

• With a team member who *says no* to everyone's idea, your goal should be to move from fault finding to problem solving, from negativity to creativity and innovation. Toward this, be aware that trying to convince an employee that an idea will work often encourages him or her to become even more critical. Think of one of those B-Westerns in which a horse and rider are sinking in quicksand. The harder the horse struggles to get out, the more embedded he and his rider become.

With people who can only say no to others' ideas (carriers of Not Invented Here syndrome), it is better to ask them to research a subject. Use them as smoke detectors or warning devices to alert you to real problems. If your no-person rejects your idea or that of another, suggest that he or she come up with a better idea. You never know—the person may come up with a winner.

The person also may rethink that no-position if you allow time. While you may be tempted to exclude the individual from further discussion of a problem and the proposed solution, the wiser course of action may be to give the person time to think so he or she can come back in when in agreement with you and the team. You might say, "When you think of a solution, get back to me," or "Why don't you think about this for awhile and report back to me with any ideas that you have for overcoming the problems you see with our solution?"

• With a *whining individual*, here's a word of warning: be alert that the condition doesn't rub off on you. Your problem performer can cause you to agonize about his or her presence on your staff to colleagues—in other words, whine about your staff whiner. To support the whiner's efforts to change his or her behavior, don't agree with his or her complaints. Neither should you disagree with them—that will only compel him or her to repeat his or her problems or feelings. If the whiner has a personal problem, send him or her to the employee assistance counselor; don't try to solve his or her problem.

Don't discount everything that a whiner says. For instance, if a whiner has a complaint with operations, listen for the main points of the complaint. Like naysayers and know-it-alls, and others mentioned in this chapter, the whiner may actually be on to something worthy of your attention. Take command of the conversation and get specific, asking for the whiner's help. Ask questions that will clarify the whiner's viewpoint, then see if you and the whiner can come up with some real solutions.

If this effort does not produce any real change in a whiner, and you have met often to counsel him or her about the impact this behavior is having on the operation, then it may be time to issue a warning that termination may be necessary owing to the impact of that behavior on workflow and staff morale.

In situations involving troublesome and troubled employees, there may be strong temptation to lose your temper and rant and rage. Instead, think about the consequences of such actions. Even in an organization with employment-at-will, termination done in anger can have serious legal consequences. Better to calm yourself, seek advice from your human resources department, and then prepare for a counseling meeting to demonstrate that you made an effort to turn around the behavioral problem. After that, follow the instructions in this chapter and the ones before and the one after to ensure that you made a serious effort to save the employee.

If you have no other option but to terminate the employee, do so but demonstrate a caring attitude toward the person. It will minimize the likelihood of litigious action against your organization or you.

Counseling Dilemmas: Traps and Pitfalls to Avoid

THE TRAPS ASSOCIATED WITH COUNSELING fall into three categories. First, there are the traps and problems associated with counseling itself. Second are the traps encountered as you move beyond counseling to the warning stage and the likelihood of termination. And third are the legal traps that may be set when disgruntled employees follow through with a threat to sue as a result of termination. Some of these pitfalls have been noted in the earlier chapters in this section on counseling, but they are discussed more fully here because they deserve emphasis.

Counseling Pitfalls

Acceptance of Poor Performance

The biggest mistake that managers can make with problem performers—whether due to poor performance or discipline matters—is to ignore the problem. You may realize that the best step is to get together with the problem performer and discuss the matter and develop an action plan to improve the employee's performance. Depending on the nature of the problem, such intervention may put the problem performer back on track or even salvage his or her career. And by intervening in this way you will come across to your staff, peers, and boss as someone who is in control of your operation.

But, given the problems that counseling can create and the commitment of time it demands, it is easy to convince yourself that you are too busy now and can address the problem later (for instance, during the next appraisal review), or that the problem isn't serious enough for you to hold a counseling interview with the employee (you can handle the task that the employee isn't capable of doing or look the other way when he arrives late or leaves early regularly), or that the problem will disappear in time when the employee moves elsewhere in the company or to another firm. But are you only rationalizing your own unwillingness to confront the employee?

Over the years, I've met many managers who procrastinate when it comes to counseling a troublesome worker. Their arguments range from "I need the person"—that is, that the poor worker is indispensable, since the job he or she holds is a hard-to-fill one (better a warm body than no body), to "That would be punishing someone whose work is all right almost all of the time," to my favorite, "Now I'll have to admit to my boss that I have a serious staff problem on my hands." Each is a lousy excuse for not counseling someone, and if counseling doesn't work, for not firing the employee. Poor performers, regardless of their unique skills, never justify their costs. Counseling isn't punishment; it's an opportunity to turn the poor performance around. Enter into the counseling optimistically. If there's no improvement after two or three meetings, you can know that you've done all you could to salvage the individual.

And, as far as clueing your manager into the existence of a problem, think for a minute. In most instances, your boss may not know the exact nature of the performance problem, but he or she will know that there is something wrong with your work group. And the sooner you come to grips with the situation, the better. Level with your boss, review the steps you've taken, and ask your manager for time to undertake counseling—if you haven't begun it already—and together set a timetable for taking action. The last will rule out any unfairness factors like discrimination, in the event that termination is called for.

Do you have a problem right now that demands your attention? Ask yourself:

> Do I truly plan to discuss this problem during the next appraisal review?
>
> Is that too long to wait to discuss the problem?
>
> Until the problem is solved, or the employee moves on, do I have the time to do a portion of this employee's work for him?
>
> Is it fair to expect all my other staff members to arrive on time and put in a full day's work for a full day's pay?

Is it fair for me to put another manager, either within this company or outside, in the position of having to address this problem because I didn't?

And, maybe the most important question is: "Who besides me knows about this problem?" Likely, it's your staff members, peers, and boss. Management is the art of getting work done by others, and your performance as a manager will be measured by the performance of your staff—all of them, even your problem performer. Don't apologize for confronting the troublesome or the troubled employee. Your responsibility is to maintain acceptable performance for all your employees.

Failure to Get the Message Through

Often, when employees reach the warning stage, they argue that they had no idea that the problem with their performance was that serious. In some instances, it is an excuse; in others, unfortunately, it is because the employee's manager never made clear the nature of the problem and the consequences of its continuation.

So it is important that, during counseling sessions, you be very specific about the existence of a work problem and its nature, *and,* even more important, the consequences if the employee does nothing about it. Document your counseling sessions and share a copy with your problem performer, including the action plan you both agreed on to address the problem.

Disagreement About the Existence of a Problem

Sometimes an employee will deny the existence of any problem, and the manager will have to prove that one does, indeed, exist. Unless you can point to specific incidents, a discussion with an employee with only a single performance problem can take the form of a "Yes, you did" "No, you didn't, prove it" conversation. This is where those management textbooks are right: You must document employee performance, both good and bad. As I will show later in this chapter, documentation of an employee's performance is important not only to defend in court any decisions you make about an employee but also to support your statements during counseling that there is a serious work problem requiring your attention and the employee's.

Documented observations particularly have the advantage of helping you during counseling to pinpoint both the nature of the problem and the steps to take to correct it. Mike, for instance, had an employee who did a spectacular job except for her behavior when working with staff from this advertising firm's art department. Carla, his copywriter, refused to accept Mike's statement that she always came into the art department with a chip on her shoulder. As he cited specific incidents he had been witness to, Carla found it harder and harder to deny that her manner made it difficult for the artists to work with her. Mike was then in a better position to find out the reason for her rudeness and come up with ways that she could mend fences.

If you expect the kind of opposition to your assessment of a problem such as Carla first gave Mike, you may want to have your records on the employee with you and to have highlighted those incidents that support your remarks. If the individual's work is bad enough for you to consider putting the person on warning, you should also consult earlier performance reviews in which these issues were discussed. They prove that you have gone over these problems with the employee before. Have them with you when you sit down with the employee.

Disagreement Over Standards

Employees may agree that your assessment is accurate, but then argue that the expectations, standards, goals, or outcomes themselves aren't fair. You can counter this argument in two ways. First, if others who report to you have similar standards and have met them, you can remind the employee of this fact. Alternatively, if that is not the case, you can point out that over the years you and this individual have discussed the performance goals and at no point in the past did she raise this issue, as shown by your documentation of those earlier appraisals. With the appraisals readily available, you can even show the staff member that she signed the appraisal form or other document you use in your company's performance appraisal program agreeing to pursue these goals.

The ADA Excuse

Since passage of the Americans with Disabilities Act (ADA), many managers suddenly discover during a performance appraisal in which their employee is poorly evaluated that that employee has a previously undisclosed disability that is covered by the ADA. For example, after working with Marty for several years and tolerating chronic tardiness, Jack decided to do something about it and brought up the problem with him. Marty didn't deny that he was always late, nor did he argue that other staff members also came in late and that it was unfair to come down on him alone. Rather, he told Jack that he had a sleep disorder, took medication that made it difficult for him to wake up when his alarm clock rang, and consequently couldn't do anything about being continually late. Jack knew his staff members well and kept his ear tuned to the department grapevine, yet he had never heard anything about Marty having a health problem, so he doubted Marty's claim. Whether he believed him or not, though, he knew he had to hear him out. And if Marty did indeed have a sleeping problem, Jack would have to make *reasonable accommodation* for the situation. But Jack knew that he had the right to ask for confirmation of Marty's allegation, which he did. He asked Marty to bring in a letter from his doctor or to see the company's medical office. If Marty was an insomniac who had to take medication to fall asleep, Jack would accommodate the condition by putting Marty on flextime; Marty could arrive an hour later than his peers, but he would have to work an extra hour after they left. But being protected under the ADA didn't mean that Marty could get a full day's pay for less than a full day's work.

The Emotion Trap

Besides denying either your assessment or the validity of the goals, or coming up with a heretofore unknown illness, employees may respond emotionally to your comments about the need for them to improve their job performance. The responses run the gamut from tears to shouts to threats of violence. Some may show no reaction at all; they may listen quietly, then get up and leave, which can be equally unnerving.

The emotion trap is twofold. First, knowing that your troubled or troubling employee will get emotional when you confront him or her about the need for improving performance may discourage you from ever bringing up the existence of a problem. Some managers would rather tolerate poor performance and even violations of corporate rules than have to stand before an employee who, they know, is likely to sob—or, worse, shout at them or, worse still, threaten to go over their head to personnel or their boss or to take them to court or, worst of all, promise to beat them up. However you expect the problem performer to respond, you can't let this person distract you from your course, which is to get her performance back on track.

Second, should an employee get emotional during a counseling interview, you should not let it sidetrack you from your mission, which is to get agreement with the employee that a problem in performance exists, what the nature of that problem is, and the actions you will have to take should the problem continue. If the employee does cry as you expect, you can offer both compassion and Kleenex.

Let the employee have some time to compose him- or herself; you might even want to reschedule the meeting for later in the day, when the employee is more composed, or excuse yourself for a few minutes while the employee pulls together. Once you return to the room, you can begin by reassuring the employee that you would not want to begin counseling if you did not believe that he or she was capable of improving.

Balance is critical in your discussion with the employee. While you want to communicate your faith in the person's ability, you also want the employee to realize that failure to improve will end in his or her termination. Sometimes, employees show a little improvement and then lapse into poor performance or misbehavior again. They may even say to you, "The problem is no big deal." You have to make clear to your staff member that it *is* a "big deal." For instance, if the problem is attitude and your initial follow-up shows no change in behavior, you may want to give the worker another chance. Meet with him or her to re-emphasize the need for improvement. "Otherwise," you might say, "I'll have no choice but to fire you."

Beware that you don't get caught up in one follow-up meeting after another and another without any positive change in performance. Based on my conversations with managers, I suspect that one reason—beyond the unpleasantness of having to fire someone—is that no one wants to admit that his or her good-faith efforts have failed.

Also, shouts or threats about going over your head or to a lawyer should be handled professionally. Let the employee vent. If the person is out of control, you might want to suggest that you get together later when the individual has had a chance to regain control and you can talk more calmly. Usually, after giving the issue some thought, the employee will return in a more subdued mood, ready to discuss the problem and set goals for improvement. At this stage, few employees carry through with their threats to go to a lawyer. At worst, they will go to your boss or Human Resources to complain. And if you have kept your boss informed of your situation with Employee X and alerted Human Resources about the need to undertake counseling, the employee will be met only with professional courtesy.

If you have the kind of hotheaded employee who might actually get violent, you may want a second person in the room with you. If the employee does hurl threats or suggest violent acts against you or the company, call security. Even if the situation doesn't escalate to the point that you feel physically threatened, you should report the threats to either Human Resources or your boss. And if you ultimately have to fire the individual, you should have a second person with you, even a security person nearby, should the worker try to make good on the threats.

Misunderstanding Your Role

Too often in the course of counseling, managers wrongly take on the role of sympathetic parent or professional psychologist. It's critical to maintain your focus as a manager, which is to get the employee to do fully and well the job for which he is paid, and to recognize your professional limitations. Not only are professional counselors better at identifying problems and helping individuals to solve them, they are also better at spotting phony sob stories, as in the following case study.

ALICE: WHEN TOUGH LOVE IS NEEDED

Zack had never been late until his mother was placed in a nursing home. Afterwards, he was late several days a week. Worse, Alice had noticed that he seemed a little confused and groggy when he walked in. She wondered if he were drunk. When she asked Zack to meet with her in her office, she raised the two issues with him. Zack told her about the pressures he felt in working to save the family home and that he had had to visit a doctor for medication to help him cope with anxiety. He denied he was drinking, since the doctor had warned that alcohol and Xanax—the medication he was taking—were a dangerous combination.

Alice believed him. As he sobbed out his story, she also found herself feeling extremely sorry for him. His situation reminded her so much of the stress she and her own brother had experienced when their father was placed in a nursing home. She was tempted to tell Zack that she understood and leave the situation at that, or to tell Zack about her family and advise him to see the same lawyer she and her sibling had used. Fortunately, she fought the temptation. She didn't let herself get so involved in Zack's problem that she was unable to separate her feelings of compassion for the hurt he obviously was experiencing from her management responsibility to ensure that all members of her crew were at work on schedule.

Instead, she stressed how a continuation of his tardiness could lose him his job, which would only add to the pressures on him. She told Zack that she felt he had reason to be upset, but he could not use it to justify his chronic tardiness. She also was worried about the effect of the medication on his ability to work and asked him to visit his doctor to discuss other medications that would not leave him so drowsy during the day.

Instead of tolerating Zack's situation until he got his act together, as he asked her to do, Alice told him that she expected him to get his act together by Monday of the next week or she would suspend him for a week. She also wanted him to visit the employee-assistance program and said she would make an appointment for him. They could suggest to Zack a financial adviser to help him get through his financial troubles. Alice did give Zack the option of taking some time off to straighten out his problems, but he told her he felt better being at work.

For those of you who wonder what happened to Zack, let me tell you that he was able to find a lawyer who helped to secure the family home; he wasn't forced to sell the house he lived in. The government agreed that the property, while not in his name, was his sole residence and that he had maintained its upkeep since his father's death, when he moved in to keep his aging mother company.

Preconceived Notions

We may think that we know our employees well enough that we don't need to ask them the cause of a performance or disciplinary problem. This is a mistake. We should not enter into counseling sessions with preconceived notions about the cause of a problem because we may be wrong. And if we are, this would mean that the action plan we set with the employee won't work. Besides, asking the employee the reason for a problem demonstrates that we respect his or her opinion and want to hear it.

Poor Counseling Preparation

With both troubling or troubled employees, you will want to have your documentation readily at hand to point to specific instances that necessitate employee counseling. With troubled employees, however, you also should have on tap information about your company's employee-assistance program, if your organization has one, or, if not, community programs that might help the employee.

Failure to Consult Human Resources

There are legal traps in counseling, as you will see later in this chapter. Consequently, it is unwise not to check with the human resources or personnel department before you schedule your first counseling interview with the troubling employee.

In your meeting with Human Resources, you should ask for a review of your firm's policies and procedures for handling poor employee performance or rule violations to ensure that you follow each step called for in your company's performance management effort. Failure to do so can make both you and your organization liable to a charge of discrimination.

Interviewing Traps

During the counseling interviews, there are other smaller mistakes you can make, like:

- *Dominating the Discussion.* Here's where the 20/80 rule should apply: speak only 20 percent of the time and listen 80 percent of the time. You also don't want to interrupt the employee; by doing so, you can miss some key point that will help you identify the reason for the problem.

To help you monitor how much you are talking, try this trick. During the next one-on-one meeting with an employee, note each time you speak and each time the employee speaks by making a mark in either of two columns on a sheet of paper. Now compare the two. If you have more marks than the employee, you will need to learn to be quiet to give the employee an opportunity to talk. You can check if you frequently interrupt an employee the same way. Mark each time you interrupt the employee, and each time the employee interrupts you, and compare the two records.

- *Shifting Attention from the Employee's Performance Problem to Your Problems or Feelings.* You can point out how the employee's performance is creating problems for the department or organization as a whole, but you don't want to dwell on how his or her continued mistakes are making you look bad. Likewise, while it may be disappointing to have someone you trusted let you down or someone you believe has tremendous potential not use his or her capability, it shouldn't be the subject of the discussion.

- *Overempathizing with the Employee's Problem or Feelings.* You may understand how the situation could have happened—you may even have been in the same boat once yourself—but you have to remain objective. If an employee senses that you are on his side, you are less likely to get a change in behavior.

• *Dictating What an Employee Should Do.* For an action plan to succeed, the employee must be truly involved in its creation.

• *Moving Too Quickly into the Problem-Solving Phase Without First Discussing the Nature of the Problem.* Doing this is really jumping the gun. As a result, the employee may go through the whole problem-solving process while still not believing that a problem in performance actually exists. As mentioned previously, the sine qua non of successful counseling is to get the employee to admit that there is a problem. Besides, the employee should have an opportunity to share his or her feelings. This will not only let the individual know that you care about him or her as a person but will give you a better idea of how successful your counseling will be. Listen not only to what the employee says but also to what he or she doesn't say; the latter is a "third ear" or counseling gauge, measuring how effective the counseling sessions will be.

Following Through on Your Warnings

Despite the quality of your counseling, not all employees will change their behavior or improve their job performance. At this point, the biggest mistake you can make is not to take the action you told the employee you would have to take if the behavior change did not occur. If you don't act, you will prove not only to the troubling employee but to your entire staff that your warnings are meaningless, and they will act accordingly. Don't fall into the trap of holding one counseling session after another, after another, in the hope that the employee's performance eventually will turn around.

Different companies have different discipline and termination policies. But given today's leanly staffed organizations, it's unfair to you and your staff to counsel an unrepentant employee for more than two months before going to the warning stage. Remember that it only means extra work for you and a staff already carrying a heavy burden.

Even though you are at the warning stage, and the problem employee has acknowledged the existence of a problem, you will encounter some employees who will deny that a problem exists. He or she will look at you dumbfounded, surprised that, despite several counseling sessions, a problem *really* exists. You can avoid any misunderstanding by making clear from the start of counseling that it is one step removed from warning and that warning is one step removed from the individual being terminated.

Well-documented counseling sessions will enable you to prove to a third party as well as to an employee either in denial or lying that you both have discussed the problem over time. Memos to the employee should describe not only the nature of the performance problem but also the consequences of its continuation—termination—and the performance standards or goals or outcomes that will need to be met to avoid those consequences.

From the first counseling session, you should set, and write down, targets for the employee to reach in terms of both work improvement and the time by which the goal must be achieved. Be very specific in these targets. For instance, you might write about Marge, "By June 12, I expect you to revise the advertising kit." Or you might reach agreement with Will in customer service that "within two weeks, you will increase the number of callers you handle from ten to fifteen per hour." Further, because of previous complaints about his discourteous manner to customers, you might want to monitor his incoming calls and add to his target that "there will be no more complaints about being rude to customers."

If Marge claims that you never discussed the problem, or Will argues that you never suggested this was a serious problem, you will have in writing a summary of your discussion and the final conclusions. Thus if Marge fails to finish the copy for the ad kit on schedule or Will continues to fall short of standard in the number of calls he handles and you have received another call about his brusque manner, you can place the employee on warning. This is the last chance—and you must clearly mean the *last chance* to turn around performance. Once again, you set a specific goal and timetable and put these in writing in a warning memo. And you provide the employee with a copy just as the employee received copies of the counseling reports.

When Termination Is Your Only Recourse

If the individual once again fails to make that objective, termination should not come as a surprise, whatever the person might say. You will have protected yourself. And you should feel justified in terminating the employee. If you have set specific objectives and the employee has done little to achieve those objectives or made only halfhearted efforts toward reaching them, then you need not feel guilty about having to use the three-word phrase "You are fired." If your company has an intermediary warning step, you should make clear to the employee that this is his or her final chance to improve. A carefully worded memo to that effect should drive home that point. So should having to meet with you during the targeted period, during which you keep careful records of the individual's efforts.

Should the goals still not be reached, you will need to meet with the individual to terminate him or her. It's best to get right to the point. The less said at this stage, the better. Reiterate the nature of the performance problems that made you come to this decision and then send the employee to Human Resources, where he or she will receive information about vacation pay or other benefits forthcoming and his or her legal rights.

Despite the impact that termination of the employee may have on workflow, it is better to have the individual leave immediately after he or she is terminated rather than give the person two weeks' notice. Keeping the person on-site only opens you up to a fractionalized workforce as your staff members take sides between you and the terminated employee. Some disgruntled employees can also use their last days with the company to sabotage critical work.

There is much written about what the best day or best time of the day is to terminate an employee. Some experts argue against terminating anyone on Friday, since it gives individuals two days to worry before they can contact potential new employers. These writers contend that in a tight job market, with few jobs available, depressed employees may harm themselves or others over the two-day weekend. Other experts write that it doesn't matter on which day you terminate an employee, but that it's imperative to do so at the end of the day, when there are few employees around.

I think that, rather than time, it is more important that you treat the employee with respect when you terminate him or her. Keep the fact that you will be firing someone confidential, just as you kept to yourself the fact that he or she was on warning; the news will get out soon enough after your meeting.

During the termination interview itself, don't try to get even for all those times this individual created problems for you or the team, or you had to do work that he or she was responsible for, and don't express sorrow that this person is not using the potential you recognize exists. Instead, use this occasion to wish the individual more success in the next job and tell the employee that he or she will personally be missed. Review in brief what has happened. Don't be long-winded; it can only trigger an emotional response or provide substance for legal action. Tell the employee something like this:

"As you know from our past conversations, we have certain standards in the company that have to be met. I think we approached those standards on a fair and reasonable basis. Over the last few weeks [or months], I have told you that your work has not been up to those standards. I don't believe it is because of lack of effort, but it just hasn't worked out. I don't think that it should come as any surprise to you. We're going to have to terminate you as of today. I really regret this. I had hoped that things would work out just as much as you did, I am sure. Human Resources can review what checks you have coming to you, as well as any unused vacation time. Susan in Human Resources is waiting for you to call to set up an appointment to discuss the situation."

If there is a security issue involved, you can have the person watched, but marching him or her in lockstep to Human Resources and then to the locker to pick up personal belongings and treating the person like a convicted criminal can prompt him or her to lodge a legal complaint against you and the firm, and this can cause co-workers previously in agreement with your decision to change sides.

Dealing with Repeating Problems

With some employees, you may find that being put on warning is sufficient to turn around their performance over the short term, but that the problem reappears after a few months. Angela was one such person.

NORM: DEALING WITH ANGELA

Angela would sometimes be extremely passive during counseling and yet, on other occasions, become extremely argumentative. When Norm told her during counseling that he would have to put her on warning, suddenly she started making deadlines, was on time in the morning, took only an hour for lunch, and stayed until the end of the workday. But once he took the pressure off her, she returned to her old habits, slipping in after 10:00 A.M., taking ninety-minute lunch breaks, and disappearing by 4:30 P.M.

And forget about meeting deadlines. Angela was apologetic about the situation, but she would also get upset and argue that there were lots of business reasons she was behind in her work. Still, she did nothing about these conditions that she blamed for her work failures unless Norm, once again, threatened her with the possibility of being placed on warning and terminated.

Norm tolerated the situation longer than he should have because he saw the tremendous potential in Angela. But in the end he had to accept the fact that she was a lost cause, unwilling to use the potential she had if she didn't have to do so. It took longer than usual to terminate Angela because of her performance highs and lows, but maintaining a record of her inconsistent performance over nine months gave Norm sufficient information to make a defensible case for terminating Angela.

This was a concern for Norm. One reason that he had not moved more aggressively to rid himself of her was that he was afraid she might sue for discrimination. She was over forty-nine, suffered from diabetes, and had had a poor performance record over several years before she began to report to Norm, but nothing had been done about it. Norm thought he would be walking into a legal minefield. Fortunately for Norm, Angela recognized the rightness of his decision and never went to a lawyer. But not all managers are so lucky.

Post-Termination Pitfalls

If an employee is terminated for cause but the employee decides to sue, charging discrimination, then you may find yourself in court defending your decision. There are four pieces of legislation that are often the basis for court cases:

1. *Title VII of the Civil Rights Act.* This act makes it illegal for an employer to discriminate against an employee because of the individual's race, color, sex, creed, or national origin. In 1991, this act was strengthened to allow plaintiffs to have jury trials and to sue not only for back pay but also for compensatory and punitive damages.

2. *The Age Discrimination in Employment Act.* This act protects employees and applicants more than forty years of age against discrimination. In 1990, this act was amended to require employers to recommend that an employee over the age of forty seek legal counsel before signing a waiver of employee rights and gave the employee twenty-one days to consider the waiver.

3. *The Vietnam Era Veterans Readjustment Assistance Act.* Under this act, companies with contracts of $10,000 or more with the government must take affirmative action to employ and advance in employment qualified disabled veterans and veterans of the Vietnam era.

4. *The Americans with Disabilities Act.* The ADA makes it illegal to discriminate against people in hiring, in job assignments, and in the treatment of employees because of a disability. In 1997, coverage was extended beyond wheelchair users, the seeing- and hearing-impaired, and drug and alcohol users to include the mentally challenged.

These laws were enacted to prevent discrimination, however, not to force managers to accept poor job performance from an employee in a protected group. For instance, under the ADA, an employer is required to provide, unless it is a financial hardship, *reasonable accommodation,* such as an oversize doorway to a cubicle or an access ramp for a wheelchair-bound employee or a Braille keyboard for a blind word processor. However, if the individual does not do his or her job despite the accommodation, then discipline and ultimately termination are within the law. Likewise, under the ADA, alcohol and drug users are considered disabled. But if such workers are found to be using drugs or alcohol while on the job or come to work under the influence of an illegal substance, you are within the law to take disciplinary steps leading to termination.

Some managers are so frightened of the repercussions of taking action against a poor worker within a protected group that they either ignore the existence of the performance problem entirely or go through counseling session after counseling session, hurling threats at the employee who over time comes to recognize how empty the manager's words are. But, in truth, managers only create a further problem for themselves when they do nothing: Co-workers who do their jobs resent one of their own getting away with chronic tardiness or excessive absenteeism, too much socializing, or missed deadlines, or whatever the job problem is. Actually, they see the failure to take action as a form of discrimination *against them,* since they expect you, as their manager, to respond with fair, understanding, and firm measures to correct poor on-the-job performance.

Left untreated, a problem employee's performance can cause you to be judged negatively by staff members, can set a bad example that others on staff will emulate, and over time can become a topic of conversation between you and your own boss. Then it becomes a problem with *your* performance, which can affect your career, if not threaten your job.

It's unfortunate that such situations occur. You should have little fear of legal reprisal *provided:*

- You have adhered to your company's policies and procedures, which in most instances means its performance appraisal program.

- You can demonstrate that you have applied the same criteria in assessing this employee as you have with your other staff members.

- You can prove that the standards or other measurements you are using to make performance management decisions about an employee are realistic and are based on the actual needs of the job.

- You have documentation to support your evaluations and final decision to terminate the employee.

When you allow a busy work schedule to keep you from conducting an appraisal of a problem employee, when you seem to be tougher on some employees than others, and those on whom you are tougher fall into a protected group based on race, color, sex, and the like, or when you don't keep careful records of both positive and negative performance, you weaken your company's and your own defense against a charge of unfair termination. Let's look at each of these traps in greater detail.

Failure to Adhere to Corporate Procedures

It doesn't matter how busy you are, you must closely follow the steps set forth in your company's appraisal program. If you treat one employee differently from another, you may open yourself and your organization to a discrimination charge. For instance, suppose the company's policy may call for performance evaluations every three months, but you neglect to review one employee once out of the mandatory four times during the year. After all, you had to get that business plan completed prior to closure of the budget period, or you had to attend a meeting with visitors from another organization with which you are forming a joint venture, or you were invited to participate in a brainstorming session about a new product.

But let's assume that this one employee whose appraisal you don't get to is behind in his work. His performance continues to deteriorate. He spends all his time socializing with his co-workers, distracting them from their own tasks. He comes in late at least once a week. And he even talks back to you in front of other staff members. You meet with him and try to create an action plan to turn his performance around, but he denies the existence of a problem, blames you for demanding more from him than from the rest of the staff, and does not seem to care about meeting the goals you both had set at the start of the year. You put him on warning, but his performance still does not change. Ultimately, you have to fire him.

You conducted three of the four evaluations with him and have met on several occasions to discuss his declining performance, his behavior's impact on the work of the entire department, and the rudeness and disrespect he has shown you. Yet he charges you with discrimination because he, unlike his peers, missed out on that first quarterly assessment. His lawyer argues that he would have met the work goals if the problem had been caught sooner. He would have achieved his goals and behaved more properly if his situation had been given attention at the start. His lawyer tells the jury that you didn't give him the attention you gave his peers, not because you were too busy that week but because you didn't want to help him; the oversight was deliberate and attributable to a personal animosity or an age, race, gender, or other bias.

Even if the problem doesn't go so far as to lead to termination, you might find yourself in a court case. Let's just assume that the employee received a poor rating and no raise. He might go to the Human Resources Department to complain or take the case over your head to your own boss. Finally, if he still doesn't get a raise, he might take his complaint to a lawyer and together they might take you and your company to court, charging that you deliberately discriminated against him.

Non-Job-Related Standards or Unrealistic Expectations

When you sit down with an employee and together agree on the standards or goals or outcomes by which her performance will be measured, you must set standards that are based on the actual needs of the job. This is required under the Equal Employment Opportunity Commission's Uniform Guidelines on Employee Selection. They require that standards be "valid" or "job-related."

A big mistake is to hound a talented employee who fails to use all her abilities. You may know that the person is capable of much more than the outcomes on which you've agreed, and it may be frustrating to see this individual not using her full potential, but so long as the employee is achieving the outcomes you both set, then the person is doing her job. An assessment that reflects your frustrations can wind up in court and lead to a judgment against you at considerable cost to your employer.

Inconsistency in the Application of Standards

Just as failure consistently to follow your firm's policies and procedures can weaken your defense of a negative assessment of an employee, so too can evidence that one employee was allowed to get away with an infraction that another employee was not.

Let's say that an African-American employee was late three out of five workdays every week during the year. Despite your counseling and putting him on warning, he did nothing about his tardiness. In the end you terminated him, as you had several other workers of various races, genders, and ages—*except* for one white employee who is chronically late yet has not been terminated. The terminated employee's lawyer could claim that the employee might not have been terminated had he been white. And the plaintiff might well win his case.

Poor Documentation

You need to keep careful records of your employee's performance. When you can't point to specific incidents to justify a decision to pass over an employee for promotion or not to give her a raise, or to terminate her, the employee may charge you with discrimination and take your company to court.

Given your current responsibilities, asking that you document not only negative situations but also employees' accomplishments may seem too much to demand. In termination cases especially, it would seem to be enough to document negative incidents, but the courts question managers who can produce documentation only about poor performance or have only bad things to say about an employee. Critical incidents, good and bad alike, should be documented for all workers—poor, average, and outstanding workers.

That a manager has good documentation will discourage a lawyer from initiating a frivolous lawsuit. What is good documentation? Certainly, it is not a notebook filled with empty phrases like "The employee was unable to follow instructions," or "The employee lacks motivation to do the work." These lend themselves easily to contest. The disagreement can land you in court, where you will be expected to prove your case by citing specific incidents in which the employee failed to perform to standard or didn't meet objectives.

Whether coaching, counseling, or, yes, mentoring, documentation is important. Yes, you are busy but documentation is valuable evidence about actions you and the other party have agreed to take, whether it is after a coaching, a mentoring, or a counseling session. When it comes to documenting a counseling session, keep in mind that you should document the nature of the problem, not your impression of the employee's state of mind. This includes statements that the employee "willfully," "purposely," or "maliciously" did this or that. You may think that such phrases strengthen your record, but in truth it only gives the employee's lawyer an opportunity to claim that you were discriminating against the employee.

For the same reason, avoid exaggerating the consequences of an employee's behavior. Your intent, again, may be to play up the shortcoming or violation to pressure the employee about the need to change his or her behavior. In court, however, you may be asked how such and such offense lost the company an order or how an employee's repeated lateness stalled all deliveries for the day. Better to be realistic about the impact of the misbehavior or poor performance in both the counseling and documentation.

Some months ago, I sat in a staff meeting, and heard a manager discount the value of documentation since his company practiced employment-at-will. You can imagine the surprise on his face when he learned otherwise. While such corporate policy does allow a manager to terminate without cause, a disgruntled employee may choose to take the situation to court rather than accept severance or some other package offered to him or her to give up such rights. The employee will charge the company with discrimination—age, gender, race, whatever—and documentation about any performance difficulties with the employee will help justify the termination decision in the eyes of the court.

Documentation should be such that a third party reading the record will be able to come to the same conclusion you have. This individual will come to that conclusion by reading your description of what happened, not by reading your opinion of the situation. Besides, at the time of the year-end appraisal, will you know why you wrote, "Barbara did a great job on accumulating customer records," or, more pertinent to the need for counseling or justifying a poor rating or termination decision, "Dan did a poor job in investigating competitive vendors to help us purchase our new office copier," or "Nan never coordinated the new format for company invoices with marketing," or similar entries? Would you remember that Barbara spent long hours in the office making phone calls to more than one hundred customers to get e-mail and fax numbers, or that Dan interviewed only two competitive firms rather than the five you asked him to consider prior to purchase of the new office equipment, or that Nan's failure to keep in touch with marketing led to several errors on the invoices as well as some omissions? You want documentation that will support your case, so you should base it on your personal observations or, if the employee works with other managers as well, on these managers' observations too (think *matrix management* or *team participant*).

Likewise, comments from customers or vendors will also help. What if a manager or customer complains about one of your staff members yet refuses to go on record about your employee's poor performance? Unfortunately, you can't include the complaint in making your assessment of the individual's performance at the end-of-year evaluation and, consequently, in any documentation; actually, if the person sharing the negative observation refuses to be credited with it, its inclusion in the final assessment or any documentation can invalidate that assessment or documentation. Think that this is unlikely to happen? It happened to Karl.

Karl's Story

Karl was a manager in a Midwestern financial services firm. Alison was always complaining about Shari, a member of Karl's marketing department, but because Alison refused to let Karl document her complaints about Alison's lack of cooperation in a team Alison led, Shari's team participation never formed a part of her appraisals.

Based on Alison's reports, Karl felt that Shari deserved a rating of 2 (poor) or 3 (average), but because Alison refused to let Karl put her observations of Shari on paper, Alison received a 4 (outstanding). Without Alison's support, all Karl had was hearsay. And hearsay is not defensible. Even your own opinions aren't valid under the law. You may think that a person on your staff is a sloppy dresser, with unkempt hair and nails, but you can't write that in your critical incident report. On the other hand, you can describe that person's clothes and general appearance, point out that an important part of an employee's job is meeting with the public, and recount any comments from customers about the person's appearance that suggest how the individual's ap-

pearance is affecting customers' impressions of your organization or
the person's ability to do her job well.

To avoid the documentation trap, it's best to keep two kinds of documentation: (1) incident reports that document specific events, the actions taken by the employee, the results, and the consequences; and (2)
progress reports that evaluate the employee's problems and successes as
he or she works on assignments or a team project. Training can also be
included in the progress reports, as can incidents that over time show a
shift (either for good or for bad) in work behavior. You can keep the
critical incident records in a notebook that you update weekly, or you
can create a computer file to maintain employee records, regularly back-
ing up the record either on your company's network or on a disk.

Here are some other rules concerning documentation to follow:

1.   Document all counseling sessions, describing the behavior that
prompted the meeting, the decisions reached, and the date for follow-
up to discuss employee improvement.

2.   Give a copy of all counseling reports to the employee and place
one in his personnel file. Should there be no improvement in the employee's performance, issue a warning memo that describes exactly the
nature of the performance problem, past discussions about the performance, and the actions you expect from the employee and the time frame
by which an improvement must be evident.

3.   As with the counseling summaries, unless your firm has a special
form it uses, you can use a standard memo format for warning memos.

Following these rules can ensure that your assessments of employees are
fair and that you aren't accused of discrimination or arbitrary or capri-
cious decisions about an employee, from giving the individual a particular rating to recommending him or her for promotion, to that tough
decision to terminate an employee.

Counseling may be next to the toughest task that a manager has,
with terminating an employee the hardest of all. But many managers may
be able to avoid the need for counseling, and maybe even the need for
coaching an employee, if they begin early by mentoring for performance
management their average and better-than-average staff members. The
third and final section of this book should help to get you started on this
important task.

Mentoring

CHAPTER 9

What Mentoring Can Do to Help High Achievers—and You

ANY DISCUSSION OF HOW TO BOOST the performance of staff must include mentoring. You can mentor your own employees, participate in a formal program within your organization to help talented staff members advance, or mentor in both work and career particular individuals outside your organization, including relatives and friends. There are numerous candidates as mentees out there.

Ambitious managers and employees are looking for executives and other higher-level managers who will agree to help them up a career ladder that has fewer rungs than it had in the past, owing to today's flatter organizations. These individuals are searching for managers and executives who will cheer them on with "pep talks"; instruct them about the power and political framework of the organization; facilitate projects that they are working on by making available both resources and contacts inside and outside the organization; and influence the powers that be to promote them when a vacancy opens up.

The Growing Interest in Mentoring

Mentoring is a trend sweeping through corporate America—and with cause. In interviews, almost all successful individuals today have pointed to one or more individuals who had a major influence on their professional lives, if not both their professional *and* personal lives. Being mentored has come to be considered one of the great things we can all do to advance our careers. So, today, hundreds of thousands of informal relationships are occurring as ambitious employees and managers—not to mention would-be entrepreneurs—look for ways to achieve their career goals faster with the help of a more experienced advisor or counselor.

Structured or facilitated company programs are on an increase as organizations see that mentoring programs can shorten learning tracks, speed up managerial advancement, and build the next generation of leaders. Managers can also mentor their own staff members, assuming trust exists between them and their employees. Contrary to what some experts in mentoring say, mentoring takes time and effort. So it is fair for you to ask what is in it for you to mentor someone—subordinate, staff member, friend, or family member. We know that those who are mentored point to an increase in their morale and their capabilities. They also come away with an improvement in listening skills. As far as what's in it for you, you'll come away from the experience with stronger coaching and counseling skills, more access to information and more contacts within and outside your organization, and an increased sense of well-being from sharing your know-how with others. Mentors tell me that they have become better overall communicators, as well.

Unmuddying the Waters

Despite the increase in mentoring relationships, there continue to be misunderstandings about mentoring. For instance, many articles about mentoring focus only on the mentor's coaching role, but that is only one of four. Mentors are also role models, brokers (that is, contact aides), cheerleaders, and sponsors—but more about that later. Mentoring also looks at an individual as a whole person, working to help an individual with not only his or her current job but also career.

Further, a mentor need not be older than the mentee. Age isn't an issue. Someone is a mentor because he or she has knowledge or experience to bring to the relationship that the other party can benefit from. In an ideal relationship, the learning process goes both ways. The mentee also has knowledge and experience that is valued by the mentor and willingly shares that with the more experienced person.

If you are interested in mentoring, you can participate in one of the many mentoring programs that are available today. You may find one within your own company, in which you would help an up-and-coming manager or employee advance; one through a community group, local school, or college; one through an industry association or professional society; or one via the Internet designed to help a member of a minority group. In most formal programs, you enter into an agreement—a written document in most structured programs, usually a verbal discussion in informal relationships—to interact in ways to facilitate the learning, growth, and skill development of the mentee.

The existence of formal programs does not preclude more informal relationships, including mentoring relationships between managers and their direct reports. For instance, a manager recently told me how concerned he was that he didn't have the dollars to keep his best employees motivated and sustain their high performance. Mentoring is his answer, and is the answer for other managers in the same situation. Superstars who have reached a career plateau will see mentoring as a reward in place of a promotion or a big raise. From your mentoring, your talented new hires will have shorter learning curves and be more productive sooner. Under your mentoring, these talented newcomers will also be less likely to pick up bad habits from their less productive co-workers. Thus mentoring can be preventive, as is coaching.

Meetings with an employee mentee should be clear: You appreciate the super-performer's work and you care enough about the individual's future growth and advancement to devote time to his or her career. These meetings send a message to your work team as a whole as well: Top performers and those who exhibit high potential will get extra attention. Thus you give your entire staff reason to push themselves further. If your mentoring of one or two key performers has the domino effect within your entire department, you will get senior management's attention, too, and in the best way possible, as a manager who is able to get the very best from people and thereby contribute substantially to better bottom-line results.

Structured Mentoring Programs

In this chapter, I focus on the supervisor mentor, but first you might want to know something about more structured programs. In these programs, the methods used to match mentors and mentees vary from allowing the mentees to self-select a mentor to highly sophisticated Web-based programs in which mentors go online to choose from individuals who are looking for mentors. In between, you have mentoring programs in which a match is made by the program's coordinator, usually a human resources manager, or program board made up of peers. Sometimes an in-depth questionnaire is used to help with the final choices. Most programs also have protocols in case the pairings don't work out.

In structured programs, mentors and mentees also use forms on which they record goals and progress toward achievement of those goals.

The document includes the activities that will be used to advance the mentee. There is also a provision in the agreement that allows either the mentor or the mentee to end the relationship and seek a new partner.

Mentoring vs. Coaching

Often the procedure for mentoring a subordinate gets confused with that of coaching because one of the functions of a supervisory mentor is to coach the protégé or mentee. But mentoring even direct reports involves *going above and beyond* coaching. It is a relationship in which you do more than train the employees to do their job well. Rather, your focus is to share your experience, wisdom, and political savvy to enable your top performers to take on tasks beyond those designated in their job descriptions. As a managerial mentor, your fourfold purpose is to be:

1.   *Role Model.* Your behavior should be a model to emulate, just as the behavior of the first Mentor was. In *The Odyssey,* Homer tells how the adventurer Odysseus left his son, Telemachus, to the care of a servant, Mentor. For the next ten years, Mentor acted as the young man's teacher, adviser, friend, and surrogate father. He had less to do with teaching the young man the skills he might need in battle than with teaching him the values he would need to succeed as ruler of Ithaca. About 1200 B.C., when Homer told of the siege of Troy, it was common practice in Greece for young male citizens to be paired with older males so that the young person would learn and emulate the values of the mentor, usually a relative. It was recognized what a powerful influence role models can have on a person's development.

Assuming that you practice the values you and your organization preach, your mentees are likely to practice these values, too. When these values reflect the strategic mission of your department or the organization as a whole, you can expect the cooperation of your top talent in achieving these missions. Certainly they will be more alert to opportunities for achieving them and more willing to extend themselves to accomplish departmental and corporate strategies.

2.   *Coach.* In this role, you help to clarify the organization's culture, political structure, and vision to encourage your employee mentees to correctly direct their efforts and avoid the political traps that could derail them from a fast track within the organization. Mentoring includes being supportive of any ideas that the high-value employee/mentee might have on improving workflow or product design or sales. You have to be

willing to be a sounding board for the employee mentee, acknowledging the strengths in his or her ideas but also helping the individual to see the weaknesses, to overcome these shortcomings, and then to develop a strategy for selling the idea to others with the resources to make it a reality.

3. *Broker.* Your employee mentee doesn't have the contacts you do, and as his or her mentor your role is to make these available. You have listened to an employee mentee's career goals and you have served as a sounding board for his or her ideas. Now you have to draw on favors owed you by peers to get the additional information or resources that the mentee needs to make his or her plan work. You act almost as a corporate uncle or aunt for the employee mentee, clearing the path for the individual to reach those whose approval is needed for the idea to be tried.

4. *Advocate.* You become a cheerleader for your employee mentees, giving them the chance to show others what they are capable of doing. As mentor, you recommend that your mentees be chosen to head corporate projects and otherwise give them the opportunity to advance professionally. The latter includes making the sacrifice of recommending a talented staff member to another company if there is no opportunity within your organization for advancement. While you may lose a top talent, in making such a move you let other talented direct reports or team members know that your interest in them extends beyond their day-to-day jobs.

Supervisory Problems

There's much to be gained from mentoring a subordinate, but there are also potential problems. For instance, the protégé may believe that he or she deserves your loyalty, above and beyond what might exist if your relationship was based solely on positional power. Positional power itself may be a problem since the supervisor/mentor may guide, suggest, or coach but shouldn't be using power to direct actions. After all, the supervisor is responsible for managing the on-the-job performance of the staff member, not the individual's career. A mentor, on the other hand, has no involvement in a mentee's performance assessment.

Likewise, a supervisor's focus should be on the goals set by staff members and their day-to-day work, whereas a mentor will have longer-term goals in mind and focus on the protégé's development. You can tell if a problem between you and an employee mentee exists if your mentoring sessions resemble more how-to coaching sessions rather than meetings on personal development. But solid mentoring relationships between managers and a staff member do exist. They are founded on trust between the two individuals. On the supervisor mentor's part, it is a matter of making a commitment to empower the chosen staff member.

Your First Decision as a Mentor

The first, and most important, decision you make respecting mentoring is whom you will mentor. In selecting a staff member to mentor, you need to be careful. Your selection must seem fair and logical, particularly to your other staff members, as any other decision you might make about an employee, like a promotion or a coveted assignment. Otherwise, mentoring won't help spur other employees' performance. Unless your employees see in your mentoring candidate the same potential that you do, you could even be accused of showing undeserved favoritism or maybe even of discrimination.

In making your selection, consider the ten managerial benefits from mentoring one's own employees:

1. *Faster Learning Curves.* Taking a new and talented staff member under your wing, even for a short time, puts that person on a high-performance fast track.

2. *Increased Communication of Corporate Values.* Not only will you be able to communicate the company's values—values having to do with quality of customer service, the kinds of relationships expected among co-workers, the sense of teamwork expected of everyone, and shared responsibility for corporate profitability—but you will be able to explain the strategic importance of these values. If you share with a newcomer how important these values are to the company's success, and in some instances, to its very survival, the talented new recruit, with her fresh perspective, may come up with an idea for achieving one.

3. *Reduced Turnover at a Time When New Recruits May Be Hard to Find.* Right now companies have begun to pay hiring bonuses, even for entry-level employees in certain fields. Increased sales and profits have enabled managers to fill openings that they have had to operate around for several years. Once you find a talented employee, and he or she has agreed to work for you, you want that person to stay. If you can't offer a bonus, you can promise the individual that you will set career goals and

mentor him or her to enable the person to achieve those goals. Having an adviser and friend in a higher position in a company can be more valuable than the financial compensation of a bonus after one, two, or three years with a company.

One-on-one communication between a manager and a talented new hire that shows every likelihood of continuing and that could include discussion of a role the new hire might play in future corporate plans can reassure the talented newcomer that he or she won't disappear into the corporate woodwork once the honeymoon is over. The individual won't worry about a lack of visibility and begin job hunting immediately after getting a job with you.

4. *Increased Loyalty.* Mentoring efforts tell your employees that you care for them beyond their ability to complete today's work assignments. It lets them know that you are as concerned as they are about their future employability.

5. *Improved One-on-One Communication and a Sense of Team Within Your Work Group.* Time spent with the mentee in which you discuss your plans for his or her future can reduce the feeling of uncertainty the corporate grapevine may have created. Further, with your approval, your mentee can correct rumors that are demotivating the rest of the department and enhance communication within the department or division as a whole. As you learn about group concerns from the mentee, you are also in a better position to focus on group gripes in team problem-solving sessions or other departmental meetings.

6. *Increased Employee Productivity.* The extra instruction that mentees get can motivate them to work harder, to take on challenging assignments, and to operate outside their boxes with some direction from you. Thus you tap the potential of your talented workers. Mentoring is particularly helpful in maintaining the top performance of your superstars. These individuals can easily become frustrated when they realize that their hard work isn't going to get them quick promotions in today's downsized organizations. When that happens, they will quit. Worse than move on, they may stay but start doing below-standard work, qualifying them for counseling.

You want to give your top performers a reason to continue to outperform their peers. Your mentoring tells them that there is someone who is concerned with their professional growth and advancement; the personal coaching that will help them in their careers is a fair trade for their exceptional performance.

7. *More Time for Yourself.* Your mentees can take on projects that are important to your department or division but for which you don't have the time. You can pursue ideas that could increase your operation's bottom line while being assured that many of these more traditional projects are being handled. You can even delegate some of your day-to-day work to mentees since, in taking on this work, they are increasing their own skill levels.

Parenthetically, this use of mentoring works only if you monitor the work being done. This shouldn't be a problem because a major part of your meetings with mentees would be devoted to reviewing their progress on these assignments. Don't fall into the trap of many mentors and refrain from asking for updates either because you have convinced yourself that the employee won't have problems with the work—after all, you don't—or because you don't want to identify any causes for criticism.

8. *Additional Corporate Information.* The more information you have about what's happening in your organization, the better positioned you are to respond to your professional advantage as well as to the advantage of your organization's bottom line. Your mentees can see that you are kept informed of developments outside your departmental boundaries. Through their contacts with others in the company, your mentees become like listening stations, picking up key information that you might not otherwise be privy to.

9. *Creation of an Innovative Environment.* There is a very powerful, albeit subtle, relationship between mentoring and creativity. Mentoring, in essence, releases top talent to work outside their boxes. You, as a mentor, provide a safe, secure culture in which staff members can develop their ideas and innovations. And you see that they get the rewards their efforts deserve.

10. *Allies for the Future.* Over time, as your mentees advance in their careers and gain influence within the organization, they can also be the friends you turn to for key resources or support for your own ideas.

Let's assume that you choose to mentor someone from your own staff. Knowing the ten benefits of mentoring, whom should you choose? Do you have a talented but plateaued employee who could get off that plateau if he or she had stronger interpersonal skills? Maybe the individual needs to take a course or two or have an opportunity to participate on a team in which he or she can practice the skills. Or you might have a top team member who could speed the team effort if he or she had project-management skills. Should this person take a training program in Total Quality Management techniques? Does that newly hired talent need a better understanding of corporate values or the department mission? Or does one of your more talented staff members have an idea for a new product and need you as advocate to get the critical resources to make the idea a reality?

How a Mentoring Relationship Develops

Most traditional mentoring relationships begin informally—usually after a request by the less senior person, albeit not necessarily the younger person, for advice or counsel or for resources to complete a project. But since you plan to use mentoring to boost employee performance, you will need to take the initiative. The next time the employee you want to mentor comes with a question, problem, or need, you should offer to be available to help the individual on a regular basis. An affirmative response would signify the beginning of a mentor relationship.

Make a commitment to meet with the employee one or two times a month to discuss his progress as team leader and to offer suggestions based on your own experience on how to get critical resources; or to discuss with another employee her efforts to streamline work processes and to share your political savvy on getting cooperation from key managers. Let's look at a typical mentoring relationship and how it develops: the case study of Bob and Faith.

BOB AND FAITH: THE MENTORING RELATIONSHIP IN PRACTICE

Faith had been hired as administrative assistant to Bob, the head of purchasing. Faith had held only secretarial positions before she applied for the administrative assistant position in Bob's department, but Bob was more than willing to hire Faith for the job. In his opinion, based on her training, previous job experience, and accomplishments in past jobs, Faith not only was qualified for the vacancy but also ultimately could move up to assistant purchasing manager if she applied herself.

Bob decided to give her assignments that better reflected her capabilities than her job title, and in each instance she excelled. Each of these projects required stretch on Faith's part, and she recognized that. So one day she asked Bob if she could come to him if she ran into any problems with her assignments.

"Of course," he said. "You have lots of ability you have yet to use, and I want to give you every opportunity to use that potential." At this point, Bob decided to offer to help Faith advance in her job. Toward that end, he promised to put her in charge of several projects of her own—assignments that would make her more promotable in the future.

"If you take these on, I'll be free to work on other tasks," he said, looking at the papers stacked on his visitor's chair. "I'll help you if you run into any difficulties," he promised.

Faith was delighted with the offer. She had left her previous employer because she hadn't felt appreciated. Bob clearly recognized her potential and was willing to help her realize it. Bob didn't formalize his promise in a written agreement because he didn't see this as a formal relationship. He'd help her and she, in turn, would help him. That was all there was to his offer.

Bob identified a number of the skills Faith would need to develop the ability to handle the projects and ultimately to become a buyer or an assistant purchasing manager. These included how to use cost and price analysis techniques to rationalize the total cost of acquisition strategies and how to resolve common problems in negotiating contract terms and conditions, and what red flags to look for in contracts and supplier agreements.

Bob promised Faith that he would meet with her every second week in his office at lunchtime—he'd pick up the sandwiches at a nearby deli himself—and that at each meeting she could give him an update on her progress on the projects he would assign, and he would offer her feedback as well as any advice he might have based on his experience with the people Faith would be working with.

In examining what happened, it's important to note two things. First, and foremost, Bob never promised Faith a promotion. As her manager, it would have been a violation of corporate policy to do so. As a mentor of a direct report, you can only offer to help the individual increase his or her employability. Given the volatility of today's workplace, realistically that is all you can offer, anyway. Equally interesting, as is usually the case at the start of mentoring relationships, the word *mentor* never came up. Indeed, the term wasn't used until two years later, when Faith's husband had to relocate and Faith therefore left the company.

Faith's daughter Raquel came to the office on her mother's last day there, and she was introduced to "Bob Andrews, my boss and mentor."

Faith's husband wasn't the only person with a new job in the new city; Faith had one, too. Through Bob's network of contacts, she had landed a job in which she would be assistant manager of purchasing in her new location. Her experience had built up her self-confidence to the point that she had no trepidation about her new career move.

The use of the word *mentor* had surprised Bob; he had seen the relationship more as a partnership: in return for the free time he gained from Faith's assuming projects he would otherwise have had to oversee himself, he helped Faith with advice about the assignments he had given her and also recommended opportunities for training that would move her out of her current job track. But in retrospect, he had to agree that he had been her mentor. He had taught her a lot and advised her on the training she would need to get the new job. But it had been a win/win/win arrangement.

Faith had developed the skills she needed to succeed in her new job, but in the process she had also uncovered a vendor scam that would have cost Bob's and Faith's organization more than $50,000. She had learned about the ruse during one of the evening courses she had taken. Bob's boss had nominated her for an individual achievement certificate, which she received along with the $5,000 bonus that went with it. And Bob hadn't done poorly, either. Freed of the more mundane projects he had responsibility for, he had been able to complete a reorganization plan for the purchasing department, thereby saving the company another $100,000. His reward from the company had been an upgrading and a salary increase.

How a Mentoring Relationship Succeeds

What made Faith and Bob's mentoring relationship work so well? To answer that question, we have to consider the two individuals. Looking at what Faith brought to the relationship will give you some idea of the kinds of staff or team members who can get the most benefit from mentoring.

Faith's Promising Background

Faith had a track record that showed she was willing to assume responsibility for her own growth and development. Raquel was three years old when Faith had returned to college to complete her studies toward a bachelor's degree in English. With no real job skills, she had entered the job market as a receptionist while attending business school to learn the latest software programs, accounting and business law, and office management. She had gone to secretarial school and then entered the workforce because of the family's need for a second income, but she had wanted to continue school and get a master's degree in business administration, she had admitted to Bob.

With some careful probing, Bob discovered that Faith's father had been against her attending college right after high school. Her decision to return to school when Raquel was three had upset her parents, who felt that she should be sufficiently happy as a housewife and mother. Her husband supported her decision, but Faith's parents tried to discourage her, pointing to the damage it might do to her marriage and relationship with her young daughter. Although she made light of it, their lack of support had made her less confident about her decision—and any future endeavors. Still, her job record demonstrated that she thrived on challenges.

A Dynamic Career

In her first job, as a receptionist, she had done the clerical tasks for the head of office services while manning the outer desk. Because the manager had seen how knowledgeable Faith was about a new software program the firm had installed, she had asked Faith to give an overview of the program to the firm's secretaries, and Faith had put together a training program and followed it up by instituting a user's group within the company. If there had been a position as secretary available for Faith, she would have been given it, the office manager had told Bob when he did a reference check on Faith. "We just didn't have the budget to create the position, and there was no likelihood of a vacancy in the near future."

Faith's first secretarial job was with a marketing manager. Soon after starting, she was not only opening his correspondence but writing much of it, as well as completing market research reports under his direction. And so it went. Faith had worked as secretary for two companies before being hired by Bob. In each instance, she had actively sought challenging assignments and taken on greater responsibilities. She was continually learning because she accepted feedback and coaching well, learning from those who were willing to share their know-how with her.

An Eye on Self-Development

Bob was particularly impressed by Faith's participation in their discussions about her developmental needs. On her own, she contacted several local universities to get course catalogues, and then she reviewed their contents with Bob to determine which courses would most help her become more familiar with her department's responsibilities. While attending a course, she would ask Bob a question about what she was learning to better understand its application to their department.

In summary, Bob recognized Faith's abilities and she, in turn, was willing to take on additional responsibilities in return for his helping her to advance in her career. She knew she would have to assume more work than her peers, but she recognized that her relationship with Bob would work only if it benefited him and the organization as well as her. She used her semi-monthly meetings to increase her employability and ability to complete Bob's assignments. While Bob had agreed to help her, Faith knew that she was still responsible for her own development and she took the initiative in working with him to meet her developmental goals.

All wasn't rosy with Faith's performance. On two occasions, she failed to complete projects on schedule, and Bob was annoyed, although he tried not to show it as he explained to her that she would have to learn to balance her time. Yes, he understood that she had a home life as well as her new studies and job responsibilities, but he gently reminded her about the developmental plan. He suggested that she talk over some of her home tasks with her husband to see if he would lend a hand when she had a critical office deadline.

Faith followed Bob's advice, and found her husband entirely supportive of her career advancement goals. Most important, Faith recognized the importance of mutual respect, trust, and openness. This is why Bob learned about Faith's need to relocate immediately after the family decision was made. She could have waited at least two months to let him know, but she didn't, and thereby risked not going on her first business trip as a representative of the firm. Bob appreciated the advance notice, and was able to get approval for replacements—yes, he discovered that he would need two people to replace Faith—and, in return for her openness, he sent her and one of the department's buyers on the trip as planned.

The Characteristics of an Excellent Mentee

What made Faith such a good mentee? The answer is multifaceted but clear:

- She had a track record of success.
- She had demonstrated her intelligence and initiative in previous jobs.

- She was loyal to the organization and committed to its values.
- She shared with Bob a desire to achieve results.
- She enjoyed challenges and willingly accepted greater responsibility.
- She took responsibility for her own career advancement and growth. To this end, she planned the action steps 'hat would lead to achievement of her career goals.
- She valued feedback even if it wasn't always positive. She realized that she coul ¹ make mistakes, but rarely did she repeat them because she listened to and followed the advice more experienced individuals gave her.
- She welcomed Bob's help in identifying her performance deficiencies and setting developmental goals.

The Characteristics of an Excellent Mentor

What about Bob? What made him such a good mentor?

• *He had strong interpersonal skills.* Although Bob liked to work with numbers, which is why he chose to work in the purchasing field, he also liked working with people. And he had good communication skills, which means he was not only articulate but also an active listener. A practitioner of the 20/80 rule, he listened 80 percent of the time and talked only 20 percent in most communications with his staff members. He knew how to ask open-ended questions—that is, questions that require more than yes or no answers—and he listened to the responses, nodding and moving toward the speaker in a manner that demonstrated he wanted to hear more.

For example, Bob often paraphrased what he had been told to ensure that he understood what the other party said. Rather than answer all Faith's questions, Bob also found it worthwhile to ask her more questions to force her to think through situations and come up with the right answers herself.

• *He had contacts both within and outside the organization, and tremendous influence wi⁺hin the company.* Bob shared with Faith the insights about the company's long-range goals and strategic intent he had gained from the movers and shakers within the organization. This knowledge allowed her to identify those who might be obstacles tc completing the projects assig ed her and to develop plans to gain these individuals' support. Consequently she was able to develop an impressive track record that was attracting the attention of senior management. Clearly, with access to Bob's extensive network of resources, Faith was positioned to apply for the next assistant managerial position that opened up within the organization. And she would have been made an assistant manager had she not had to relocate. Still, Bob's contacts in the field meant that she was able to get a comparable job in purchasing in a company in her new location.

• *He recognized others' accomplishments.* Bob had learned how motivating this could be. So he went out of his way to acknowledge the accomplishments of those with whom he worked. He never took credit for the work of his employees. But neither did he praise them unless it was deserved, because he understood that praise that is not legitimately earned has little or no value; it even undermines the value of the giver.

• *He was an excellent supervisor.* That he is able to give feedback that clearly reinforces the desired performance and to coach to improve performance makes Bob not only an excellent manager but also an excellent mentor. He knows how to delegate tasks, determine adequate time for completion of the task, communicate clearly what needs to be done, estimate resource requirements and see that they are forthcoming. The list goes on, but the bottom line is that a good mentor is someone who manages people successfully.

• *He knows his field.* Since Bob's competence in purchasing is acknowledged by those in his organization, his recognition of Faith's accomplishments carried weight. Bob maintains his expertise through his attendance at local and annual meetings of associations in his field and industry. Since he has spoken at several industry conferences, his prestige extends beyond the boundaries of his organization, which gives him leverage both within and outside the company—leverage that he can use to help a mentee.

• *He accepts the risk that comes with mentoring.* There is no guarantee that each time a mentee steps outside her box she will be successful. A mentor has to have the courage to know that the person he is sponsoring may sometimes fail and to be willing to be there to support that person should she be beyond her depths. A mentor is someone who says enthusiastically to the mentee "Go to it!" but who also is prudent about the risks he lets the employee take on. After all, the mentor wants the mentee not only to build new skills but also to increase her self-confidence from a stream of wins.

• *He is willing to be available to help another advance in the organization.* Bob was willing to commit both his time and his emotional energy to Faith because he felt she was worth the effort. He wasn't threatened by the thought that one day Faith might even surpass him. He realized he could move her career forward by sharing with her the unwritten rules about the organization, wisdom he had gained the hard way from breaking the rules himself. But if he hadn't, Faith could easily have been a bull in a china shop in trying to complete the projects Bob assigned her.

During his meetings, Bob also had to listen to her insecurities and help her answer "What if . . ." questions. He had to let her test ideas, listen to them objectively, advise on the wisdom of pursuing them, help Faith adapt them as appropriate, and then help Faith to present the idea to others in the best light.

In short, Bob had to be willing to devote time to Faith's career—two hours every two weeks or four hours a month. More than this would have been too much, making Faith overdependent on Bob. On the other hand, even four hours, given the time pressures on most managers, represent a major commitment. After all, four hours are the equivalent of one team meeting or two vendor interviews, or two lunches with his own boss, or a review of a stack of requisitions. Regardless, it was a commitment Bob had to keep.

Consider what might have happened if Bob had not kept his promise to meet with Faith regularly over lunch to discuss her progress, even if he had had legitimate reasons for not being available. It's likely it would have done just the opposite of what he intended: his superstar's performance would have faded.

Your Prospective Mentoring Relationship

Let's look at that high-value employee you identified. How successful will you be in mentoring this person? To measure the likelihood of success of your entering into a mentorship, on a sheet of paper list in one column the resources (skills, abilities, knowledge) you are willing to give to the relationship, including your commitment of time and attention. In the other column, list your prospective mentee's needs. Now review the two lists.

Begin with your prospective mentee's list. First check those occasions for spur-of-the-moment interventions like a review by you of the mentee's proposal, prior to his or her presenting it to the team, to help the talented but inexperienced public speaker identify any trouble spots. The items remaining would be those developmental needs that demand a greater commitment from you. For instance, maybe the employee mentee has great ideas but can't sell them and needs someone to provide ongoing coaching to enable him or her to stand out from the team.

Now look at your own list of skills, abilities, and knowledge, including political know-how, that you can use to assist your mentee. Draw lines across the two columns where you can link your competencies very specifically with the employee mentee's developmental needs. Use a yellow marker to note those instances in which the mentee might be better off with another mentor, either because the need demands more time than you are able to give or because you lack skill in that area.

Now examine the two lists as well as the number of yellow marks on the finished sheet of paper. Needless to say, the more yellow marks there are, the less likely it is that the mentorship will help the mentee, and the more frustrated both you and the mentee will be from getting together for talks that produce no real return. On the other hand, the more linkages there are between your mentee's needs and your resources, the more productive the mentorship will be. Even if the mentee has a high need for help, so long as you have sufficient time and skills to satisfy the individual's developmental needs, the relationship should work well for both of you.

And assuming that you have entered into the relationship with a clear idea of its benefits to you—from reducing the learning curve of a new hire to making a talented employee into an informal assistant or project leader, to keeping a champion in top form—there should be every reason for you to commit yourself to this person's professional and personal development.

• • •

One caveat: Be honest about the time you can commit to the individual. We all have a tendency to underestimate the amount of our work and to overestimate the time available. So reduce by at least one-third your estimate of available time to help the mentee employee. While mentoring someone isn't as time-intensive as some people suppose, it should still be obvious that a very needful mentee with an overloaded mentor will not work well together.

CHAPTER

10

Mentor as a Role Model, Broker, Advocate, and Career Counselor

IN CHAPTER 9 YOU SAW how mentoring a staff member can be used to boost the performance of your best performers or help a new hire with lots of ability to hit the ground running. Much of this stems from coaching. This chapter offers more insights into how to keep top performers at their current levels. But let's look first at the other roles of a mentor: role model, broker, advocate, and career counselor. In fact, let's start with *you* as a role model for your mentee, whether a subordinate, a staff member, or individual with lots of potential you want to help.

The Mentor's Many Roles

Mentor as Role Model

A role model is a person so effective or inspiring in some professional or personal way that he or she is a model for others. When the role model is also the individual's mentor, he or she is someone whom the protégé admires or looks up to, a person the protégé would like to be more like. The mentor has reached a level of accomplishment in a role that the protégé aspires to with qualities and attributes that the mentee wishes to acquire.

When people assume the role of mentor, they know that they will be role models, whether they like it or not. It will be their behavior that

172

people will watch and emulate. It is their leadership qualities that they will study and want to duplicate. This puts tremendous pressure on you as a mentor to be a good role model. After all, your mentee will hear about how you interacted with someone or how confident you seemed in a specific situation. You can never fully relax in the workplace—you are always a mentor, and your behaviors will be assessed and emulated by the person with whom you are mentoring.

Let's assume, for instance, that you have a research project to complete. You want to be sure that you do a good job. Otherwise, you will be sending a poor message to your protégé about the work he or she should be turning out. If you give the impression that you believe you can just wing things, well then, your protégé is likely to figure that's all right—and he or she will do it, too. So, do you practice what you preach? Just as failure to live up to the behaviors you profess will be emulated, so too will the values that you practice. Consequently, when you mentor employees within your organization, and your values reflect the strategic mission of your organization, you can expect the support of your protégés in achieving these missions. Certainly, they will be more alert to opportunities for achieving them and more willing to extend themselves to accomplish corporate strategies.

Since your behavior will influence your mentee's behavior, consider how you would appear if someone were to take a video of your behavior over a day. Would you be proud of your behavior and of your mentee if he or she emulated your behavior? Ask yourself these questions:

- Do I act in ways that are ethical, earning the respect and trust of others with whom I do business?
- Do my remarks show consideration for the feelings and convictions of others?
- When I make a promise, do I make an effort to keep that promise?
- Am I a phony, putting on airs to impress others, or do I come across as the person I *really* am, regardless of my job title?
- Can I be trusted not to reveal information told to me in confidence?
- Do I have the strength of character to be the bearer of bad news when that is my responsibility, and do I do it with sensitivity?

Once you are a mentor, ask yourself another question: What impact have my actions had on others—in particular, my mentee?

Mentor as Broker

Your protégés may not have the contacts you do, and as their mentor, your role is to make them available. To be a broker to a protégé, you have to have solid contacts. That means that you have to be skilled in building a network of individuals to whom you can go to help your mentee. If you want to have a strong network—not only for your protégé's career but for yours, too—here are some steps to follow:

• *Develop a 25-second infomercial about yourself.* Be prepared to introduce yourself and to answer the question, "What do you do?" in 25 seconds or less in a clear, concise, and memorable way. Remember, first impressions count, and you have a limited time to make a good impression. Don't just give your job title; tell the other party what you do.

• *Do your research.* Know more about the people you will be meeting and their interests. This will enable you to plan in advance how to enter into conversations with the individuals you will be meeting for the first time. Let's say that you are at a professional association meeting. You might ask someone, "What brought you to this meeting?" Or another good opening line might be, "What business are you in? How useful do you find these meetings to be?" Still another question might be, "This is my first meeting. How does this compare to others you've attended?"

Did you notice that each of these questions is open-ended; that is, they require more than a one-word answer? The trick is to get the other person talking and to start a conversation—to break the ice.

• *Introduce yourself to the speaker.* Tell him or her how much you are looking forward to the talk and mention something specific about the topic or speaker. You will be able to do this because you have prepared in advance. After the presentation, follow up by sending a note saying how much you enjoyed the talk and mentioning a helpful piece of information you took away.

• *Have a list of "get to know you" questions.* The focus here is on the person you are speaking with. Depending on the circumstances, here are some questions with which you can start a list: Why did you come to this session? Where do you work and what do you do? What other sessions have you attended? What do you do when you aren't working? What do you love about your job? What types of projects do you get involved in? What have you done recently? After you've introduced yourself, transfer the focus from yourself to the other person. Since people love to talk about themselves, this should sustain the conversation for as long as you wish.

• *Listen to determine how you can help the other party.* Always be ready to give information, resources, or help to others. If someone says, "I'm ready for a vacation!" answer by saying, "I have a terrific travel agent. Would you like her name?" If they mention a work problem and you know someone who had a similar problem and found a solution, offer to bring the two together. Put aside thoughts about your phone calls at the office (and don't forget to turn off your cell phone), and pay attention to the here and now and the needs of those around you.

• *Demonstrate your trustworthiness.* For individuals you meet to remain a permanent part of your network, you need to demonstrate to them that you are reliable. If they ask you for something by a certain time, meet the deadline. Don't take advantage of their kindness—respect their time. If you promise someone that you'll call her on Tuesday, do it. That's how you teach someone that you will do what you say you will do. If you promise someone that you'll provide x items for an auction, provide x-plus items. That way, you will demonstrate that you will go that extra mile for the person.

• *Network within your organization.* Never forget to increase the contacts you have nationally and internationally within your own company. Review your firm's organization chart. Do you know people at all levels of the organization? Do they know your name and what you do? Do you know all the people whose work intersects yours in any way? Are you involved in any cross-functional efforts or interdepartmental activities (temporary assignments, committees, task forces, special projects, volunteer activities)? Do you take every opportunity to meet face-to-face with others about trends that will affect your job in the future and the tools to get the job done today? The stronger your own network— particularly if you are mentoring a staff member or other colleague inside your organization—then the more you can do as broker for your protégé.

Mentor as Advocate

As advocate for your protégés, you are their cheerleader, offering positive feedback to others about their work to ensure they are given the chance to test their wings. You recommend that your mentees be chosen to head corporate projects and otherwise give them the opportunity to advance professionally. If the protégé has a desire to set up his or her own business, you help the individual find the venture capitalists to finance the project, assuming that you think the business idea is sound.

We discussed your rating as a role model and discussed your trustworthiness. As an advocate, that issue becomes relevant: will others trust your recommendation about a mentee based on your previous endorsements? To be an advocate, you have to be known to others as someone whose judgment can be trusted. This means that you yourself should not have the reputation as someone who goes around praising everyone he comes in contact with, using grandiose terminology without reason.

At a recent meeting with individuals from another organization, I listened as the group's leader spoke glowingly about his team members. He did, indeed, have a good, solid team, and I was delighted to work with the group over time, but that first meeting left a lot of doubt. He spoke about how each member did the greatest work imaginable, that they were the best staff ever. He pointed to the manager with him and told us, to the manager's embarrassment, that she was the best supervisor since the creation of bosses.

If you were mentee to such a mentor, at first it might seem great. You'd think at first that you'd have no more to do than sit there and bask in his or her praise. Not so. Once you become a protégé of an exaggerating congratulator, you come to realize that the new mentor isn't really very helpful—any praise out of his or her mouth is questioned. Worse, during coaching sessions, when this kind of mentor said complimentary things about your performance, you would discount it as exaggerated praise and lip service and lose respect and confidence in the mentor. Eventually, you would come to view the mentor's comments as a joke if all he or she gave was praise.

Why do some managers give praise whether it has been earned or not? Some executives and managers feel that their supervisory responsibility includes acting as public relations representative for their team. They believe that as long as the group seems happy, the organization will believe that the department or division is running smoothly. Some managers don't want to confront a problem in performance and consequently prefer to be blind to its existence. This behavior carries over to their relationship with their protégé. So, if you want to perform your role as advocate, you need to have a reputation for giving praise that is genuine and sincere. When you speak to others about your protégé, you have to be specific, not talk in generalities. Be prepared to cite specific instances in which your protégé demonstrated his potential.

Being an advocate isn't as simple as it seems. For instance, if you put your recommendation in writing, keep in mind that it will be a lasting document, one that many people other than the individual to whom you sent the letter will see. So you want to be sure that this permanent document reflects well on you, as well as on your protégé. If you have some reservations yet believe that your protégé deserves a chance to test her skills, you may prefer to phone in your recommendation, with praise about the mentee. If you believe that a personal conversation will help you to make your case, you may want to use the phone to set up a time to meet with this third party to talk face-to-face about your protégé.

When talking to someone about your protégé, you may want to "sell" your comments by speaking in a manner that will enhance acceptance of your remarks. For instance, some individuals may be interested in only the big picture. What did your protégé do that is relevant to his or her need? Once they hear that the person is skilled at leading IT projects or getting a new product to market on time, they will be satisfied and ready to decide whether the individual can help him or her. No further details are needed. They would only muddy the discussion. On the other hand, there are people who are very detail-oriented. They want to know the specifics. If you are selling your protégé to one of these individuals, you may need to fully paint the picture for them, from A to Z. What specifically did they do? How long did it take them to complete the work? How was his relationship with others on the project?

Mentoring Skills in Action

As a mentor-supervisor, there's another positive impact that you can have—one that extends beyond the impression that you make on your mentee employee, as Erik learned.

ERIK: REAPING UNEXPECTED BENEFITS

When Erik decided to assume the role of Maria's mentor, he expected good things to result for Maria, himself, his engineering department, and the company. But he never expected the mentoring relationship to bring about a cultural change for the better in his department.

Maria was one of Erik's best performers. She always came up with great ideas for improving the company's line of electronic components or less expensive ways of producing them. Since the market was undergoing one of its shifts, and dollars were short and sales down, Maria's creativity was an asset. It was an asset that Erik had begun to worry about losing.

Maria had come up with a system improvement, but management had turned down her suggestion because of the short-term costs. The company would have to pay the costs of terminating a contract with a supplier and change several plant processes, but over the long term the new components would be cheaper to produce. There was also a ready market for the new components. Erik had heard that Maria was so disappointed about having her idea rejected that she had begun to talk about leaving the firm for a company that could see beyond the first or second quarter.

Although neither Erik nor Maria had ever used the word *mentor* during their once-a-month lunches, Erik had assumed that role with his superstar. And Erik felt that he should do more than merely commiserate with her, particularly if he didn't want to lose her to the competition. Consequently, he prepared a memo for his boss and others in senior management in favor of Maria's proposal, putting his ten years in the industry on her side. A patent holder many times over, Erik was known both for his creativity and for the ability to implement his ideas. He put that reputation on the line for Maria. And he got management's approval for her idea.

It worked. Management took the financial hurt during the first two quarters, but once the new component was on the retuned production line, the numbers quickly turned around. Costs declined 15 percent while sales jumped almost 30 percent. And Maria was so delighted with her bonus that she confided to Erik that she had no desire to leave. Besides, she had other ideas for further perfecting the line that she wanted to try.

But there is more to the story than Erik's acting as advocate for his mentee. His support of Maria had an effect throughout the engineering department. Morale rose as the news of what Erik had done spread. The engineers began to come to Erik with ideas that they had developed but had never shared with him before. Erik found himself mentoring more people than Maria when he discovered several potential superstars on his team as these former mediocre performers found that their creativity would be recognized. Erik's engineering group became the benchmark for innovation in the industry. There also was a decline in turnover. As the engineers learned that Erik had put his own job on the line for one of his engineers, and saw that he was willing to go above and beyond his responsibility as their manager to help his employees, the employee loyalty that had been lost as the result of a deep downsizing about a year before he returned—not to the organization but to Erik.

SANDY: AVERTING PROBLEMS THROUGH MENTORING

Both Chan and Clint reported to Sandy Lester, head of the marketing division for Acme Assets, a California-based financial services firm, and both were marketing managers at the time. Clint had been with the company for only a little over a month, whereas Chan had been there for three years. Chan was overdue for promotion, but there was nowhere within the organization he could go. Both men were excellent workers, but it wasn't their current performance that was Sandy's concern, but whether they would continue to produce at their current high levels. They both represented problems on the verge of happening if Sandy didn't avert them—through mentoring.

Clint asked to meet with Sandy to find out if he had made the right decision in leaving his previous employer to take a job with Acme. Since he had joined the company, Clint had heard rumblings from his colleagues about the likelihood of a downsizing. Clint's decision had been financially beneficial, but he had not known about two downsizings in other areas of the organization; he was concerned that the rumors might be true and that there would be cuts in marketing and he might be one of the first to be let go. As one of his new peers reminded him over lunch, "Last hired, first fired." Clint was also concerned because he might not be able to do his job well if the company was tightfisted about the money it laid out for marketing efforts. Consequently, besides making an appointment to meet with Sandy to discuss the situation later in the day, Clint also tried to reach his boss at his old company to see if his job there was still open, just in case.

Chan had an appointment with Sandy to talk about his plateaued status. He also wanted to find out if it was true what he had heard from a friend in Human Resources: Clint was making $10,000 more a year than he was. Chan, one of Sandy's stars, was hurting because he had thought his work was respected. That a new hire might make more than he did made him wonder if he really should be putting in all those long hours and weekends. Chan was being courted by one of Acme's competitors, and until now he had rejected their overtures. But he was considering visiting with the company's marketing VP to discuss the offer.

Sandy found herself in the position of possibly losing two of her best performers in one and the same day if she didn't come up with acceptable answers to their career concerns. She suspected that Chan was frustrated about his promotion prospects, but she had no idea what was troubling Clint. Since they were her two top performers, she was concerned about the impact their declining morale would have not only on their own work but on the performance of the team as a whole.

Clint's Meeting

A very direct person, Clint got to the point of the meeting immediately: Why hadn't Sandy mentioned that there had been layoffs before he was hired? Sandy was taken aback. "Yes," she said, "there have been downsizings within the organization, but none has occurred within this operation. Actually, this division has been given approval to hire because it is launching two new products in the coming year." One of these products had been assigned to Clint; the other had gone to Chan.

Further, because the company had high hopes for both products, Sandy told Clint, he had "no reason to be concerned that the budget would be cut. There had been some objections raised to the marketing campaign, but its cost certainly wasn't an issue," she continued. As Sandy fielded each of Clint's questions, she realized that he had been listening to the wrong people. She had thought Clint was experienced enough to be able to steer his own way through his new company's political byways, but judging from his comments he clearly wasn't. It looked as if he needed her help to separate the truth from the rumors and to identify whom to trust and whom not to trust. Since it was likely he would encounter some small opposition to his marketing plans for the new product, it was certainly worthwhile for her to serve as his adviser and broker until he had gained the respect his past job history suggested he deserved. Sandy answered each of Clint's concerns, and as she did so, she noticed the muscles around his mouth ease and his body relax into the chair.

"I'm sorry," Clint stammered. "I guess I was jumping to lots of conclusions. Next time, I'll talk to you before losing my head."

"Yes, please," said Sandy. Then, after thinking for a minute, she suggested that she and Clint meet over lunch once a week for the next few weeks while he better familiarized himself with the operation. "I can help you through some of the traps you could encounter working with the product managers here," she said. "Besides, we have just installed several new systems. Even our old-timers are having a hard time adapting. I'd like to see that you get off on the right foot."

Clint was flattered. At his previous company, he had had to find his own way around during his first few weeks. But his new boss here was offering to help him over the political obstacles and to give him any support he might need to get his new marketing campaign off the ground. Sandy told Clint to ask her assistant to schedule lunch with Clint every Wednesday for the next two months, and Clint promised to be ready to show Sandy the design for the new product's campaign over lunch in two days. He then scurried back to his office to schedule meetings with a designer and copywriter.

"One problem down," thought Sandy. "I hope I can be as successful with Chan. He's usually so upbeat and enthusiastic, but lately he has been sullen, glaring at me if not avoiding me entirely."

Chan's Complaint

When Chan entered Sandy's office, he looked almost in pain. His humorous manner and twinkling eyes had made meetings with him over the past three years pleasurable, but Sandy seemed unable to get even a smile from him now. "Are you angry?" she finally asked.

"Yes, I'm angry," he said, clenching his teeth so the words barely came out.

"About what?" Sandy asked, trying to defuse the situation by making light of it.

When Chan only grimaced, Sandy realized she had to change her tactics. She quietly moved her chair from behind the desk so that she was sitting at right angles to Chan. "Tell me what's bothering you," she asked.

"It's everything. I know that we have had only one opening in the division and it was a lateral—at least, I thought it was until I heard about Clint's salary."

"Oh," said Sandy.

"Yes," said Chan, gaining courage. "I hear he's making at least $10,000 more than any of us. I've been here three years, and am long overdue for a promotion. Why didn't you offer me the position?"

"It was posted," Sandy said defensively, then calmed herself. "But it is the same grade as yours. Clint's salary is only slightly higher than yours—certainly not $10,000 more—and he is getting what he is getting because that's what the market demands. You know all about compressed salaries and the like," she added.

"Yes, sure, but how come he is being put in charge of our newest financial offering?" he continued, still upset.

"We have two products that senior management has targeted for major marketing campaigns," Sandy explained. "Although Clint is new to the firm, he's familiar with the targeted market, so I gave him one. I gave you the other. Both are so important that it would have been unwise to assign both to a single marketer," Sandy said.

"Sandy," Chan complained, "I don't know. Maybe I shouldn't be as upset as I am, but I've been in the same position now for three years. I'm good—really good at what I do—and yet we both know there is nowhere in this office right now for me to advance to." When Chan finished his lament, Sandy admitted that all of what he said was true. She then said, "I haven't really shown you how important you are to our operation, have I?

"You're right that since our de-layering of the organization, there is no opportunity for advancement for you right now," Sandy continued. "But there are a number of critical assignments you could take over that would tell others within the organization how highly regarded you are. Would you be willing to take over one or more of these? These are projects I have been asked to spearhead, but if you are willing, I'd be delighted to have you handle one yourself and work with me on another. What do you say?"

"There wouldn't be a raise in this, would there?" Chan asked.

"No, I can't promise that. But if you do a good job, it will certainly be reflected in your performance appraisal and the regard with which others in the company and industry hold you. In fact, you'll likely have people within the company knocking down your door to get you to help with projects of their own—and I don't even want to think about how involvement in these projects will increase other companies' interest in you."

Suddenly, Chan smiled. "I like working for you, Sandy. Money isn't really as important to me as knowing that my work is appreciated," he said. Sandy knew Chan well enough to know that he was telling the truth.

"Tomorrow is Tuesday," Sandy said, thinking out loud, "let's arrange to get together after 4:00 P.M. so we can discuss the two projects. Let Marie know," she said.

"I may need to meet with you during the project to ensure that everything goes well," Chan said as he headed for the door.

"Of course. After I've explained the projects to you tomorrow, we can decide on how frequently we need to get together to monitor project progress. And, Chan," Sandy added, "if you ever again have doubts about how important you are to this organization, please put them aside. You have some of the most creative ideas in the department; even P. T. Barnum couldn't have come up with such audience-grabbing ideas."

As Sandy readjusted her chair behind her desk, she signaled Marie at her desk. "Marie," she said, "note on my calendar that I should ask Chan out for lunch in about two weeks. I'm putting him in charge of Project Phantom, and he'll need me to advise him on how to get through the political minefield so that he gets all the resources he'll need." As she leaned back at her desk, Sandy thought about the afternoon. Not only had she stopped two performance problems from occurring but she had motivated two of her top workers, and very likely she would see even greater performance from both in the future. "I'm a darn good coach," Sandy thought, making the mistake of many managers in confusing mentoring with coaching.

In essence, Sandy was offering to mentor Clint's orientation in the organization when she offered to help him become comfortable with the firm's new systems and to guide him with the political issues he might face in getting his new marketing campaign off the ground. That included acting as a broker to ensure that he had the resources he would need to make his ideas a success.

Whereas Sandy needed to mentor Clint for only a few weeks, she had to spend longer with Chan, providing a sounding board as he learned new project-management skills under her direction, skills that had nothing to do with his current job. With both Clint and Chan—but for different reasons—Sandy had to provide sketches of both the organization and its members, providing information that the new mentees ordinarily would not have been privy to or been able easily to discover on their own.

How to Generate Discussion

During her later meetings with Clint and Chan, Sandy answered lots of questions, but more important were the questions she asked to help her new mentees develop personal and professional insights. The questions were thought-provoking, prompting her mentee employees to begin thinking about the kinds of situations or issues that might arise and how they would handle them. If they didn't have the skills they needed, the questions were designed to prompt them to ask Sandy about future developmental efforts.

Mentoring can be a preventive of performance problems and an effective tool in performance management, but only if the mentor is skillful in getting a dialogue going with the mentee. Interestingly, the secret to getting a productive mentoring discussion going is not to begin with a question but rather with a statement that tells the mentee the direction in which the discussion will go. The mentor's opening statement tells the mentee what page the mentor is on; it also spotlights the issue that will be discussed. For instance, in Sandy's meeting with Chan at 4:00 P.M. on Tuesday, she began with a statement that focused the subsequent discussion on one of the political issues that Chan would have to address to complete Project Phantom on schedule.

> Sandy: Chan, you have worked with Tim Gilmour?
>
> Chan: Yes, I've been on some teams with him recently. When I first came here, I had to lend a hand when his marketing manager took maternity leave.
>
> Sandy: What have you learned about how he works?
>
> Chan: He is very numbers-oriented.
>
> Sandy: How did the numbers he demanded differ from those that Larry Nichols regularly asks for in connection with marketing his product line?

Sandy was encouraging Chan to compare work styles so as to help him work successfully with Tim on Project Phantom. But she was far from through. She had to continue to probe to be sure that Chan saw specifically why Gilmour operated as he did ("How is Tim cost-conscious?") and that Chan appreciated how he would have to adapt his own work style to work effectively with Gilmour ("When you work with Tim, what will you be doing differently from the way you currently work?").

Throughout that first meeting, she used statements followed by provocative questions to get Chan to develop an action plan for handling his new project:

> Sandy: You did a good job introducing our new mutual fund offer, but you'll need to move more quickly with Project Phantom. The CEO understands it is your first time heading up a project.

Chan: Will Gilmour help me?

Sandy: Would you feel comfortable asking him?

Chan: I think so. Do you have some suggestions for how to introduce the topic?

Sandy: You've worked with Tim before.

Chan: Yes. He likes being asked for help.

Sandy: How would you ask him to co-lead the project?

And so that meeting and subsequent meetings went. Few of the questions that Sandy raised in her first meeting and in subsequent sessions began with *why* because *why* questions seem to put people on the defensive, making them feel as if they have to justify their actions. Sandy wanted to encourage an open discussion, and she knew that *why* questions might have put either Clint or Chan in a guarded frame of mind.

Advice vs. Feedback

Although mentors act as advisers to their protégés, they should more often provide feedback than advice. Unsolicited advice only draws resentment, whereas feedback, when offered correctly, instructs the person getting the feedback. A secret to getting someone to *really* listen to the feedback you are offering—and helpful in any mentoring situation—is to make clear to the mentee that he or she would have discovered and addressed the problem without your help. Your purpose in offering the feedback is to speed the developmental process.

As you give feedback during mentoring, remember the advice I gave in connection with coaching: give the feedback in a straightforward and honest manner. Ask yourself how you would like someone to assess something you have done. Very likely, you would want that feedback to be clear but empathetic. You wouldn't want to be told something in a cruel or hypercritical manner. On the other hand, you don't want to feel that the person responsible for giving you feedback is holding back. You want to feel that you can trust this person not to wimp out because he or she is uncomfortable with being open or honest with you.

In many ways, a mentorship is a form of friendship. Consider how you would give advice to a close friend.

Christine Mentors a Friend

Christine, a manager, recently heard from her friend Taylor that she had been passed over for a promotion, and Taylor wanted to complain to Human Resources about the failure of her boss to give her the pro-motion. As Christine explained, "Taylor was furious. She felt a principle was involved." Taylor had applied for a job in a company that claimed that internal candidates would get first consideration; yet Taylor had learned that her boss had already interviewed several external candidates before meeting with inside applicants. Further, the boss had not noted all the requirements for the job, and while Taylor met these requirements as well, she had focused only on those in the posted notice.

Taylor wanted to report her boss to Human Resources and even to senior management. Yet she still worked for this individual and had no prospects for a job outside!

"Yes, it was unfair," Christine said. "But Taylor had to be made to realize that going to Human Resources in her present mood would do her no good." Interestingly, Christine did exactly as Sandy had with Clint and Chan. She asked her friend questions both to calm her and to get her to consider her various options and the consequences of each. Ultimately, Taylor went to her boss and discussed what had happened, but she decided to wait several days until she had calmed herself.

Christine didn't tell her friend what to do; she didn't even tell her what she would do in a similar situation. Rather, she asked gently probing questions that helped her friend find a way to address the "principle" without alienating her boss.

To measure your communication skills as a mentor, ask yourself the following questions. The more often you can answer no to them, the better able you are to mentor someone—particularly a subordinate—to increased individual effectiveness:

- Do you jump in with solutions before you have heard out your employee about a problem he or she is having?
- Do you believe there is only one way to handle a situation?
- Do you remain calm even when someone in whom you had faith lets you down?
- Do you get visibly annoyed when you have to go over the same issue time and again until the individual with whom you are speaking understands why the subject is important?
- Do you tell people what to do rather than lead them by asking thought-provoking questions?

- Do you have a reputation for avoiding awkward conversations or addressing sensitive issues?

- Even though you can't guarantee it, do you make promises to staff members about getting them a promotion or giving them a bonus if they do such and such?

- Do you allow others to interrupt while you are meeting with employees about their career concerns?

- Do you lie occasionally about the realities of career advancement in your organization and recommend unrealistic paths to advancement to avoid addressing the limited opportunities available?

- Do you toss individuals into the water of new experiences without being present to throw them a lifesaver?

- Do you gab over lunch with colleagues about the weaknesses of your employees?

Three Mentoring Success Stories

You may be wondering what happened to the marketing managers Clint and Chan, who worked for Sandy at Acme Assets. Actually, all three stories have a happy ending. Clint remained as marketing manager with Acme for four years and ultimately moved up to take Sandy's job when she was promoted to senior management. On the other hand, Chan, despite his close ties to Acme, left two years after his meeting with Sandy, but they were two years of tremendous success for him and the company—and for Sandy. Why do you think she advanced to senior management?

Sandy's friendship with Chan continued after he left, so she was delighted to find Chan at her promotion party. At that meeting, Chan listed the many reasons why he enjoyed working with Sandy. Interestingly, several reflected her mentoring style more than they did her managerial style. For instance:

- *Sandy allowed him the freedom to do things his own way.* Chan noted how Sandy recognized when he needed help to advance in his career, but she didn't let him become dependent on her by doing all the thinking for him. Rather, she asked him questions that made him think. The projects she gave him were within his reach, but they also required him to stretch.

"Yes, she had solutions that she could offer. But," Chan said, "she led me through a thinking process to help me choose how best *I* should handle the situation. Sandy can be very explicit when she knows you are confused about what to do next, and you seek her out for direction," he told the group. "But she also encouraged me to try new approaches to a situation. Sandy made me aware of the various paths I could take to achieve a goal, but she let me choose my own routes."

• *Sandy gave him a developmental plan with individual goals to aim for.* Chan told the assembled group how he and Sandy had set goals for him that would make him a more skilled project manager. "I looked back on those goals," he said, "and I discovered something. Each one was designed to move me forward—each small win built my confidence and prepared me to achieve my next goal. The developmental plan we created," Chan observed, "built on my strengths as well as addressed my development needs."

• *Sandy acknowledged she wasn't perfect.* "I knew I was going to make mistakes leading the projects I handled," he told the assembled group, "but I was surprised when Sandy admitted to mistakes she had made during the first times she headed up a project."

Employee mentees need to know that their mentor made errors along the way as well as to hear about the mentor's accomplishments. This prepares the mentee for the problems he might encounter while pursuing a goal. Parenthetically, it also makes a mentee (or, for that matter, someone being coached or counseled) more receptive to negative feedback; after all, in most instances, the person offering the feedback gained her wisdom the hard way.

• *Sandy always followed up on tasks assigned others.* "Sandy followed up as she promised," Chan observed. Too often a mentor will give an employee a project and then fail to monitor his work to see if he completes the assignment or to ask about the nature of the problems he is having. Some mentors don't want to follow up because they are afraid they will find problems, which will put them in the unenviable position of having to criticize the mentee. But the reality is that problems can arise, and a mentor isn't doing her job if she doesn't raise these issues.

Everything Chan said ties in closely with the most important elements in a mentoring relationship: trust and mutual respect. These are the cornerstones of a successful mentorship. The mentee has to trust the mentor to keep their conversations confidential and to be honest about any problems either in the relationship itself or in the mentee's work. And both mentor and mentee must respect each other and be able to carry on open communications with one another without concern about hurting the other party's feelings.

Let's Talk: Face-to-Face and E-Conversations

WE'VE TALKED ABOUT HOW MENTORING can be used to boost performance or help individuals advance in their careers, or make it possible for new hires with lots of ability to hit the ground running, thanks to your support. But mentoring can also be used to address problems experienced by these same mentees.

Successful Mentoring

Admittedly, solving a mentee's problem can take up a lot of your time as a mentor. But it comes with the responsibility, and, if done well, it can strengthen the mentor/mentee relationship.

The secret to successful mentoring is to listen not only to the words being said by your mentee about a workday but also the feelings that underlie those words. Sometimes the mentee has a concern, or is uncertain about how you might be able to help, and therefore doesn't say anything specific about the situation. There are also times when your mentee may have a difficulty but may be embarrassed to bring it up because it concerns a problem with his or her supervisor or a colleague or family member. Let's look at how to address these kinds of situations.

Operating Matters

Jay had joined his company's mentoring program. The program's coordinating committee is responsible for pairing mentors and mentees, and Jay was fortunate to get Patrick, the warehouse's shipping manager. The company had its eyes on Patrick, so it also had its eyes on Jay as Patrick's mentor.

Jay had set up a meeting for lunch, and he was a little annoyed when Patrick didn't come on time. Patrick was a half hour late, and Jay began to worry about what might have happened. Suddenly, Jay saw Patrick dashing through the cafeteria line, grabbing at food. As soon as Patrick saw Jay, he headed for his table, nearly knocking a tray out of the hands of a staff member on the way. "I'm sorry I'm so late," he told Jay as he caught his breath. "It's been a busy day. First, one thing went wrong and then another. But the real reason behind my lateness for lunch was a delay in getting a shipment out. It's really annoying—we keep losing track of finished parts in the warehouse."

"Should I become involved in this issue?" Jay wondered. On one hand, it wasn't Jay's area of expertise—Jay was head of product engineering at the plant. Patrick, as shipping head, should be addressing the situation, Jay thought. On the other hand, he reasoned, if the situation is a recurring one—and Patrick had indicated that it was—then its continuation would reflect poorly on both Jay and Patrick. So Jay decided to find out more about the matter. At the very least, he thought, he could teach Patrick about how to handle work problems when he experienced them. "How often does the problem occur?"

Patrick, reaching for the menu, replied: "Too often. I just wish I knew what was happening."

"This could suggest that a parts management problem exists, right?" Then Jay paused in order to let his remark set in. He wanted to give Patrick the opportunity to think about what had happened today, a few days ago, and the previous week—incidents he knew about because Patrick had told him about them at earlier sessions. Jay thought that there was a pattern here, but he knew that Patrick wouldn't learn to recognize problems like these if he told him. Patrick had to learn to identify patterns for himself.

"You know, Jay, I think you may be right. I've been so busy finishing my operating plans and budget lately, I never realized that the warehouse might need a better way to keep track of raw and finished parts."

Jay now had two options. He could let the matter drop and move on to the purpose of the meeting—Patrick's progress on his operating plan and budget. Or Jay could probe further about the shipping problem, inquiring how (or if) Patrick planned to investigate the situation further. Since the installation of such a system would need to be included in the next year's plan, it wouldn't be odd to inquire further about it, after all. Surprisingly, Patrick decided to drop the issue.

"Gee, Jay, I have no idea what to do. I'll pass the problem on to the plant manager at our next meeting. Now, let's talk about this operating plan . . ."

Jay decided to help Patrick, not only about his operating problem but also about his attitude toward the problems he encountered. "Patrick, before we do that, what do you plan to say to the head of the plant? As the head of shipping, don't you think you have some responsibility to identify the problem?"

"I do, but you know how experienced Steve, our plant manager, is at resolving problems. He'll know what to do."

"But he'd be more impressed with you if you presented him with the facts, if not a solution, at your meeting, right?" said Jay.

Patrick thoughtfully responded, "Yes, you're right. So, how do I begin?"

Jay realized that Patrick was still trying to pass the problem on to someone else—this time, it was him. Jay's goal as Patrick's mentor was to develop his professional abilities, not to be a crutch for him. So, rather than answer Patrick's question, he asked him one: "Jay, if you were in Steve's place, what would you want to know about the problem?"

"I guess he would want to know when the problem occurs and what might be behind the situation. If I think that a new system needs to be installed, he'd ask me what it might cost.

Jay, happier, said, "Yes, you're right." Again, Jay paused, passing the decision about the next step that needed to be taken back to Patrick.

"Wait a minute. I was on a project team and we used several sophisticated problem-solving tools to identify the reason behind a shortfall in sales. Do you think I could use some of those tools to help here?" Patrick asked.

With a smile on his face, Jay responded, "It sounds like they might be valuable."

Caught up in the idea, Patrick mentioned the techniques he had learned to use: Pareto analysis, scatter diagrams, workflow diagrams, cause-and-effect diagrams, and variance analysis. "Look. I'm not as knowledgeable about these techniques as I should be. I had better go to the project leader of that team to see if she can lend me a hand. Can we reschedule lunch for another day?"

"Sure," answered Jay.

As Patrick's mentor, Jay had done his work well. He had helped

Patrick see a problem in the making, helped him begin to think about solving the problem, and even taught him how to use the colleagues with whom he had worked in the past to help him with the current situation. As Patrick walked away, it suddenly occurred to Jay that there was something that Patrick could do for him. "Hey, wait a minute. Let me come along. I'm not familiar with all those techniques, and this might be a learning opportunity *for me*."

This conversation between Jay and Patrick is instructive in two ways. First, it shows how mentors should *not* solve mentee problems. Rather, they should use questions and statements to help their mentees think them through and come to reasonable solutions. Only if the answer is wrong should the mentor intervene. Second, as you no doubt noticed, this story demonstrates how helping a mentee with a situation can be a learning experience for you as a mentor.

The First Steps in a Mentoring Relationship

Jay was fortunate in that he had a protégé who fell into the category of high potential; that is, he was an individual who, with minimal coaching, had the ability to move up. As a mentor, when you are paired with a protégé you don't know well, even before you discuss the person's goals you must be clear about his or her skills, abilities, and knowledge, as well as career objectives. If your mentee is like most people, he or she may want to advance but may not be sure what that means in real terms. In other words, what would the individual like to be doing in the next two years, maybe five years, ten years from now? How prepared is the person for the first big career move?

So these are the first questions that you, as a mentor, need to address with a new protégé. At the very least, you should ask your mentee to make a prioritized list of ways you can help him or her move to the next level. Sometimes, you may be surprised to discover that a talented and conscientious mentee, with all the skills he or she needs for advancement, may lack self-confidence.

Opening Up Possibilities That May Not Have Been Imagined

There are countless kinds of fears that people have, and many of them show up at work. While you won't find your mentee running and hiding under his or her desk, you might find other signs, like depression or anger, when you talk about career advancement. For example, Cindy, an accountant at a small accounting firm, was irritated because she thought that the only way that she would advance in her career would be to put in overtime every night and also work weekends. A single mom with two daughters, Cindy felt that such a commitment was out of the question for some time to come.

Phoebe, Cindy's mentor, worked in a publishing company's financial department. She felt that she had the responsibility to make Cindy aware of her capabilities and also to encourage her to take the risk that comes with making an effort to gain the attention of those who make hiring decisions, like those in Phoebe's company. Phoebe knew that the head of her department was looking for an assistant director, which was a logical career move for Cindy. All Cindy needed to do was to update her resume. Phoebe knew the department head would like Cindy's background and conscientiousness. But Phoebe also knew that Cindy needed a makeover to make it past the HR department.

Phoebe first had to talk Cindy out of the belief that she had to leave her daughters in the hands of a sitter every evening and put her nose to the grindstone to take an advancement. As far as the job was concerned, Phoebe felt that all Cindy needed was to project a more professional image that would get people to know and recognize her potential. What would this entail? Phoebe's first step as a mentor was to encourage Cindy to discard that outmoded image of herself, as well as to discard any outmoded habits.

For instance, Cindy, a young mother, seemed to carry all the trappings of motherhood with her—from clothes that wouldn't spoil from milk spills to stuffed toys, coloring books, and crayons in an oversized bag. Even more important, Phoebe had to overcome Cindy's reluctance to imagine a better position than the one she currently had—to visualize herself ultimately as the assistant director of finance for the publishing firm. Cindy had to think of herself as receiving the position and diving successfully into the new job and all she could learn in the job.

> Phoebe: Cindy, you know that there is going to be an opening as assistant director in my company. Would that be a goal of interest to you?
>
> Cindy: I don't know, Phoebe. I've got Jennifer and Jessica to care for. I don't know if I would have the time.
>
> Phoebe: You once told me that you enjoyed many of the administrative tasks that you have in your job. About 50 percent of this job is administrative.

> Cindy: Really. And I'd be working with more people in more complex situations.
>
> Phoebe: Well . . .
>
> Cindy: I don't know [pausing]. Oh, nobody would take me seriously as a candidate for the position.
>
> Phoebe: First, Cindy, you have to take yourself seriously as a candidate for the position. If you did, then we could work to make others do the same.
>
> Cindy [enthusiastic]: Do you really think I could get the position?
>
> Phoebe: I can't promise anything, but you won't go anywhere in your career if you don't give it a try. How about it?

Phoebe was able to get Cindy to think about her aspirations by urging her to think about those things she really enjoyed doing—that is, what tasks truly made her happy. To trigger such thinking, as a mentor you might want to ask your mentee to recall one or two moments in the near past that were especially satisfying. When you meet with your mentee, you would talk about these. As you question your mentee, you would get insights into your mentee's thinking about the next rung on the career ladder, as Phoebe had.

Encouraging a Realistic View of Advancement Potential

Your goal as a career counselor is to determine not only what rung your mentee believes that he or she is qualified to reach but also what specific rung is in your mentee's mind. If you work in the same organization as your mentee, you are best qualified to judge how realistic the mentee's goal is. If you are not colleagues, but you are familiar with your mentee's company and/or industry, then you may be able to assess how realistic your mentee's plan for advancement is. Is the organization growing so there is room for your mentee to rise in the organization or is the company currently held back by the economy or state of the industry?

If you are mentoring a colleague, you may not want to discourage him or her if you see no opportunity for promotion at this time. On the other hand, you need to be honest with your mentee. If now is not the time to shoot for that ideal position he or she wants, you may suggest that your mentee seek a promotion that would position him or her for consideration at a later time. Some mentees are reluctant to consider an alternative to their ideal job, but zigzagging within the ranks is an option that should not be ignored, particularly in tough economic times when companies are running lean with little opportunity for promotion.

Sometimes, it will help if you send the mentee out to do research about available positions and the requirements. For example, Linda wanted to move up to assistant marketing manager yet she lacked some critical skills for the position. Her mentor, Tom, knew that, and realized that Linda needed to make a commitment to some on-the-job training, maybe even a semester at a community college, to qualify for the position. He suggested her need for training, but she was resistant. Rather than fight over the matter, he suggested she have a heart-to-heart talk with both the head of marketing and the human resources manager to get a clear idea of the qualifications for the position.

Linda came back with a much more realistic view. While she still was enthusiastic about her career goal, she realized it would take longer—and some extra training—and accepted her mentor's advice.

• • •

Phoebe and Tom both worked with their respective mentees to write vision statements that identified their mentees' specific job goals and also the action steps that would need to be taken to achieve the objective. Remember how in corporate planning we develop SMART objectives— that is, Specific, Measurable, Achievable, Realistic, Timely (scheduled) goals? Likewise, the development goals that you and your mentee should set should be SMART.

The Mentor's Tough Talks

In the previous chapter, I took you through a couple of coaching sessions. Sometimes, such sessions aren't as simple as the ones described in textbooks. When you are mentoring and the results aren't as they should be, constructive feedback isn't enough. The advice you offer may be rejected. Clearly, the problem with giving criticism—even something we call "constructive feedback"—is that some people just don't take kindly to it. Criticism is evaluative and judgmental, no matter how much you might try to sugarcoat it.

Most people feel threatened by criticism. For some, it can even prolong the problem. What should you do? To avoid giving the criticism would mean accepting the defeating behavior, so that is not the right response. When a mentee's behavior isn't up to snuff, you need to address it. Remember, your goal is to bring around change rather than continually criticize what the mentee is doing. Giving the same criticism over and over when a mentee makes a mistake repeatedly will accomplish nothing.

The most effective way to handle a problem or a disagreement between a mentor and mentee is to look at what happened and try to analyze the source. In most instances, you will discover that you will need to switch from coaching to counseling mode. This means that you and your mentee need to do two things:

1. Win the mentee's agreement that there is a need for a change.
2. Agree on the specific actions that your mentee will take to correct the mistake or behavior problem.

If you were your mentee's supervisor, you would be able to use the threat of termination if there is no change in behavior. But as the individual's mentor, you have to rely more on the trust between you, the respect the mentee has for your past experience, and your ability to influence his or her thinking. This last point is critical. Influencing isn't about manipulation or the misuse of power. It is about using your good relationship with your mentee, and the trust he or she has in your know-how, to change the individual's attitude about the situation. Present your ideas logically and persuasively, spelling out clearly and honestly how your mentee is going to personally benefit from doing as you suggest.

Begin by clarifying in your own mind what your objective is. What do you want to achieve? The second step is to actually plan your campaign. Ask yourself how you will discuss the situation with your mentee in a manner that is most likely to gain his or her agreement. For instance, when you next meet with your mentee, perhaps you should listen before you say anything. Ask open-ended questions (e.g., How? Why? What? When? and Where?) to discover any concerns that may be behind his or her past refusal to accept your suggestions.

You also have to be prepared to answer any questions you are asked by your mentee.

Finally, and most importantly, you need to spell out the benefits if your mentee shifts gears and behaves as you suggest. Use open and friendly body language (e.g., maintain eye contact, keep arms in a relaxed position) to communicate, nonverbally, your good intentions.

Your mentee may be refusing to accept your opinion because he or she feels threatened, is frightened of making a mistake, or believes you are overselling your concern about the impact that continuation of such behavior will have on the individual's career plans. Of course, it could also be that your mentee doesn't really understand what you are suggesting. What should you do? Rather than tell you, let me show you how Michael handled such a situation with his mentee, Gene.

MICHAEL: CONSTRUCTIVE CRITICISM

Gene refused to accept Michael's remark that he needed to change his leadership style. As head of the new product development team, Gene interrupted members, refused to consider others' ideas, and demanded members make unrealistic deadlines. Even if the team was successful with the idea that Gene was pushing down the throats of his teammates, Michael felt that senior management would not be pleased. It knew that Gene wasn't a team player, a value highly prized at their organization.

When Gene joined Michael for lunch, Michael began the meeting by telling Gene, "Gene, there's something that's concerning me and I need to talk to you about it." Having heard Michael raise the issue of his behavior in the new product development team, Gene told him, "Let's not go over that again, Mike. Management respects strong leaders."

"Yes, management respects strong leaders, but," he continued, "it is looking for leaders who listen to their followers and gain their support, not those who badger and harass those with whom they work." Michael then went on to describe the management styles of several recently promoted managers. Each had gained senior management's attention by their leadership skills, yes, but these skills included a willingness to listen to their staff members, an openness to others' ideas, and creation of a strong team. "Would you agree, Gene, that these are qualities that separate these managers from others?" Michael asked his mentee.

"Yes," Gene said, "but that's not me. I'm not sure I could handle that style effectively."

As far as Michael was concerned, this admission from Gene was a critical turning point in the discussion with his mentee, "I'll help you," he offered. Michael and Gene then sat down and worked out an action plan that would help build the leadership skills that their organization expected in its leaders. The development plan that they completed included specific steps that Gene should take to open up the discussion in the product development team and make the final product recommendation a product of everyone's ideas. Michael had sat through several sessions in the past as a guest of the team, and he promised to sit through several more to observe Gene's change in behavior and offer constructive feedback after the fact.

Since Gene lacked self-confidence about his ability to change his style, Michael suggested that he try to re-visualize his behavior. "Think about how you would act and what you would say," he suggested. Michael knew that the picture Gene would create in his mind would help create a real-life change in his behavior. This didn't mean that the problem was done and solved. It took several more meetings before Gene had fully bought the idea of changing his leadership style. But Gene did stop fighting with Michael and moved to accepting his viewpoint and even asking for feedback on his behavior. Michael invited questions and answered them patiently and thoroughly. He knew that Gene had to make a big style adjustment.

Michael was successful because he followed a four-step process:

1. He made sure that Gene heard the message. As a mentor, you have to overcome mentee objections that can range from having a different agenda from yours to disbelief that your idea is not in their best interests, to an unspoken fear that giving up one behavioral style for another could lose them control of a situation critical to their advancement.

2. He worked to be clear. As a mentor, you need to be sure that you are clear to your mentee about what change in behavior you expect—and why.

3. He realized that the process was useless unless Gene was agreeable. This is your goal as a mentor. Just as in counseling an employee, you can't expect a change in behavior until your mentee acknowledges that a continuation of the current behavior can impede career advancement. It's your responsibility as the mentor to communicate the cost to your mentee in a manner that isn't threatening but convinces him or her to change behavior.

4. Michael sat down with Gene and agreed on changes to the vision statement and action plan. When there is a glitch in achieving a career goal, the development plan needs to be revised to address the problem. Thereafter, you and your protégé need to make sure you keep track of your mentee's progress. Be patient—your mentee may not change overnight. What you want to see is effort in the new direction you have both set.

What if your mentee *announces* to you that he or she has had a confrontation with a peer or, worse, a manager above him or her and plans to let the individual know how he or she feels. A trick that many communication specialists suggest is an "I message confrontation." Yes, your protégé wants to tell the boss off. What should you say? An "I message" generally contains three parts:

1. A neutral description of what you perceive the mentee intends to do.
2. A statement of the possible negative effects on the mentee or other people.
3. The feelings or emotions you are having about the mentee's plan.

Note that nowhere have you told the mentee how to behave. The mentee still makes the final decision. However, your mentee knows the following from your "I statements."

1. "I believe that you are so angry at your boss that you will march into her office and lose your temper as you tell her off."
2. "I believe others will observe your behavior and consider you unprofessional for losing your temper, no matter how justified."
3. "As your mentor, I am concerned about how such an act will impact your reputation as someone who is cool, calm, and capable of addressing numerous problem situations."

Can you see how these three statements might discourage your mentee from pursuing her original intent?

E-Mentoring

Office technology has created opportunities to mentor individuals off-site. Mentors and mentees can communicate via e-mail, supplementing their face-to-face meetings. Where mentors and mentees are located in different states, even different countries, e-mail, phone calls, and teleconferencing may even replace face-to-face meetings. Software can set up discussion boards where mentors and protégés can have ongoing dialogues. And let's not forget cell phones for emergency calls for advice.

E-mentoring is on an increase, as is mentoring itself. After all, in today's busy world, a virtual mentoring program provides for greater flexibility in regards to time—on a practical side, when two people are separated by multiple time zones, the number of hours they may be available to each other decreases—it allows individuals from very different parts of the country to partner, which can make the experience broadening for both.

At the same time, there are drawbacks to virtual mentoring. The experience can lack the spontaneity of interpersonal communication that usually develops in face-to-face mentoring. This shouldn't discourage prospective mentors from considering this mode of mentorship, however. Those who have engaged in virtual mentoring programs report that their experience was a fun challenge. They felt they had grown themselves, since the process put a little greater demand on their communication—in particular, e-mail skills.

There are four key steps in most mentoring relationships, and they are as applicable in distance mentoring as in traditional mentor relationships:

• *Building the Relationship.* If possible, both the mentor and protégé should meet in person to share their objectives from the relationship prior to the start of the e-mentor relationship.

• *Setting Clear Expectations.* The mentor has to ask the protégé if he or she has specific concerns or career goals. The mentor, in turn, needs to describe how he or she hopes to assist the mentee. At the same time, the mentor needs to be clear about his or her commitment to the protégé. Some protégés assume that their mentors will be more accessible since they are both communicating via e-mail, but that may actually not be the case.

• *Monitoring the Results.* Some mentors and protégés communicate exclusively via e-mail, others limit e-mail communications to the posting of non-time-urgent questions to the mentor, requests for meetings with the other party, and summaries of conclusions drawn from the last communication. All other communications are handled via phone.

Those who run phone meetings kick off these phone sessions with a review of the protégé's last assignment or outcome of the planned activity discussed during the last phone call. What did the protégé accomplish? Is there something new that the protégé tried that was successful? What challenges did the protégé overcome and what challenges does he still feel need to be met? What did the mentee learn about not only how to handle a new responsibility but also him- or herself?

The mentor and protégé should also review any unexpected situations that arose since the last phone call. What were they? What impact have they had on the opportunities or challenges facing the protégé in the near future? How can the mentor help? Finally, the two should discuss those activities the protégé will be doing until the next phone call. The protégé should be prepared to identify the next learning opportunity, and together the mentoring partners should decide on an appropriate assignment as a learning experience. Before the two hang up, they should agree on a date when the two will talk again—and the protégé will offer an update on the assignment.

•   *Providing Feedback.* Since distance management doesn't give a mentor the same interaction with a protégé as face-to-face communications, the mentor has to rely on the remote control that comes from respect for the mentor. The mentor can begin to foster that trust by showing trust him- or herself in the protégé. That means that the mentor only questions the protégé when there is real reason to do so about the results of an assignment.

Should you mentor someone on the phone, it's important that you listen not only to what is said but also what is not said, like the silence after a question is asked. Likewise, consider what the protégé isn't saying. Sometimes that can tell you more than what the mentee does say. Keep your ear tuned for a rising or lowering of voice, a change in tone, and a quickening or slowing of speaking pace as well.

In face-to-face communications, you can rely on body language for additional insight into how the coaching session is going. In phone communications, you will need to tell your protégé what you are "hearing" or "sensing." Check on feelings by asking your protégé how he feels about a remark you make. Also, push for specifics—don't settle for generalities. Ask that your protégé express thoughts and opinions clearly. After all, you have to understand where your protégé is coming from to make the mentoring relationship worthwhile for him or her and make the most effective use of your time. Certainly, don't hang up before you have both summarized in words of your own what you feel has been agreed to, testing the accuracy of your perceptions.

What about e-mail? Just as with the phone, you should be focused on the communications under way. Don't let co-workers distract you from the flow of the communication. Certainly, in providing constructive feedback, think first before you press the "Send" button with your message.

Also, you may be tempted to respond immediately to a message, either via an e-mail or on an instant messaging system. Don't. Avoid knee-jerk responses. Electronic communication is quick—that's why we use it. But its greatest benefit can also be its greatest drawback. When you sit down at the keyboard to respond to your e-mail, your mindset is typically to get through it all—to empty your mailbox and free yourself for other tasks. That mindset can generate snap judgments. It's unwise to allow this to happen with any e-mail, but it is particularly wrong if you allow it to happen to some mentee who is asking for opinion or advice. So be mindful of speed when you are answering e-mail from your mentee—a quickly worded response to a critical question can destroy the considerable time you have taken with your distance mentee to build a positive relationship.

The Knack for E-Mentoring

No question, e-mentoring takes a certain ability. One manager I know told me about a problem that arose. Anna, who was located at headquarters, was mentoring Travis, a newbie at a regional office. Anna had offered some advice to Travis about his handling of his first focus group. To her surprise, the next e-mail she received flamed with CAPITAL LETTERS indicating his annoyance with her remarks and—worse— criticism of Anna as a mentor. Anna told me how she was just dying to press the "Caps Lock" key as she began her reply, but she resisted because she knew that doing so would only escalate the e-argument.

She took her hands off the keyboard and went for a walk. She left Travis's emotionally charged message in her e-mail for a full day before she felt calm enough to respond to his message. "I had to remember that there really was a live person on the receiving end of any message that I wrote," she told me. "He was young and he was upset that the focus panel didn't go as well as he had expected. I hadn't told him what he did wrong. I only asked him to think about how he might better handle certain aspects of the process, but I guess 'the list' ticked him off."

Anna continued, "The message clearly was misunderstood, too. I wasn't telling him that he had done a poor job. Rather, I was telling him that he did well for his first effort. And I was listing some points that he might want to consider the next time. But Travis saw the entire e-mail as critical of his effort." She continued, "Fortunately, I realized that by flaming back, I would only keep the communication gaffe alive. I've been the recipient of unintended hurt feelings, so I could appreciate how Travis might be feeling."

After considerable thought, Anna replied by e-mail. Her response began with acknowledgment about Travis's need to flame. (Even though it was unjust, acknowledgment of Travis's feelings under the circumstances seemed fair.) She then went on to explain her intent in sending the list of suggestions. People are usually reasonable if they feel they have been treated sincerely and honestly—which is how Travis responded to Anna's reply.

Tone, Rhythm, Persuasion

Anna's reply exhibited a much friendlier tone than her earlier message. As a recipient of Anna's e-mail, I know that they can be a little officious, so I believe that she made an extra effort to duplicate a conversational style in her e-mail without erring on the side of being too informal and conversational. She used words and phrases that came naturally. She also kept her message short and to the point. "The most important point that I wanted to make in my reply," Anna told me, "was that Travis had my support."

What if the e-mail reply hadn't worked? Then Anna would have suggested a phone call to discuss the matter further. The sooner they resolved the disagreement, the better. Its continuation would simply have impeded the mentee's development. And that's something that a mentor never should do.

12

Mentoring Traps to Avoid

NOT ALL MENTORING EFFORTS work out as planned. Like all human relationships, they have their ups and their downs. Fortunately, some of the downs, or traps, can be prevented. Just as forewarned is forearmed in coaching and counseling, so too it is with mentoring. You can maximize the benefits of mentoring top talent and avoid potential problems by being aware of the problems that can arise in mentoring. Formal mentoring programs even go so far as to acknowledge this possibility. Often, such programs include, as a part of an agreement between mentor and protégé, an "out clause" that allows either party to put an end to the relationship without any needed explanation.

Breaking Up: When It's Time for the Mentee to Move On

Interestingly, one major mentoring trap is the belief of the mentor that he or she can't end the relationship—that only the mentee can do that. Not so. There are several reasons a mentor might want to end the mentoring relationship, including the possibility that the top performer has outgrown the mentor. Yes, it is possible for you to mentor a talented employee to the point where he or she needs challenges that you can't offer. Then you may want to recommend that the top employee find another mentor—maybe a manager with a growing department in which opportunities for promotion for your talented mentee might arise.

It might seem that you are making an unnecessary sacrifice, but consider the reality. If your mentee is as bright and as hardworking as you believe, he or she probably feels a little restless. The mentee may be thinking of career opportunities outside your organization. Better to keep the individual with your organization. And while you may lose an outstanding employee, you could find that department productivity and morale increase as staff members see what your efforts on their co-worker's behalf have brought.

Needless to say, it is easier to end mentoring relationships built on a few brief meetings than it is to write *finis* to a long-term relationship with an exceptional staff member with whom you have probably built good rapport. In a short relationship, you can continue to show interest but also look for opportunities for that person to meet with and seek answers from others in the organization. In time, you will find that the employee comes to you for help less frequently.

In any event, it is best to explain your decision to end the mentorship with your top performer, regardless of how formal or informal the relationship was. The employee needs to know why you feel you can no longer continue to contribute to his or her career advancement. That you're too busy only sends a message to the mentee that he or she is not as important as you initially made the individual believe. It will only demotivate the mentee and lower his or her level of performance, whereas you entered into the mentoring arrangement to further increase this talented employee's contribution to the department or company as a whole. Instead, point out those developmental gaps that the employee still has and the skills that a new mentor must have to help close them—areas in which you are not expert. Then, together with your staff member, develop a list of prospective new mentors that have these strengths.

If a mentee has the talents that attracted you in the first place, it should be possible for you to find another mentor for the person or for the mentee to locate one for him- or herself. Even though you end the mentorship with a staff member or other mentee, you should make clear to the employee that your door is always open for those times that the employee needs help—the same as it is open for any other employee.

When Mentoring Hurts Rather Than Helps

What kinds of mentorship problems should cause you to dissolve the relationship? Some mentors have found that mentoring their subordinates can inhibit their employees' development rather than support it. The talented employee becomes so dependent on his or her managerial mentor that there is actually a decline in performance. This is particularly a problem in mentoring relationships between a mentor and his or her subordinate. For example, rather than trying to resolve problems on his or her own, the mentee continually runs to the mentor for help. But, worse, rather than begin to build his or her own network of contacts, this talented employee becomes dependent on the mentor to use his or her network of contacts both within and outside the organization. The employee will be giving so much attention to the mentorship that he or she won't be developing connections with others who are important to success, and perhaps even focus more on the mentorship than on routine work.

Evidence of this is cause to end the mentoring relationship, regardless of its nature. Overdependence on a mentor is a major trap, and the only way it can be addressed is by severing the relationship as soon as there is proof of its existence. After all, the purpose of mentoring a top talent is to increase individual or organization effectiveness. Your mentee can become complacent unless you take action—which is to take that little chick you put under your wing and kick him or her out of the nest.

Another trap that mentors can fall into is to become so concerned with their protégés' careers that they lose perspective about their role. Alex almost did this when Jenny, his protégé, told him about her marital problems.

ALEX: AVOIDING JENNY'S MARRIAGE PITFALLS

Jenny probably would not have brought up the situation regarding her marriage except that Alex had mentioned her disinterest in her work over the previous few weeks. When he asked why, Jenny told him that she had found out that her husband was having an affair with a woman in the office. When Alex heard the story, he told me how he had been tempted to offer Jenny advice based on his relationship with his stay-at-home wife. "Fortunately, I didn't, however," he said. "That isn't the advice and counsel I promised to give Jenny when I agreed to mentor her. Nor does my home situation or my wife's life goals compare to those of Jenny."

Alex felt that the only help that he could offer was to suggest that she seek a family counselor. He then went on to discuss with Jenny how they could work together on achieving her mentee goals despite her personal situation.

If your protégé is experiencing family difficulties, drug or alcohol misuse, depression, or other potentially complex or even life-threatening situations, then all you can do is to recommend that the individual seek the help of a psychologist or personal counselor. The best reply is as follows: "I care very much about you and want to support you as you deal with this. When we agreed to work together on advancing your career, we discussed how we might run into some circumstances about which I'm not an authority. I believe that this is one of those situations. Can we discuss available services within the community or through the company's EAP to help you?"

Personality Conflicts

Another reason for ending a mentorship, even with a talented staff member, is that you just don't like the person. You offered to mentor someone and was given an individual by your company program whom you first liked but since have found that you are always at odds with. Yes, he is a hard worker and very talented. But your mentoring sessions with him are only turning into debates that seem to go on from one session to another. Time spent with this individual could more productively be spent with another, equally talented person within your organization who would be more willing to listen to your feedback. Let the person know that you want to see him grow, but suggest more suitable candidates as mentor for this individual. If you can't recommend someone, suggest that your mentee meet with the program coordinator to identify suitable candidates for the role.

If you are thinking of mentoring a staff member, you can avoid such a situation by waiting through a get-acquainted period before extending an offer to be available to mentor the person.

A Mentee with an Achilles' Heel

Still another reason to get out of a mentorship is a mentee who is unable to develop the new skills important to her career advancement, despite the time you've spent with her. Generally, it's not a matter of the person's developing new abilities or knowledge but rather one of acquiring political savvy or adapting to the corporate culture. This was the problem with one mentee, her mentor told me.

SAL: A MISMATCH WITH SARA

Sara had done a terrific job on a business proposal, which was why Sal became aware of her and offered to mentor her; he envisioned her working with him on numerous projects. Sal knew that Sara came from a more traditionally structured organization, but he didn't think she would have any difficulty working on the team-based initiatives he often became involved in. Not so. Rather than work with him on these projects, Sara buried herself behind papers stacked two feet high on her desk. When she wasn't e-mailing someone, she was issuing reports that no one was reading.

Sal tried hard to get her to change her work style, but to no avail. She was deaf to his pleas to involve herself in the team initiatives. He ultimately decided to devote his time to another individual whose work habits were more culturally in tune with his own work and the organization's new approach to the work. Clearly Sal and Sara were a mentoring mismatch. Since Sal's organization was moving toward a team-based structure, Sara was probably a hiring mistake to begin with.

I believe that Sal had another reason for wanting to sever his mentoring relationship with Sara. Like some mentors, he was concerned that he might be viewed as a failure as a mentor, based on Sara's minimal interest in team dynamics. Some mentors even worry that rather than help the up-and-comer, they may be hindering his or her development by offering the wrong advice. The reality is that many people contribute to the professional development of a new or an advancing employee. You need never worry that a less-than-perfect mentoring effort will prevent your protégé from becoming the next Bill Gates.

Mentorships That Can Cause Problems

Before sharing some mentoring problems that can be remedied, let me address two other situations that can create problems and that may—but not always—lead to dissolving the relationship. Of these, I would agree with Harry Truman that "If you can't stand the heat. . . ."

Cross-Gender Mentoring

Rumors can arise if you are a male manager and you choose to mentor a female employee. The situation is likewise if you are a female manager and choose to mentor a male employee. The likelihood of a sexual relationship between a manager mentor and an employee mentee can easily become subject of discussion on a corporate grapevine, regardless of the parties' personal or professional reputations. One manager was warned by his boss that he might not get a promotion he clearly had earned because of his mentoring relationship with a female staff member, despite her fine professional reputation. The office rumor mill said that he was spending so much time with the young woman that they had to be having an affair—which they weren't!

The manager was happily married. The woman wasn't married, but she was engaged. Their meetings were always in his office. Neither had ever been the source of office gossip in the past. Yet the manager had to choose between continuing to help his administrative assistant achieve her goal of becoming a CPA or ensuring his promotion.

The press recently contacted me on this very issue. One question that was asked was, "Should a female mentee always keep the door open while being counseled by a male mentor?" My reply at the time was that no woman should find herself in a mentoring situation with a male in which she feels she has to keep the door open to protect either herself or her reputation. But in retrospect, that reply was too simplistic. Cross-gender mentoring can be open to misunderstanding in today's sexually conscious world. Those who enter into it need to be prepared to find that some people, often jealous of the special attention the mentee is getting, may spread rumors. Should you find yourself in such a situation, the good news is that the gossip mongers usually get bored when they see no fire and move on, looking for other signs of smoke.

Despite his boss's warnings, the VP of finance in our story got his promotion, although he continued to help his assistant advance in her career. Rather than dissolve the mentorship, he extended it to include another staff member—another woman—who took his job when the manager moved up. As for the administrative assistant, she received her degree in accounting, got married, and now works for a tax return processing company.

Reaching Down Below

An equally awkward situation occurs when you mentor a subordinate of one of your direct reports. Don't say you would never think of it—it could happen. Maybe one of your direct reports has an employee who has lots of potential. If you decide to mentor that individual, recognize the impact that it will have not only on your new mentee's relationship with his or her boss but also on your relationship with your direct report.

Unless you see the mentorship as a short-term step before promoting the individual to the spot you have in mind, meet with your direct report and discuss his or her mentoring the individual. Such involvement will clarify the roles and responsibilities of everyone involved in the mentoring relationship. Otherwise, any problems between the mentee and his or her boss will become exacerbated as the mentee reaches out to you to resolve the problems. And new problems can arise between you and the boss as the boss sees him- or herself losing control over that direct report.

Problems in Mentoring That Have Remedies

So far, I've identified problems that might cause you to dissolve the mentorship and situations that can easily turn awkward. Now let's discuss some mentorship problems that are remedial.

Failure to Live Up to Expectations

Either mentor, mentee, or both may be guilty of this. You may have selected among your staff members a top performer whom you thought you could make into a project leader or an informal assistant to you, but the person hasn't lived up to your expectations. That potential may still be evident to you, but the employee hasn't been following any of the developmental suggestions you have made. The employee might have misunderstood your offer to be available to provide feedback, or to serve as an advocate; instead, he or she might have interpreted it as a fast track to advancement without the need for any further effort to develop the competencies you originally saw. If this is the case, then it is time to make clear to the individual that the extra effort you are making in the form of mentoring has a price, and that it is increased performance, development of new skills or abilities, leadership of a team effort, or whatever developmental goals you both agreed on.

Of course, you, too, could be letting down the partnership. Maybe you meant it when you told your staff member that you would be accessible any time. But now you find that your calendar is too full to accommodate the time your mentee needs. Rescheduled meetings over time suggest to the mentee that he or she is a low priority for you. This is a frequent problem for managers who agree to mentor an employee.

Too often, mentors assume that initiating the mentoring relationship is more than sustaining it. Not so. Expressing your intention to mentor someone is, perhaps, at most only 10 percent toward building the partnership; the day-to-day effort—the ongoing communication and support—is the other 90 percent. When the continuous effort isn't forthcoming, no matter what your assertions about how important the employee and his or her career are to you, the greater likelihood is that the protégé will become frustrated. He or she will become disenchanted about the relationship, even question your motives—maybe even doubt his or her own worth.

You have two options here. You can seek out someone else to mentor your employee, perhaps a peer who has more time than you do right now. Or you can find the time—maybe meet during lunch if your calendar is so busy that you can't meet in your office during the workday. Or suggest that you and the employee meet before the start of the workday or after everyone else has left.

But here's one warning: some mentees may have an expectation beyond reality as to your availability. So it is best to be clear at the beginning about how much time each month you can devote to the individual. Give too much time, and the mentee can become dependent on you. Or you may both find yourselves sitting together in the office with nothing to talk about but your wife's new job or the mentee's child's report card. If you can, commit your calendar ahead of time to meeting with the mentee as a way to ensure that you always have the agreed-upon time available.

Expectations of Perfection

Another reason you may want to end your mentoring relationship is that, thinking about the two of you together, you realize that you are continually too hard on your mentee, asking more of him or her than you might do if the person were a staff member. Let me share with you an example.

JACK: CUTTING ROY A LITTLE SLACK

Before he retired, Jack enjoyed the satisfaction he got from mentoring the techies in his firm. Jack was a human resources manager, and he believed that he could broaden the perspective of these individuals, contributing to their advancement to management. In most instances, the relationships worked well. Then Jack offered to mentor Roy.

If you heard Jack, Roy couldn't do anything right when it came to working with staff. Roy even put together a training program for staff to familiarize them with new software programs, but it didn't impress Jack. Fortunately for Roy, Bob—a friend of Jack—intervened. Bob suggested that Jack join him for lunch. During the meal, he casually asked how the mentoring was going. "I'm sorry I agreed to help Roy," Jack said. "I've mentored many young people in his field," he said, "but this is the only time when I feel as if I'm wasting my time. I feel as if I should tell Roy that he'll never be anything more than what he is now."

Bob replied, "Would that be fair to Roy?"

Jack was surprised to hear this from his friend. "What do you mean? I spend several hours a week with him, and he acts more and more like a geek."

Bob answered, "I've seen him when you aren't around and he seems pretty comfortable with people. He doesn't have the management skills he'll need to take on a job like yours or mine, but he has the interpersonal skills."

Jack started to laugh, "You're kidding, right?"

But Bob replied, "No, I'm not. For some reason, you're a tough taskmaster with Roy. Could it be that he reminds you of yourself when you were his age? I seem to recall that you weren't so smooth with people—it took another of our old buddies to make you the smooth HR manager you are today."

"You mean Bill; yeah, good old Bill," Jack said, smiling. "I was a lot like Roy when I think of it."

Jack reassessed his thinking about Roy. He realized that he made Roy uncomfortable, which explained his manner with others while he was present. They discussed the situation, and Roy agreed to give Jack a second chance. Today, Roy is a software consultant, and Jack points with pride to his finest accomplishment in a fifty-year career: Roy.

Communication or Stylistic Managerial Weakness

Sometimes the problem is bigger than that which could have destroyed Jack's effort with Roy. Some managers just lack the communication or managerial styles critical to mentoring. For instance, a manager may criticize, rather than listen, or may provide the mentee with answers rather than risk the mentee's making a mistake. Or the mentor may become more than an advocate for the mentee by assuming the role of press agent, perhaps selling the mentee for a team leader role, not because this person is right for the assignment or has done a good job in similar positions but largely because of the relationship between the mentor and the individual.

GLENDA: WHEN ADVICE BECOMES CRITICISM

To understand the impact that such mentor behavior can have on the relationship, consider that between Glenda and her staff member Martha. Martha was one of Glenda's top engineers. Twice monthly Glenda met with Martha to work with her on her project-management skills. It was a promise Glenda had made to Martha when she persuaded her to join her division rather than go with a competitive firm. Martha's division had been downsized, but her technical know-how had caught Glenda's attention in planning discussions that had included Martha and her former boss, Howard. So when Howard's division was dissolved, Glenda immediately had sought out Martha and offered her a slot in her division.

At that time, Martha told her about a job offer she had received from a competitive firm, so Glenda went out of her way to point up the opportunities for advancement in her own area. When Martha mentioned that she was worried about her weakness in project skills, Glenda had jumped at the opportunity to offer to help Martha if she stayed with the company and agreed to join Glenda's operation. Although the word *mentor* was never mentioned, Glenda's offer encompassed all the roles of a mentor—role model, adviser, broker, and advocate—for the purpose of making Martha more at ease in project situations.

Six months passed. As Glenda promised, she continued to meet with Martha every second week. At these sessions, Glenda shared with her new staff member her own experiences in overseeing projects and critiqued Martha's efforts at improving her people skills. During the first few sessions, Martha seemed receptive to Glenda's suggestions. Since Martha and Glenda both attended several meetings together, Glenda could comment from firsthand observation, not simply listen to Martha describe situations and how she had handled them. Martha had even seemed grateful when Glenda called a break at one meeting Glenda was heading when Martha seemed to be at a loss for words in defending an idea for improving the division's intranet setup.

On the other hand, Martha showed little interest after the fact in hearing Glenda's suggestions for how Martha could have better handled the situation. Or how embarrassed Glenda had felt for Martha. "I never found myself in such a bind," she had told Martha. "You really have a problem in leading project teams. But don't worry. We'll find some way to help you." Martha at this point sometimes seemed to go out of her way to do just the opposite of what Glenda told her to do at their mentoring meetings.

A Helping Hand from Howard

No longer delighted with Glenda's offer to help, Martha had now become visibly angry about having to give up her lunch hours to meet with Glenda. It was clear to Glenda that something was wrong. So when she spotted Howard in the hallway, she asked him to come to her office to talk. When his division had been eliminated, Howard had been relocated to the company's Houston office.

"What's up?" Howard asked as he closed Glenda's office door. "I was glad to see that you were able to keep Martha. I've seen your operating numbers, and I bet some of those savings were due to her systems improvements. That woman is a technical genius."

"If she could only be as good working with project teams," Glenda said. "Martha doesn't know a thing about project management. But it shouldn't be affecting her work. Right now, the way she is acting, she would probably be happier tinkering with computers, off by herself." Glenda decided to tell Howard about her promise to Martha.

"I'm surprised she admitted her lack of project-management skills, but I'm delighted that she recognizes it as a weakness," Howard observed. "But if she could master the knack, she would be in line for a team leadership or supervisory position."

"That's what I had in mind," Glenda continued. "But the time I am spending with her isn't giving her the confidence she needs to lead a project group. In fact, she seems to have even more trouble directing the project groups she works with."

Howard then listened as Glenda described how she had instructed Martha in how to behave with the other members of the team. "I've reviewed what she has done wrong after each meeting, and I've told her how I used to handle such situations in the past. Yet she doesn't seem to change."

. . . And a Finger on the Problem

Howard was silent for a moment. "I hate to say this, but the problem may be as much with your handling of the problem as with Martha's lack of know-how."

"What do you mean?" Glenda asked, sincerely interested in Howard's view of the situation. "I thought I was giving Martha constructive criticism."

"There is no such thing," Howard said. "The two words just don't belong together when you are talking about giving an employee feedback to help her deal with an obstacle to career advancement. You may have thought you were helping to build her up—that's the constructive part—but all that the criticism has really been doing, from what you say, is tearing her down. From my own experience as a supervisor and manager, I know that employees don't listen if you give them feedback in the form of criticism.

"By criticizing Martha all the time about her work with others and always advising her about a better way or, worse still, coming to her rescue," Howard continued, "you are telling Martha that you think she's hopeless in project settings. You aren't building her self-confidence, you're destroying what little self-confidence she had about working with others. And she's resentful because she thought you were a friend. Instead, you've become her toughest critic." [Sounds a lot like Jack, right?]

Glenda thought for a moment. After her first meeting with Martha, Glenda had to admit, she had assumed a more directive approach with Martha. Rather than ask a series of questions to help Martha identify for herself how she might better have handled situations, Glenda had jumped in with advice and lectures. In considering the situation, Glenda realized she needed to go back to the consultative approach she had used earlier if she was to rebuild her previous rapport with Martha.

Giving advice, extricating the mentee from a potentially embarrassing situation, and focusing on the "how to" rather than the reason something should be done might seem to be faster ways to mentor an employee, but these behaviors do little to build the individual's self-confidence. At a point when you, as mentor, might want to empower your employee mentee, instead you wind up disempowering him or her.

Unrealistic Developmental Goals

Glenda may have had an unrealistic expectation about how quickly Martha could learn how to interact more effectively with people. Actually, this is a problem that can go both ways. While a mentor may demand more of the mentee over a shorter time than he or she is capable of, so too may a mentee expect more, besides time, of the mentor than he or she has the ability or willingness to provide. For instance, a mentee may expect the mentor to protect him or her from organizational pressures, perhaps even a downsizing. But the mentor may be unaware of the political problems the mentee is experiencing or, in the case of a potential layoff, the mentor may lack the clout to save the mentee from the corporate axe.

Whatever the misunderstandings, they can cause hostility to grow between the mentor and mentee. The mentor may have set goals with the mentee, and the two may have much in common, but the mentor can become an easy target if a promotion that the mentee expected isn't forthcoming or the mentee blames the mentor for a mistake, even though the mentee made it him- or herself. While the goal was to boost the mentee's performance, the emotion between the two can affect the mentee's performance and even cause it to decline.

Because such problems can arise, you have to be very specific in discussions with a prospective mentee about what you will provide. This is particularly the case when mentoring a staff member. The employee shouldn't feel that he or she will be favored over other staff members because of your extraordinary relationship.

DAN: CARL—THE STAR WHO BLAMED HIS BOSS

Carl had been relatively new to the automobile company when Dan, a vice president, made him his protégé. Only a few months later, an opening occurred in Dan's department, and Carl thought he had the position sewn up. At home, he told his wife that they would celebrate when the announcement was made.

"Carl, you're jumping to conclusions," Cindy said.

"I have no reason to worry," he told her. "If Dan didn't think I was suitable for promotion, he wouldn't have chosen to mentor me," he replied.

"Just don't be surprised if someone else gets the job," she answered as she cleared dishes from the table.

But Carl was so sure that he even told one or two of the fellows in the plant about his expectations. Put yourself in Carl's shoes when the word got out that Dan had chosen Tony for the job. Carl's pals looked to him to see what he would say, but Carl was speechless for the first time in the time they had known him.

Dan had recommended Tony for the promotion because he had the experience that Carl, a newbie to the firm, lacked. The decision was logical to everyone but Carl, who felt that his relationship with Dan gave him special privileges like being the first to be asked to lunch or to go to a ball game or to be offered a promotion.

Carl couldn't ignore the "slight" (Carl's word, not mine). He sought Dan out and asked him at the cafeteria table, "Why not me?" Dan didn't understand.

"Why what?" he asked.

"I'm your protégé, Tony isn't. How could you pass me over?" Suddenly, then, it occurred to Carl what the nature of the problem was. "I know what the matter is. I've told you all about me. You know what I think I'm good at and what I'm not. You have watched me like a policeman and you know even the smallest mistake I have made. You used that knowledge against me. That's why Tony got the job and not me."

Dan was shocked, but fortunately he was understanding. "No, Carl, that isn't the truth. Tony has had more experience and was ready for the promotion he received. You have more to learn before you are qualified for the job. You're young, and you have the potential to advance in your career. I wouldn't be mentoring you if I didn't truly believe that."

"But, Dan, I told my wife!" moaned Carl.

"Your wife, huh. I'm sorry. But you can tell her for me that she's got a pretty smart husband and, if she is as patient with you as I am, you'll be a VP in time."

"You believe that, truly?" Carl asked.

"Yes, I do," Dan replied emphatically.

I heard this story about a year ago—from Carl. He's vice president of purchasing at one of the largest automobile companies in the United States. His favorite story to new mentees is that one about the time he didn't get a promotion!

Identifying Problems as They Occur

If you suspect that there is a problem in your mentoring relationship, you may want to use this list of ten questions to set matters straight:

1. Are we addressing your needs?

2. Do you feel a sense of satisfaction from our ongoing meetings?

3. Do you have expectations that are not being met?

4. What could be done to improve our conversations?

5. Do you feel that we are spending more time together than you now need?

6. Are there some special issues that we should put on the table and address? (For example, the likelihood of co-worker jealousies, ethnic or cross-gender communication problems, or mistaken impressions about the relationship.)

7. Do you see the same need for my help as you did originally?

8. If we have achieved our initial goals, what would be the next goals?

9. Am I still the person to help you reach your next level of accomplishments?

10. Is there someone else within the organization who would be a more appropriate mentor at this stage in your development?

The discussion may identify problems with the current relationship, but if they are ones that the mentee believes are remediable, he or she may want to continue to come to you for career advice and developmental help. The decision then falls on you to decide whether to try to improve the situation or to discontinue the relationship.

Under these circumstances you may want to walk away, but you owe it to the staff member to make an effort to revitalize the mentorship. This includes a willingness to accept responsibility for the problems that still exist. But you must also demand the same honesty and responsiveness from your protégé.

Assuming that you identify changes that you believe will turn the situation around, give the partnership a month. Then ask the same ten questions once again. If there has been no change, you are justified in ending the relationship.

Your Role as a Leader

EVERYONE ADMIRES THE MANAGER who has a great staff of employees. His or her workers are both productive and cooperative. There are even one or two superstars in the department or work team. Guess what? That manager could be you as you apply the information in this book to your working relationships with your employees. As you demonstrate your coaching and mentoring skills, and as you turn around poor performers via counseling, you will be thought of as a leader as well as a manager.

If there is one thought you should take away from reading this book, it is this: people problems, whatever their nature or level of seriousness, shouldn't be ignored. Avoidance is the fastest way to make an employee situation get worse, even allow it to become infectious, expanding beyond the single worker to encompass an entire department. The situation can grow so large that it can hinder your relationship not only with the rest of the staff but also with your own boss and other managers, and even bring you to the attention of senior management for all the wrong reasons.

Even before coaching, counseling, and/or mentoring, there is a major step you can take. You can create a positive work environment in which employees are highly motivated to meet and exceed performance standards. Managers tell me how their own supervisors discourage performance by creating a bureaucratic organization in which they feel no motivation to demonstrate their creativity or show their initiative. They find themselves held back by an obsession with processes that leaves little opportunity for flexibility and responsiveness to today's fast-changing business conditions.

How can you begin to create the environment that can complement or supplement the performance-management system described in this book? The answer lies in fostering communication with your staff. Actively solicit feedback about your own communication as well as exchanges within the organization. Ask your staff members questions like, "When we talk, are you clear about what I'm saying?" or "Do you think we communicate well around here?" or "Do you have any ideas about how we could communicate better?" In other words, open the door to critiquing the suitability of the workplace to generate the kind of performance you and your organization need to achieve competitive advantage.

Because it is repeated so frequently, the phrase "People are our most important asset" may seem only like rhetoric. Certainly the behavior of some companies has caused many employees and even managers to regard the statement as nothing more than corporate propaganda. But it is a fact of business life, and as a manager, your role is to increase the worth of that human capital. Consider the impact that competent, highly motivated employees could have on achieving your department's mission and making its contribution to the bigger corporate mission as well as your organization's strategic intent, not to mention your career.

Admittedly, you're very busy. And people situations can be tricky. But the kind of attention to people problems that this book proposes should take no more than 10 percent of your time. On the other hand, failure to allocate that 10 percent when you first see a performance problem can cost you 50 percent or more of your time when the problem grows beyond coaching or mentoring to counseling. At best, you will have to pick up the slack from an unproductive employee. If the problem continues, you will find yourself taking time away from bottom-line assignments to justify the individual's termination. And if you have failed to be upfront with the worker all along, you may find yourself preoccupied with fear of a lawsuit brought by the disgruntled employee whom you could have salvaged with some effort earlier on.

Not responding at the first signs of a problem can allow enough time for a small molehill of a people problem to grow into a mountain that you professionally never get over. Better to demonstrate your belief in the phrase "People are our most important asset" by coaching all your employees, counseling your poorer performers in order to turn their behavior around, and mentoring your superstars to keep them shining than to stand with your peers and look covetously at those managers with high-performing teams who are recognized and rewarded by senior management for all the right reasons. That's the WIIFM (What's in It for

Me) in taking action to boost employee performance when you become aware of the need.

Aside from the personal pride you will take in building and then overseeing a highly productive work group, you will have the knowledge that your team's successful track record is reflecting well on you.

Index